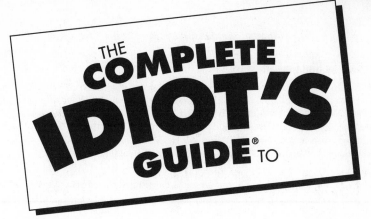

THE COMPLETE IDIOT'S GUIDE® TO

Shamanism

by Gini Graham Scott, Ph.D.

ALPHA

A member of Penguin Group (USA) Inc.

To the traditional shamans; may they never be forgotten.

Publisher: *Marie Butler-Knight*
Product Manager: *Phil Kitchel*
Managing Editor: *Jennifer Chisholm*
Acquisitions Editor: *Gary Goldstein*
Development Editor: *Jennifer Moore*
Production Editor: *Billy Fields*
Copy Editor: *Cari Luna*
Illustrator: *Jody Schaeffer*
Cover/Book Designer: *Trina Wurst*
Indexer: *Amy Lawrence*
Layout/Proofreading: *Angela Calvert, Mary Hunt, Sherry Taggart*

Contents at a Glance

Contents

Foreword

When European explorers first encountered shamans, they were shocked. Their letters back home described them as uncivilized savages who were doing the work of the devil. Religious authorities attempted to convert them, and if they objected, shamans often found themselves tortured, burned at the stake, or skinned alive. But shamanism survived. The colonial governments banned shamanic rituals, dances, and music. Colonial families were forbidden to see shamans or use shamanic herbal remedies. Frequently, missionaries took native children away from their parents and from their pagan practices. But still shamanism survived. When Western psychology and psychiatry turned its attention to shamanism, experts in psychopathology diagnosed shamans as schizophrenic, hysterical, or severely neurotic. It was assumed that enlightened tribal members would soon realize the folly of following the old superstitions. But shamanism still survived.

Finally, shamanism is being taken seriously again, and Gini Scott has written several pioneering books on shamanic practices and their relevance to contemporary life issues. Contemporary social scientists describe shamanism as a body of techniques and activities that enable its practitioners to obtain information not ordinarily attainable by members of their social group. Shamans use this information to meet the needs of their community and its individual members. Originally, shamans were active in hunting, gathering, and fishing tribes, and this is where they can be found in their most unadulterated form. However, contemporary shamanic practitioners also exist in nomadic, agricultural, and even urban societies.

Shamanism takes on different forms wherever it is found. Sometimes a community may recognize several types of shamans. Among the Gold Eskimos, only the *siurku* shaman is allowed to heal, while the *nyemanti* shaman performs special rituals over a deceased person's soul after his or her death, and the *kasati* shaman conveys the soul of the deceased to the spirit world. When I visited the Cuna Indians of Panama, I was told that the *abisua* shaman heals by singing, the *inaduledi* specializes in herbal cures, and the *nele* focuses on diagnosis.

Readers of this remarkable book will learn how to work with power animals, how to initiate rituals, and how to use their imagination to take shamanic journeys. This is not a shamanic cookbook; shamans undergo years, sometimes decades, of tests and trials before their community gives them shamanic status. However, Gini Scott has given her readers an inspiring account of the shamanic process. Every shamanic tradition is different, and every reader of this book is a unique individual. The information and exercises in this book will motivate its readers in diverse ways. But this diversity and variety has always been at the very roots of shamanism.

Stanley Krippner

Stanley Krippner, Ph.D., is professor of psychology at Saybrook Graduate School in San Francisco. He has worked with shamans from six continents, and is the co-author of *Exceptional Dreams and The Mythic Path.* His co-edited book, *Varieties of Anomalous Experience,* was published by the American Psychological Association, which gave him their award for Distinguished Contributions to the International Advancement of Psychology in 2002.

Introduction

I have long been intrigued by one of the oldest skills in the world for gaining knowledge and healing—shamanism—which I first encountered in 1980 while I was studying the growing interest in spiritual growth, alternative religions, and humanistic/transpersonal psychology in California in the late 1970s and early 1980s. I had already spent a decade going to assorted workshops and seminars on altered states of consciousness, hypnosis, and dreaming, including at Esalen, a thriving Big Sur retreat center at the heart of this movement, and had studied some of the new spiritual growth, pagan, and Wiccan groups. I first learned about shamanism from an adventure travel brochure. It featured a group trip to Ecuador, led by anthropologist Joan Halifax, to meet with shamans and other traditional healers. In Ecuador, we visited four different shamans, two located deep in the Amazon jungle, one in the central city of Quito, and another on the coast. One night we even took part in an all-night healing ceremony, which included ritual drinks of ayahuasca, a powerful hallucinogenic drink made from a brew of jungle vines.

My interest in shamanism goes well beyond a social scientist's academic interest, though. A few years after my return from Ecuador, I met a shaman who had drawn on a number of shamanic traditions and practices to create the Order of the Divine Flame, then based in Los Angeles. I soon became one of a small group of his students in the San Francisco Bay Area. Frequently, we went out into nature—from local parks to the nearby beaches and mountains—to work with the elements of nature and call on the spirits.

Eventually I adapted some of these techniques for everyday self-help and personal and professional development. I combined them with visualization and mental imaging techniques I had previously written about (*Mind Power; The Empowered Mind*) to create workshops and write books (*Shaman Warrior, Secrets of the Shaman, Shamanism for Everyone*, and *Shamanism for Personal Mastery*) to help others learn how to use shamanic practices for their own empowerment and personal mastery. In retrospect, I would describe what I was doing as part of the modern stream of popular shamanism, where we were using shamanic practices, rather than actually being shamans as the term is usually used to describe traditional healers. But at the time, I didn't make such distinctions, and the modern shamanism movement was too new to understand these developments.

The term shamanism, as you'll discover, has many meanings. In its most traditional form, shamanism is the practice of entering into an altered state of consciousness to contact the spirits to help and heal others. The original shamans were healers and counselors in small hunting-gathering, pastoral, and agricultural villages. In the last few decades, though, shamanism has undergone numerous changes, as its practices have been adopted by psychologists, medical practitioners, and by those, including myself, involved in various combinations of New Age practices, humanistic psychology, and business, educational, and personal development.

This book is intended to provide you with a broad understanding of shamanism today and how you can use it in your own life. I start with an overview of the nature of shamanism and how it has developed. Then, I look at how you can apply it to your own life, focusing on the use of journeying, self-understanding, personal and professional development, and everyday guidance. Because the use of shamanism for healing is more specialized, I don't delve too deeply into that area, though I provide an overview of it, should you be interested in seeking more guidance.

After reading this book, you will be able to use shamanic practices in your everyday life to increase your awareness, make better decisions, improve your skills, and otherwise attain empowerment.

How This Book Is Organized

This book is designed for both the newcomer to shamanism and the person already familiar with it who wants to know more. Feel free to skip to those sections that are most of interest to you, whether that's the early chapters on the nature of shamanism and how it developed or on how to apply shamanic practices to your daily life.

The book is organized in four sections:

Part 1: "Shamanism: The Ancient Skill of Knowing and Healing"

Take a self-guided tour of the world of shamanism. The tour starts with a basic definition of the essence of shamanism, which is based on seeing and entering the world of spirits and working with them to attain knowledge, energy, and power to help and heal. Then, this section traces the development of shamanism from Paleolithic times to today and looks at the many varieties of shamanism around the world.

Part 2: "Power, Shaman Style"

The focus in this section is on the many different techniques that shamans use for gaining power and getting information and assistance through entering an altered state of consciousness to contact the spiritual world. You'll learn how to work with three of shamanism's most powerful tools: power animals, power objects, and teachers and spiritual guides. Then, you'll discover other ways to harness shamanic power, such as working with the four elements of nature, and using songs, chants, prayers, and dancing. This section also considers using rituals and different types of power places to enhance your shamanic experience and make the practice of shamanism more powerful.

Part 3: "Pack Your Bags, We're Going on a Journey!"

Next, we turn to the heart of most shamanic practices for both gaining information and guidance and for healing: journeying. You'll discover the many ways to take a journey and how to journey safely. This section also considers the way journeying parallels and can be used with other self-help techniques, such as hypnosis, visualization, and self-talk. You'll be introduced to the different types of journeys to the lower, upper, and middle worlds. And you'll learn ways to maximize your journey experience, no matter where you go. Finally, we'll look at the method of using journeying to go even more deeply within yourself, an approach developed by some psychologists.

Part 4: "The Well-Traveled Shaman"

Now that you have a general understanding of journeying and where to go, this section more carefully maps out the three worlds and the kinds of journeys you can take. You'll learn about the traditional lower, upper, and middle world associations and how to use them or incorporate your own associations. These chapters also include many tips for enhancing your journeys to each of these worlds, along with examples of workshop participants who have traveled to and gained insight from each of these worlds. In the final chapters, we'll take a look at the many forms of modern shamanism and consider what's in store for the future of shamanism.

Signs You'll See Along the Journey

On your journey through the world of shamanism you'll encounter many signs. Watch for them to receive guidance on your trip:

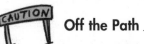
Off the Path
Try to avoid these roadblocks and dead ends as you journey to other worlds.

Shaman Says
You'll be talking like a well-traveled shaman by the time you read all these definitions.

Bon Voyage
Make the most of your journeys by following these travel tips.

Wise Ways
Shamanism is full of interesting insights, as you'll find out by reading these boxes.

Oh, One More Thing

I'm setting up a page on my website with the latest information on shamanism and lots of interesting links. Just go to www.giniscott.com/shamanism.html.

Acknowledgments

I want to extend my special thanks to Dr. Stanley Krippner, who has served as both technical editor and written the introduction. He has helped to remind me of the many nuances involved in describing the varieties of shamanism both in the past and today, and I have appreciated his wisdom as someone who has worked with shamans, consciousness, and healing for several decades.

Secondly, I want to thank my agent, Giles Anderson, who brought the idea for this project to me.

Also, I want to extend my thanks to Dr. Laurie Price, an anthropologist at California State University of Hayward, where I am currently pursuing a second M.A. in anthropology. Her class on medical anthropology provided many insights on the use of shamanism by medical practitioners. Additional thanks go to Jason Coleman, an archaeologist, who guided me in my studies of the Maya when I studied with him in his Maya, Aztec, and Inca class at Merritt College in Oakland, California.

Additionally, my thanks to Michael Fairwell, as he preferred to be called, when I studied shamanism with him as one of his students in the Order of the Divine Flame and later wrote about his teachings in *Shaman Warrior* and *Secrets of the Shaman*. The work we did in learning about seeing, going out in nature, and working with power objects and the elements helped to set the stage for my further explorations about shamanism over the years.

Finally, my thanks to many others, who provided other resources and assistance, from writing about it to organizing conferences and putting up websites devoted to shamanism past and present. I especially want to acknowledge Ruth-Inge Heinz, who has been organizing an annual conference on shamanism in Northern California for 19 years, several of which I have attended.

Unless indicated, all photographs are by Gini Graham Scott; clip art is from Broderbund and Corel Gallery

Special Thanks to the Technical Reviewer

The Complete Idiot's Guide to Shamanism was reviewed by an expert who double-checked the accuracy of what you'll learn here, to help us ensure that this book gives you everything you need to know about shamanism. Special thanks are extended to Dr. Stanley Krippner.

Trademarks

All terms mentioned in this book that are known to be or are suspected of being trademarks or service marks have been appropriately capitalized. Alpha Books and Penguin Group (USA) Inc. cannot attest to the accuracy of this information. Use of a term in this book should not be regarded as affecting the validity of any trademark or service mark.

Part 1

Shamanism: The Ancient Skill of Knowing and Healing

Why is shamanism so old? Why is it a global phenomenon? And why are there so many different types of shamanism? We'll answer these questions and others in the following chapters.

Part 1 is like a guided tour through the world of shamanism. First, it clears up what shamanism really is by describing how shamans see into the other world of spirits, contact spiritual beings, and work with that knowledge and power to help and heal others and themselves. Then, it looks at how shamanism developed from Paleolithic times to today, becoming many different varieties of shamanism in different cultures around the world. By having this broad view of shamanism, you'll be better able to tap into its power and use shamanic practices more effectively in your own life and in helping others.

Chapter 1

The Power of Shamanism

In This Chapter

- ◆ All about shamanism
- ◆ What shamans can do and see
- ◆ Stepping into another world
- ◆ Working with energy and power
- ◆ The healing power of shamans
- ◆ Learning from a traditional source of wisdom

The age-old wisdom of *shamanism*, which reaches back to the Stone Age (called, more technically, the Paleolithic) is alive and well today. It is still used by traditional healers around the globe, but the ancient methods have also been put to contemporary, everyday personal use for self-help and self-healing. Even medical practitioners, psychologists, and counselors have adapted the techniques and traditions of shamanism. You, too, can draw on the powers of shamanism for healing and personal growth.

In this book, you'll learn about the power of shamanism, including its early roots in ancient healing practices and traditional cultures and its modern adaptations. You'll find out how to harness the powers of the spirit world, meet power animals and guides, engage in rituals, and journey to other worlds. But before you adapt shamanic techniques for your own purposes, you probably want to know what shamanism is all about.

What in the World Is Shamanism?

Shamanism is a deeply rooted traditional system for healing and solving personal and community problems, in which a spiritual or healing practitioner, called a shaman, contacts spirits for wisdom and advice, usually by going into an altered state of consciousness. In this altered state, the shaman can see deeper truths and gain insights for understanding and healing. Sometimes this activity is referred to as shamanizing.

These images from early rock art dating back to Paleolithic times, perhaps to about 40,000 years ago, show what might be early shamans leading rituals or calling on their power animals.

In different cultures, the shaman can range from an ordinary individual who practices healing and spiritual guidance as an occasional activity to a specialist or professional, much like a doctor, healer, or counselor. In some cultures the shaman is regarded as a holy person or priest, who is part of a religious system. Shamans have practiced in traditional rural and village cultures—and still do in some of the few that remain—as well as in some modern urban societies.

Shaman Says

Shamanism is a deeply rooted traditional system for healing and solving personal and community problems, in which a spiritual or healing practitioner contacts the spirits for wisdom and advice, usually by going into an altered state of consciousness.

A modern day shaman practicing in his local community in Java. This shaman, known as Dalan, was once a successful businessman who received a call from the spirits. He moved into a cave on the beach, which he furnished with ordinary furniture, but no electricity, where people come to him for consultation and healing.

(Courtesy Stanley Krippner)

A traditional shaman from a Native American tribe leading a healing ceremony.

(Broderbund Clip Art)

Recently, a type of modern shamanism has emerged. Sometimes referred to as *neoshamanism*, it involves the use of traditional shamanic practices, such as drumming, dancing, and chanting, to go into an *altered state of consciousness* in order to engage in personal self-development or self-healing.

> **Shaman Says** _____
>
> An **altered state of consciousness** is a nonordinary state of consciousness that can range from light meditation and hypnosis to deep trance. A **trance** is an altered state of consciousness in which an individual loses touch with everyday reality and enters another world.

The preparation for becoming a shaman can vary widely, too, from an individual participating in an apprenticeship as a child with a practicing shaman to a middle-aged adult learning on his or her own. Some individuals grow up in a family where a parent or close relative is a shaman who passes on the family tradition; others receive a personal call, similar to the religious calling many ministers, rabbis, monks, priests and nuns experience. Still others, who live in closely knit tribal groups or villages, may be recognized by the local community as destined to be a shaman based on unusual personal traits, such as a propensity to be alone and a deep interest in spirits.

Despite the variety of ways one can become a shaman, the essence of shamanism remains the same: The ability to invoke the power that enables an individual to see or step into a nonordinary world of spirits. This contact and communion with the spirits imparts an unusual type of wisdom or healing power, one which enables a shaman to divine what is wrong with and heal someone or find the solution to a range of personal problems, from locating lost property to coping with an unfaithful mate.

John Grim, author of a classic book called _The Shaman_, describes shamanism this way:

> The transformative power that the shaman invokes is experienced as an all-encompassing presence that is mysterious but as real as the wind or as breath … It evokes the awesome feeling generally associated with the holy … The sacred is remarkably different from the routine or the mundane, and … manifestations of the sacred bring human beings into contact with an order of reality that is different from their ordinary world.

Is Anybody Out There?

The spirits the shaman contacts and calls on act as intermediaries between the cosmic power, or the power of the universe or cosmos, and the individual; if they respond, they

> **Shaman Says** _____
>
> **Shamanic healers,** often referred to as "curanderos" or "paje" in Latin America, are a specific kind of shaman who might engage in rituals with a patient or a group of patients.

become the shaman's allies or personal helpers. In some cases, the shaman contacts these spirits through a contemplative state, in which he or she asks for advice from a teacher or guide. In other cases, the shaman enters a deeper trancelike state and goes on a journey to meet spirit helpers. In still other cases, shamans go into a trance in which they become so close to the spirits that they experience "incorporating" these spirits as they take over and possess the shaman's body and speaking through him or her.

Shamans might dance, chant, drum, work with symbolic objects, or use herbs and medicinal substances, such as tobacco juice or smoke and *ayahuasca*, which comes from plants that grow in the South American tropical rainforests.

Shaman Says

Ayahuasca, sometimes called *yage*, is a hallucinogen, which is brewed from the *Banisteriopsis caapi* vine that grows in the Upper Amazon basin. It is often mixed together with other plants, such as the chacruna, technically known as *Psychotria viridis*. It helps to induce visions during a shamanic session, so that the shaman can see into nonordinary reality. The active chemical ingredient that causes this change in consciousness is called *harmala*. Ayahuasca is commonly used in shamanism in South America, as part of a healing ceremony that includes the use of a staff, bundle of leaves, gourd rattle, and sacred objects, such as rocks and carved statues. Some of the other substances used to alter consciousness include *huanto*, technically known as *Datura* spp., which also grows in the Upper Amazon basin, and *parica* or *yupa* snuff, technically known as *Anadenanthera peregrina*, which grows in the Lower Amazon basin (Sharon, 1978, 153).

Shaman Superstar, at Your Service!

People seek the assistance of shamans for a wide number of reasons. Shamans not only act to heal diseases and injuries—the primary activity of most traditional shamans or modern shamans using traditional methods—but they may also:

- Interpret dreams and visions.
- Guide the souls of the dead to the afterlife.
- Divine and foretell the future.
- Offer sacrifices to appease offended spirits.
- Find lost animals, children, or property.
- Initiate new shamans.
- Participate in various forms of community problem-solving.

Traditionally, a shaman conducted a ceremony for an individual patient or group of patients, and often friends or relatives attended. Sometimes these ceremonies were put on for all of the members of a small tribal community or village.

Today many modern New Age or neo-shamans apply these traditional techniques of shamanism for their own personal development, self-growth, and self-healing, or they teach these techniques to others, such as in ongoing groups and at workshops, seminars, and conferences on shamanic techniques.

A Shaman by Any Other Name ...

Modern practitioners using shamanic techniques usually don't call themselves shamans, because this is considered a very special term of honor. Normally, it is reserved for traditional shamans or modern shamans engaged in traditional practices to help and heal patients in the community.

> ### Shaman Says
>
> The words **shamanic** and **shamanistic** have different meanings, although I use "shamanic" to refer to both to simplify things. The basic difference is that the word "shamanic" describes what shamans do, whereas the word "shamanistic" refers to adaptations of shamanic practices – in other words, they are like the rituals, songs, or other activities of shamans. So generally, if you are not a shaman yourself, you are really engaging in "shamanistic" practices, rather than "shamanic" practices. But now that you understand the differences, it's simpler to use "shamanic practices" throughout.

But the term "shaman" is becoming more widely used today, and some New Age practitioners are claiming this title, although not without controversy. Many practitioners using shamanic techniques regard this action as inappropriate for someone who has not gone through the long period of training normally required of a shaman. It's like calling yourself a priest or nun after attending Catholic mass a few times. In fact, many modern shamans from traditional cultures, particularly Native Americans, resent New Age practitioners adopting their traditions and using them for personal healing. But that's another story, to be discussed in Chapter 21.

> ### Shaman Says
>
> Shamans are known by various terms in different places. They have been called:
>
> - **Kam** in Eastern Siberia
> - **Curandero or paje** in Mesoamerica or South America
> - **Peaiman** among the Macusi people in British Guinea
> - **Lhapa,** or "god-man" in Tibet
>
> as well as many other region-specific terms.

Regardless of all this variety, the essence of shamanism is that an individual practitioner is able to go into an altered state to communicate with or obtain help from spirits and to cross over into the spiritual world to gain visions. The shaman then directs this spiritual power, usually for a positive, healing purpose, through diagnosing and treating illnesses and other problems. While traditionally shamanism has been used to help individual patients or the community as a whole, it is also now used to help oneself to heal or resolve everyday problems. You can do this, too.

The Dark Side of Shamanism

While most shamans use their abilities for the good to help and heal, to do so, shamans must sometimes confront negative forces, power, or spirits—such as spirits who cause diseases and problems. Such encounters can be dangerous, and there is always the risk that a shaman could be taken over or possessed by this negative energy in whatever form it takes.

A shaman might also use the power he or she has gained for negative, destructive ends, such as harming a perceived enemy. The process is much like what happens when a good doctor, priest, politician, teacher, or any other authority figure goes bad. Just as in the rest of society, as a shaman's misuse of authority and power becomes known, he or she will be rejected or punished by the community. Often malevolent shamans are known as *sorcerers*, who work with these negative, destructive forces, and use them to harm others, such as by causing them to suffer an illness, lose their job or loved one, or even die.

Shamans are not only different from sorcerers, but they are not to be confused with a variety of other practitioners. Here's a short guide to what shamans are *not* and how they differ from them:

- **Sorcerers**   These characters usually use spiritual energy and forces for destructive, harmful ends. Shamans use their powers for the good, though some might be drawn to engage in sorcery—and eventually become sorcerers if they continue to do so. Some sorcerers will use their powers for healing and divining, but only because they have been paid to do so, not because they see it as a service to the community.

- **Witches**   Traditionally, the term "witch" has been used to refer to someone who does evil, though the term is often used to refer to the wise woman or wise man of the village who can use his or her talents to know or heal both positively and negatively. More recently, though, practitioners of the pre-Christian pagan traditions or the "old religion" have called themselves "witches," as well as "Wiccans" and "neopagans" and conduct religious services in which their stated motto often is "Do as you will, but harm no other."

- **Mediums**   These practitioners incorporate various spiritual entities, eventually losing control of their bodies and voices to these entities, which speak and act *through* their hosts. Shamans, even when incorporating spirits, remain in control of the process during the time they contact and communicate with spirits. Both shamans and mediums are sought after for advice, but the medium generally serves individuals rather than whole communities.

- **Channels**   Some practitioners prefer to be called "channelers" rather than "mediums," stating that mediums primarily contact deceased relatives of their clients, while channelers contact sources of high wisdom, often ancient spirits, or entities who never lived on Earth. During the incorporation process, channelers' bodies and voices become a vehicle for the spiritual entities, who speak *through* them. By contrast, a shaman may share some of the information received by these spirit forces, but he or she acts more like a messenger who speaks *for* them. Also the shaman stays in control of the process and so shares only what he or she decides is appropriate.

Because of the power of negative forces, and of the individuals like sorcerers who work with them, shamanic ceremonies often become spiritual battles. For instance, a healing shaman might have to fight against the spirits believed to have been sent by a sorcerer to harm his or her patient or even the shaman. If this happens, the shamanic ceremony turns into a pitched battle for the soul and the health of the patient, or in cases when a shaman is trying to heal an entire community, the fight could be waged on behalf of the community as a whole.

If the shaman wins the battle, the disease is vanquished; the problem is overcome. But sometimes the shaman doesn't prevail; he or she doesn't have enough power in that particular situation to combat the negative forces. In some cases, this may lead the shaman to make a referral to another practitioner who may be better able to deal with the problem—such as a Western physician asked to combat a serious disease. But in other cases, the shaman may keep trying—and if the shaman repeatedly fails, he or she can lose his or her reputation and the trust of others, much like any other professional.

Shamans can lose their powers for other reasons, too, such as aging; as a result, they don't have the energy and strength to engage in shamanizing. Or their interests may lead them in other directions; some former shamans have become successful artists or musicians or have gone into business for themselves. Shamans might also lose their power due to sudden fame and the temptation to enjoy the attention, money, and sexual favors offered to them. This is a relatively new problem due to the increasing popular interest in shamanism today.

A New Way of Seeing

Being able to *see* into the world of spirits is essential to shamanism. It is this gift of seeing that enables shamans to peer past the veil of everyday reality into other realms of nonordinary or spiritual reality.

Shamans are able to see these alternative realities by altering their ordinary, everyday states of consciousness. Shamans in different areas use different techniques or different combinations of methods, which will be discussed in great detail in later chapters. Most of these methods are used in other disciplines, as well—from working with magic to religious practice to participating in different forms of psychotherapy and healing. What makes this special way of seeing or perceiving a part of shamanism is the way it is used in combination with other shamanic activities to help and heal.

Some basic methods that promote nonordinary seeing include:

♦ **Meditation or contemplation**   This is a type of focused and relaxed concentration, where someone is in a receptive mode, letting in whatever thoughts and perceptions come, but not interpreting or holding on to any of them.

♦ **Hallucinogenic plants**   These plants have the ability to produce altered states of consciousness characterized by visions and insights. Some examples of these drugs are ayuahuasca, peyote, and psychedelic mushrooms.

♦ **Drumming and rattling**   This is the repeated use of a percussion instrument to make a recurring, rhythmic sound that helps to transport one into an altered state of consciousness.

♦ **Singing, chanting, whistling, or prayer**   The shaman and sometimes others in a shamanic ceremony make recurring rhythmic sounds that help to produce an altered state. Often these songs and chants indicate what the shaman hopes to see or the results he or she hopes to produce through the ceremony.

♦ **Tobacco smoke**   Altered states can be produced by either ingesting or blowing the smoke of tobacco leaves. This is a common practice in the Upper Amazon and elsewhere throughout North, South, and Central America.

No matter how it is achieved, the ability to see is fundamental to working as a shaman. It is the essential building block on which all else rests, because a shaman has to be able to look at and be aware of this other reality before he or she can begin to work with it to gain information or power. If you want to practice shamanic activities yourself, you, too, need to learn how to see like a shaman.

Bon Voyage

Decide your main purpose, goals, or objectives in learning about shamanism. Keep them in mind as you read this book.

Getting Started

Try to think of shamanic seeing as looking at the spaces around things. Rather than seeing things directly, look for the auras or energies around objects and people. It is a type of unfocused seeing, during which you are looking off in space, rather than at concrete forms. Or alternatively, it is the kind of seeing in your mind's eye that occurs when you are in a relaxed, receptive, meditative state and perceptions freely enter your mind.

Do Try This at Home

To get the feeling of seeing yourself, try the following unfocused seeing exercise, which I learned when I studied with a shaman. It's taken from my book, *Shamanism and Personal Mastery:*

> Pick out some object or point on the wall and stare at it for about five minutes. You will find that soon your vision will start turning fuzzy and unfocused, and you may notice changes in the object or point you are staring at. You may see an aura emerge around it, or you may even see it disappear. Or possibly it may change shape or vibrate.

> For an even more intense experience of this process of seeing, try looking at another person for five or ten minutes. Pick a point in the center of the person's forehead, but don't look into his or her eyes, because that is too intense. Again you may notice some interesting changes, as you shift from direct looking to seeing into this other space. Sometimes, you may see the person's face turn into a mask. Or the person's face may seem to disappear. From these changes, you may pick up insights or information about the other person.

Stepping Into Another World

By seeing, shamans are able to not only contact and communicate with spirits from other dimensions of reality, but they believe that they travel to these worlds in various ways. The shamans from Siberia travel to other worlds by riding the sound of a drum. In other traditions, shamans use drumming or chanting to create an altered state of consciousness, and then they follow a "path" to another world—such as walking along the tree roots leading down into the underworld, an approach used by some traditional Upper Amazon tribes.

Whatever their means of travel, shamans journey to other worlds for specific purposes—to get information, to get the help of various spirits, to battle with spirit entities causing harm, or to retrieve the soul of a patient who has been captured by a harmful spirit. This form of travel in an altered state of consciousness or trance is commonly referred to as going on a shamanic journey or journeying. The term soul travel is sometimes used, too.

Where shamans go can vary, depending on the shaman and the usual practices in their community. Sometimes they will travel to a remote location on the earth, often called the middle world, where spirits are thought to reside. But other times, they may travel to the upper world or higher world, which is the spiritual realm located in the air or above the earth and is often the area where teachers, spiritual guides, and spiritual helpers are found besides being on earth. Or they may travel to the lower world or underworld, which is the spiritual realm located underground or below the earth. This is often the area where power animals are found, although they may be found on earth, too.)

Where shamans go, who they go to see, and what kind of assistance they are looking for depends on the shaman, the tradition they are following, the local situation, the needs of the patient, the spiritual helpers they have acquired through their practice, and many other factors. It's a very intuitive process, developed through years of training for many shamans. You can learn to apply many of these techniques to both help yourself and others.

Working with Energy and Power

Besides using their ability to see and travel into another world to contact and communicate with spirit helpers, shamans seek to work with energy and power to gain knowledge or to heal. Shamans describe this ability in various ways, but whether they call it spiritual energy, force, or power, the goal is to gain this power to achieve their goal in shamanizing, whatever it may be—to heal, gain information, overcome a problem, and so on.

This power, in turn, can come from various sources—the assistance of teachers and spiritual helpers, the aid of *power animals*, also called *animal helpers*, and assorted *sacred objects*, also called *power objects*, that provide the shaman with spiritual energy or power during a ritual. These objects can take various forms, including staffs, sometimes made from a tree branch or purchased already made; stones; shells; feathers; or pictures. Shamans in different traditions use different objects, and often objects are selected because they have personal meaning.

Power is critical, because shamans can use it to overcome the forces causing disease in a patient, or other problems. They also need power to overcome any spiritual attacks on themselves they may encounter, such as when a shaman sucks out the disease from a patient. A shaman wants to prevent these negative forces from affecting himself or herself, much like doctors or nurses seeks protection from the illnesses affecting their patients. In turn, since shamans work with power, they have generally been regarded as very powerful, effective people in their communities, which is why community members turn to them for help. In this book you will learn to work with various types of power techniques, objects, and power helpers to achieve your goals and to help others.

Shaman Says

Want power? The various tools a shaman works with to gain and use power include **power animals**, which shamans call on for assistance when they are seeking knowledge or attempting to do a healing, and **power objects**, which are considered to have a spiritual force or energy.

The Goal: Knowing and Healing

Ultimately, put all the techniques for working with energy and power, stepping into another world, and learning to see together, and the goal is to gain knowledge and heal. Traditionally, the role of the shaman was to gain this knowledge and healing ability to help those in his or her community, and many modern shamans, particularly in developing countries or in ethnic communities in the developed world, still do that. But as noted previously, many modern-day practitioners use shamanism for other purposes—from self-help and self-healing to motivation and conflict resolution.

This ability to know and heal comes from many sources including:

- ◆ Developing your intuition
- ◆ Understanding your dreams and using them for guidance
- ◆ Altering your state of consciousness
- ◆ Projecting yourself into the future
- ◆ Becoming more sensitive to others and their needs
- ◆ Learning about natural techniques for healing, including the use of herbs and medicinal plants

> **Wise Ways**
>
> Different types of shamans specialize in different types of knowing and healing, and they learn what they are good at, much like any professional. And as appropriate, they make referrals to other practitioners, who may have more knowledge in a particular area, such as when a Native American shaman refers a patient with a serious illness he can't cure to a physician.

To develop your own abilities to employ shamanic techniques, think of where you want to focus your efforts. Ask yourself, what are your main purposes, goals, or objectives in learning these methods and what approach is most comfortable for you. Even if your goal isn't to become a practicing shaman (this path generally takes years of training—and is one for which shamans usually feel a special call followed by serving as an apprentice to a master shaman) you can still learn and apply these techniques to help and heal yourself or others.

The Least You Need to Know

- ◆ Shamanism is an age-old form of wisdom and healing that dates back to the beginnings of human history in the Stone Age or Paleolithic era.
- ◆ Shamanism is a practice of healing and solving personal and community problems, in which a shaman contacts the spirits for their help, usually by going into an altered state of consciousness; sometimes the shaman will call on the spirits or travel into their world.

- Shamanism takes many forms throughout the world.

- Shamans use a variety of methods to promote non-ordinary seeing, including meditation or contemplation, hallucinogenic plants, drumming and rattling, singing, chanting, whistling, or prayer, and even tobacco smoke.

- Although traditional shamans have used shamanism to primarily help others, many modern practitioners of shamanism have used these methods for other purposes, including personal growth, self-development, and self-healing.

Chapter 2

The Origins of Shamanism

In This Chapter

♦ Evidence of shamanism in prehistory

♦ How shamanism came to America and the West

♦ Encounters with Christians, explorers, and rationalists

♦ The arrival of the anthropologists

♦ The expansion of knowledge about shamans

Shamanism dates back 30,000 to 45,000 years ago to some of our early human ancestors. As one anthropological wag once put it: "Prostitution isn't the oldest profession; shamanism is." And research by anthropologists suggests this is true.

How It All Began

Shamanism very possibly emerged as a form of magic to help ensure a successful hunt for game or to successfully gather plants or the leavings of kills by animals. As archaeologists theorize, these early humans engaged in group rituals to raise their energy, appeal to the spirits for help, or increase their hope of success before setting out on a hunting or gathering expedition. Or perhaps they engaged in such rituals after a hunt or other expeditions to celebrate their success and hope for continued good fortune.

Compelling Evidence from the Rocks and Caves

Some of the most compelling evidence that shamanism developed at the very beginnings of modern human history comes from caves and rocks that have drawings dating back to the Paleolithic era.

One famous image, called the "dancing sorcerer" or "le sorciere," was found in the Cave of Les Trois Freres in France and might have been drawn between 30,000 and 10,000 B.C.E. Painted on a rock wall, the image features a half-man, half-animal, with the face and legs of a man, and the antlers and tail of a stag (Larsen, 1988, 9). Although this figure is called a "sorcerer," this term is really used in the sense of a shaman or magician, rather than as someone who is practicing black or evil magic today.

An image of the "dancing sorcerer" from the Cave of Les Trois Freres in France, dating back to 30,000–10,000 B.C.E.

Another very famous image of what could be a shaman depicts a man lying next to a large bison that is pierced by a spear. Nearby, is a bird on a pole. According to anthropologist Stephen Larsen, author of *The Shaman's Doorway*, this image is thought by many anthropologists to represent a Paleolithic shaman in trance, though possibly the man could be simply asleep, dreaming, or in some other altered state of consciousness. The bird, which is on the shaman's staff, is thought to symbolize the flight of the spirit.

An image from the Cave of Lascaux in France, dating back to 17,000 B.C.E.

Anthropologists have found examples of burials from the Neanderthals, a heavy-boned big-brained early human who lived from about 130,000–30,000 B.C.E., in which the bodies were buried with grave goods, including stone tools, animal bones (such as a cave bear), and even flower arrangements, suggesting a religious belief system. These examples of burials date back to at least 90,000 years ago (West, 1998, 318–319). While anthropologists aren't sure whether these Neanderthals were eliminated by the modern Homo sapiens or might have intermarried with them, this suggestion of a religious belief system and a belief in spirits means that maybe even the Neanderthals had an early form of shamanism, too. If so, shamanism goes back even further into the past—further evidence of shamanism's long-standing and enduring power.

> **⚠ CAUTION**
>
> **Off the Path**
>
> Theories about humans' earliest roots are often very controversial because of lack of evidence.

More Hunting Magic

Other more modern examples can be used to infer evidence of shamanism's early roots in hunting magic, too. For instance, when anthropologists and explorers first encountered the Eskimos in Greenland in the 1920s, they found evidence of shamanic ceremonies. As described by Walter Burkert in *Shamans Through Time*, these Eskimos used to live largely on seal hunting, and they believed that the seals belonged to Sedna, the mistress of animals, who they called the Old Woman "down there." When the tribe didn't find enough seals and felt threatened by famine, they believed this was due to Sedna's anger. So they arranged for a festival and called on a shaman to help calm Sedna's anger.

During this festival, the shaman would go into a trance. Then, in this trance state, he would travel down into the sea, where he would meet Sedna and ask her why she was angry. Most typically, her anger was due to some human failing, such as a woman breaking one of the many taboos restricting her behavior. As a result, Sedna wasn't sending any seals because she was covered with dirt because of human uncleanliness. So now it was the shamans job to clean the "mistress of animals" and ask for her forgiveness. Then, once he succeeded—the usual result of such a shamanic journey—he returned with the animals, at least in symbolic form, after which the hunters would go out hunting with renewed confidence and optimism resulting in their success.

Off the Path

Very often, human problems are traced to human failings of all types—from breaking taboos and generally not doing something right to feelings of jealousy, envy, anger, and rage. Such failings not only disturb others in the community, but they are believed to upset the spirits. Hence the need for shamans to mediate by appealing to the spirits—both in ancient times and today—to put things right again after humans have screwed up.

Anthropologists in other areas have found hunting peoples—or people who used to hunt—who have called on shamans for their help. For instance, some hunting-gathering peoples in the Amazon used to have (and some groups still do have) a medicine man or shaman, called a *payé* or *paje*, whose main role was to go into trance using certain drugs to contact the masters of the animals—the master of game in the mountains near the woods and the master of fish in the river—to ask them to send the animals for hunting and fishing.

From the Paleolithic to the Present

As early people developed and spread across the globe, they adapted, and so did shamanism. As the geography, culture, and climate changed, for example, so did the objects shamans used, the types of rituals they performed, and the purposes of these rituals. They still went into an altered state of consciousness and sought to contact the spirits for their assistance—but they sought help from different spirits and used different techniques to get into this altered state.

For instance, after the Neolithic revolution, when humans developed agriculture about 10,000 years ago in different parts of the world, people were able to grow and store food and settle down. They also began to domesticate animals and form villages, some of which expanded into the beginnings of cities. Because conditions changed, so did shamanism.

For instance, instead of trying to help hunters have a better hunt and capture more game, shamans now engaged in rituals to promote a better harvest. They might also perform rituals to find lost animals or have better weather, such as seeking more rain if it was dry or sunnier days if it was wet and stormy. And shamans were there to help, too, if people got ill or were envious of others who had more property—a development that came with the beginnings of agriculture, since now a surplus and an accumulation of goods was possible in settled villages.

Shamans also helped cure disease or bad fortune, which was believed to be caused by evil spirits or witchcraft. And although Shamans lost some power to priests affiliated with more organized religions during this time, they still played a very important role in the day-to-day healing and community problem-solving.

Shaman Says

The **Neolithic revolution** was a really big change in society that came around 10,000 years ago, when humans developed agriculture and began to domesticate animals. With these changes, people could live closer together and formed into villages, some of which grew larger and larger, until they developed into the civilization we know today.

Times, They Are A-Changin'

A good example of the way shamanism changed is the elaborate belief system that the Maya developed and which the Mayan shamans and later priests incorporated in their rituals.

A Mayan shaman or priest-shaman dressed in full finery to conduct a ritual. Rituals were generally performed at the top of one of the temples, such as the tall Temple of the Sun or Temple of the Moon in the square at Tikal.

The Mayans' predecessors were hunter-gatherers who believed in ancestor worship and practiced shamanism. They believed the world was divided into four parts, with a vertical tree running through it. The Mayan civilization emerged around 1500 B.C.E. and was a world of grand temples and pyramids, canals for irrigation, fertile fields of corn, and an intricate religious belief system based on a pantheon of gods, including rain and fertility gods and a very powerful jaguar god and sacred kings. Like their hunter-gather ancestors, they believed in an underworld, upper world, and World Tree that sprouted up between the two worlds like an ear of corn, while a cosmic serpent crossed the skies.

Shamans in this early society went into trances and traversed this world, seeking the help of the many spirits who dwelled there. Mayan shamanism incorporated the intricacies of the Mayan belief system, which had developed along with a priestly caste by at least the height of the Mayan civilization (Coe, 1993, 9). When the Spanish arrived and conquered the Maya, along with the Aztec and Inca civilizations of Central and South America, the Maya incorporated major Christian symbols, even combining the Cross of Christ with their World Tree (Friedl, Schele, and Parker, 1993, 37–39).

So today, the Mayan shamans offer a mix of techniques and beliefs from the Paleolithic world of the hunters, the Neolithic revolution, the rise of civilization, and the influence of Christianity today. The transformation of Mayan shamanism parallels the change and adaptation of shamanism elsewhere all over the world. Today, shamanism is still changing.

Shaman Says

The **urban revolution** is the third major change in the history of humanity and marks the beginning of civilization as we know it today. It began in about 3000 B.C.E. in some areas. Among the first civilizations were Mesopotamia and Egypt. Around 1500 B.C.E., the first city states developed in Central and South America as the empires of the Maya, Aztec, and Inca.

Big City Shamanism

The next big transformation of society involved the development of cities and is commonly referred to as the *Urban Revolution*. It began about 3000 B.C.E. in many areas, such as in Egypt and parts of the Middle East and Southern Asia; though in other areas, such as Mesoamerica, this revolution didn't begin until about 1500 B.C.E.; and in some areas, it didn't develop until much later. However, wherever the urban revolution occurred, the shamans adapted to that, too, now ministering to people with urban problems.

Moonlighting as a Shaman

In most communities, shamanism became a kind of specialized activity, performed by only a few members of a tribe, clan, or other group. These were the individuals who were most skilled in the ability to go into trance or other altered state of consciousness.

Shamans typically combined their spirit work with other day-to-day activities such as farming, fishing, herding cattle or sheep. As special craft occupations developed, a shaman might have become a tradesman, while practicing shamanism on the side.

With the rise of the cities, shamans might have been shopkeepers, carpenters, pottery makers, artists, or engaged in other urban occupations on the side. People still turned to a shaman when they were ill or had other problems, and the shaman would use the techniques he had developed and apply them, in keeping with the belief system of the people, to learn from or appeal to the spirits to help and heal.

> **Wise Ways**
>
> Generally, shamans were men, but sometimes women became shamans, too. Because shamans were predominantly men, I generally use the male pronouns to refer to shamans of the past.

In some cases, shamans were considered part of the religious establishment, such as priests or other forms of clergy. But more generally, shamans were individuals who were of the people, not part of an organized religious group. In fact, that's a distinction anthropologists often make, pointing out that priests get their power and position from being part of an organized bureaucratic and established religion, where they perform formalized and standardized rites. By contrast, shamans get their powers from their direct connection with the spiritual beings (Turner, 1972, 78–84). And that's what has sometimes gotten shamans in trouble—when they are seen as a threat by the religious or political establishment, leading to many persecutions of shamans. But then, that's another story, to be discussed in Chapter 21.

While shamans in most societies have developed their abilities and practice their crafts on their own, in a few societies, many members of the community have become shamans and have participated in large group healing rituals. One such group is the !Kung bushmen, in the Kalahari Desert in Botswana, Africa, where traditionally about half or more of the men of the tribe dance, chant, and sing their way into a trance to do a healing for the whole community. During such a trance, a healer can lay his hands on members of the group to pull out the sickness from individual people or the group members as a whole (Konner, 1997, 172–176). In some !Kung groups, many of the women are shamans, too.

> **CAUTION** **Off the Path**
>
> Often shamans are confused with priests, who are part of the religious establishment and get their position and authority from their training and performance of established rituals and rites. By contrast, shamans gain their position and power from being able to go into an altered state and communicate directly with spirits.

Coming to America and the West

So while traditional shamanism has roots deep in the past, it has changed with the changing times. In more recent times, starting in the late 1960s and early 1970s, once shamanism attracted the interest of people living in the Western world, and the United States, in particular, it was transformed even more. It became a New Age, self-help version of shamanism that incorporates some of the traditional elements, such as contacting the spirit world and altered states of consciousness, but with a new individual focus. This latest version of shamanism represents a kind of mixing and picking from many different traditions.

Contemporary shamanism has been embraced in different ways by various groups, including the following:

◆ Medical practitioners seeking alternative medical therapies

◆ Psychologists and psychiatrists seeking new ways to understand and treat mental illness

◆ Therapists, counselors, group facilitators, and workshop leaders seeking new paths to personal development and self-help

◆ Religious leaders and individual believers seeking a more ecstatic approach to revitalize religion

◆ Business leaders interested in spiritual methods to better motivate and inspire employees and themselves

◆ Individuals seeking to help and heal themselves, as well as find a community with other seekers and have fun

Here and there, some grumblings have erupted as some groups with long traditions have felt their beliefs, teachings, and practices have been borrowed—sometimes they say "stolen" or "ripped off"—by others who have used their methods out of context or without permission (for more on this, see Chapter 21).

But mostly, this New Age-modern Western strain of shamanism has flourished, primarily in middle-class America, and has taken on a life of its own that mixes shamanism along with other strategies for success and self-improvement.

So how did shamanism ever reach middle-class America? Well, that's an interesting story that goes back about 500 years ago, when the first Western travelers began to encounter the shamans. It's a story recounted in *Shamans Through Time: 500 Years on the Path to Knowledge* by Jeremy Narby and Frances Huxley. Here's how it happened.

The First Contact: From the Christians to the Rationalists

The first outsiders to discover the traditional shamans were European priests and explorers in the mid-sixteenth to mid-eighteenth centuries, primarily from Spain, England, France, Russia, and Germany. Most of these first observers were staunch Christians, even clergymen, at a time when church and lay authorities in Europe were cracking down on witches. Their initial reaction was to see the practice of shamanism as akin to witchcraft or consorting with the devil.

For example, when Gonzalo Fernandez de Oviedo, a Spanish navigator and natural historian, arrived in the New World, he described the Indians of Hispaniola (now Haiti and the Dominican Republic) as practicing devil worship. Writing in 1535, he complained about how their wise men used tobacco as a sacred herb to gain advice about the weather and war. To him, this was getting the "devil's opinion" (Narby & Huxley, 2001, 11–12).

The early European explorers and priests didn't understand what the shamans were doing and largely saw them as violating the principles of Christianity, at a time when Christianity was considered to be the one true faith throughout Europe.

> **Wise Ways**
>
> Other explorers who wrote about early shamanic practices in the "New World" included French priest André Thévet and Antoine Biet. Thévet, who visited Brazil in the sixteenth century, described the natives as turning to the devil's "ministers" for advice. Biet, who visited what would become French Guyana in the seventeenth century, thought that the local doctors, called piayés, were invoking the power of the devil to cure illnesses.

From Devil Worshippers to Scam Artists

Then, in the 1700s, with the arrival of the Enlightenment and the Age of Reason, Western observers arrived with a different view. Now they thought of the shamans as simply imposters or jugglers, who claimed to communicate with spirits but were really just fooling the people by using "song and dance, tricks, and slight of hand" or tapping the power of the imagination to make people believe (Narby & Huxley, 2001, 21–22).

Typical of these rational visitors was Johann Georg Gmelin, a German professor of chemistry and botany, who explored Siberia for 10 years and wrote about his observations of shamans. In one passage, he described visiting a Tungus shaman, who put on his leather shaman coat hanging with iron instruments, and began leaping and shouting, while other participants began singing along with him. But Gmelin remained unconvinced that the shaman was really in touch with any spirits or had any wisdom, concluding thus:

At length, after a lot of hocus-pocus and sweating, he would have had us believe that the devils were there. He asked us what we wanted to know. We put a question to him. He started his conjuring tricks, while two others were assisting him. In the end we were confirmed in our opinion that it was all humbug (Narby & Huxley, 2001, 28).

This rationalist view was held by many other writers, including:

♦ Botanist Stephan Petrovich Krasbeninnkov, who visited the people of Kamchatka in Eastern Siberia. He described the shamans as performing "crude tricks" for "superstitious people" (Narby & Huxley, 2001, 29–30).

♦ Well-known French man of letters and philosophy Denis Diderot, who described the shamans as "imposters" and "jugglers" doing tricks to entertain and enchant. He described them thus:

> They present themselves as interpreters of the gods. To do their tricks, they use the bones and skins of serpents … They persuade the majority of the people that they have ecstatic transports, in which the genies reveal the future and hidden things to them. This is how they persuade people of whatever they wish.

> But the main occupation of jugglers … is Medicine. Although they generally exercise this art with principles based on knowledge of medicinal plants, experience, and conjecture … they usually mix in superstition and charlatanism (Narby & Huxley, 2001, 34).

> **Wise Ways**
>
> The rationalist ideal was to be a "man of science," so the rationalists view the spirits the shamans contacted as simply fanciful creations of a superstitious mind or even fantasies used to trick others so they would believe and could be influenced by the shaman/magician/trickster/imposter.

And so it went through the 1700s to the mid-1800s. The rationalists imagined that the shamans were simply faking it, because they looked at the world in rational terms themselves. Meanwhile, the Catholic priests and Protestant ministers who encountered shamans thought they were doing the work of the devil.

A New View of Shamans

Attitudes toward shamans and their practices started changing with the arrival of anthropologists in the late 1800s. Unfortunately, the first anthropologists who arrived—mostly white men from the colonial powers such as Britain and France—approached the natives they studied as if they were exotic primitives or "savages." For instance, Sir Edward B. Tylor, one of the founders of the discipline of anthropology, writing in the 1870s, described the native peoples as members of "lower races" who believed in animism—the belief that spiritual beings exist in everything in nature.

In time, anthropologists became aware of their biases, and by the 1950s and 1960s, they were taking a much broader point of view, trying to see and explain the world as the people they studied saw it did. Initially, however, they were very much like foreign travelers enthralled by the unusual customs in new worlds.

Some of the first anthropologists to study shamans in the late 1800s to early 1900s, were:

♦ **Everard F. Im Thurn,** a British anthropologist, lived with the Macusi Indians in British Guiana. He described taking part in a ceremony conducted by a Macusi doctor called a *peaiman*, in which the peaiman waved several bunches of green branches cut from the savannah bushes, as Im Thurn and 30 other participants lay in hammocks. The peaiman roared out questions and commands to the spirits, called *kenaimas*, who appeared in the form of tigers, deer, monkeys, birds, turtles, snakes; and nearby Indians yelled, growled, and shouted back their answers. To Im Thurn, however, the ceremony was just a "clever piece of ventriloquism and acting" and he wasn't cured of his headache, though the peaiman offered to cure that (Narby & Huxley, 2001, 43–47). Still his account reflects a sea change in that he was one of the first anthropologists to actually participate in a native ceremony.

♦ **Franz Boas,** an influential American anthropologist born in Germany, spent a year in the early 1880s living among the Inuit, popularly known as the Eskimos, on Baffin Island near Alaska. In an essay, "A Year Among the Eskimos," that appeared in the *Journal of the American Geographical Society* in 1887, he described his year there, including his observations of the local medicine-men, called *angakoq*. These medicine-men used incantations to call on the minor spirits, called the *Tornait*, that appeared in the form of men, bears, or stones, to seek their help in discovering the causes of sickness and death.

Apart from the early anthropologists, the study of shamans in Siberia got an early start from the Russian and Polish revolutionaries and activists who were exiled to Siberia. It would seem that since they had little to do in these frozen, isolated areas, they began studying the indigenous people and their shamans. Later, they wrote about them, setting the stage for future study in Siberia. Their writings also popularized the term "shaman," which originally derives from an account about the Tungus of Siberia, written by Avvakum Petrovich, a Russian clergyman, in his autobiography published in 1672 (Narby & Huxley, 2001, 18).

Among these Russian and Polish exiles who ended up in Siberia studying the native peoples and their shamans were:

♦ **Wenceslas Sieroskevshi,** a Pole, who lived as a political exile among the Yakut people in Siberia for 12 years and published his book about them through the Imperial Russian Geographical Society in 1896 (Narby & Huxley, 2001, 49–50).

- **Waldemar Bogoras,** a Russian, exiled to northeastern Siberia for revolutionary activities. After studying the natives, he fled to the U.S., participated in an American Museum of Natural History expedition to study the Chukchee, and later settled in New York and wrote *The Chukchee* (Narby & Huxley, 2001, 53–57).

- **Vladimir Ilich Jochelson,** a Russian ethnographer and linguist sent to eastern Siberia for revolutionary activities, where he also studied the natives. These studies later led him to join an expedition by the American Museum of Natural History, and subsequently he published his study of *The Koryak* in 1908 (Narby & Huxley, 2001, 58–62).

The books of these exiles helped to set the stage for a growing interest in the Siberian shaman as the powerful village wise man. He dressed in animal skins and beat the drum, while singing in an all-night ceremony to summon the animal spirits to send disease and other troubles away from his village.

The writings of these early explorers and anthropologists in turn helped to open the doors to learning about shamanism. Over the next 100 years, this interest exploded, as more anthropologists, plus journalists, psychologists, and many others began to discover shamans all over the world.

The Least You Need to Know

- Shamanism dates back to the beginnings of the first modern humans, from about 100,000 to 30,000 years ago, depending on different interpretations of the early burials and rock art.

- As humans spread around the world, from Paleolithic times onward, their practices of magic, religion, and shamanism spread, too, and they adapted their practices to the changes in society and their environment.

- With the rise of cities, shamans generally practiced shamanism on a part-time basis, combining it with other everyday activities.

- Explorers and anthropologists were responsible for documenting the various kinds of shamanism throughout the world.

3

Shamanism Around the World

In This Chapter

- ◆ The expanding interest in shamanism since the early 1900s
- ◆ Shamanism from the 1910s to 1950s
- ◆ Shamanism and the hippie generation
- ◆ Shamanism goes global

Once anthropologists began investigating shamanism, interest in it spread quickly. Mircea Eliade, a historian of religion who became a University of Chicago faculty member for 30 years, wrote the first comprehensive work on the subject, *Shamanism: Archaic Techniques of Ecstasy*, which was published in France in 1951. (Its original title was *Le Chamanisme et les techniques archaiques do l'extase*; the book was translated into English in 1964.)

Eliade's book was a breakthrough in providing a broad overview of what was known about shamanism at the time. Eliade also helped to show how shamanism took various forms all over the world, citing examples from Siberia, Central and North Asia, North and South America, Southeast Asia, Europe, Tibet, China, and the Far East. (However, he did not do original research on this topic, and he misunderstood the widespread traditional use of consciousness-altering herbs and drugs in shamanism, calling the use of mind-altering plants a "degenerative" form of shamanism.)

Thereafter, other anthropologists built on Eliade's work by doing field studies of shamans, at first mainly in small isolated indigenous groups. Then as these groups were pulled into modern urban society, anthropologists began to study the shamans in the urban neighborhoods where they worked.

By the late 1950s and 1960s, journalists, psychologists, counselors and others were going to visit shamans around the world and bringing back their reports, as well as adapting shamanic techniques to create the modern New Age explosion of interest in shanamism.

But that's getting ahead of the story.

In this chapter you'll find out how shamanism became introduced to the modern world to become a worldwide phenomenon starting in the 1900s. This occurred as different forms of shamanism were discovered everywhere—and increasingly, those studying it began to participate in shamanic rituals and sought to present shamanism from the point of view of the shamans and the participants in shamanic ceremonies.

The World Takes Notice: The 1910s to 1950s

Through the first half of the twentieth century, anthropologists began to look more closely at just what shamans did. In fact, there was an explosion of interest all over the Western world, including Britain, the United States, Denmark, Russia, France, Switzerland, and Australia.

So anthropologists became the main source of information on shamans during the first half of the twentieth century, and some began to gather this information together to draw some general conclusions about who shamans were and what they did. For instance, William Howells, who focused on Siberian and Eskimo shamans, compared his findings with the research on shamans by other anthropologists in Africa, Asia, North and South America, and Polynesia.

Howells was especially impressed by the finding that shamans traveled with the help of animal souls and spirits into all three realms of nature, helped cure villagers and get back lost souls, used expert showmanship and management of self-hypnosis, relieved individual and community tensions, and gained acclaim from members of the public for his help. In his 1948 book, *The Heathens*, he wrote:

> A shaman is a medium and a diviner, but his powers do not stop there …. He can go at will to the other world, and he can see and treat with souls or spirits, meeting them on their own ground …

> Shamans seem to flourish … mainly among people whose religion is not highly organized and whose social structure is also simple and loosely knit …

> A true shaman is a lone wolf, following his own dictates.

Wise Ways

According to Narby and Huxley, some of the early anthropologists from around the globe who studied shamanism were:

◆ **Knud Rasmussen,** a Danish anthropologist who led a Danish expedition to the Artic from 1921 to 1924, where he interviewed several shaman and told their stories. For instance, he described how one shaman, Niviatsian, had a near-death experience hunting walrus, and when he recovered, as Rasmussen writes: "the walrus, which had failed to kill him, became his first helping spirit."

◆ **Sergei M. Skirokogoroff,** a Russian ethnographer who studied the Tungus and Manchus of Manchuria.

◆ **Williard Z. Park,** an American anthropologist who lived with and studied shamanism among the Northern Pauite in western Nevada in the early 1930s.

◆ **Alfred Métraux,** a French anthropologist who studied shamanism in South America among the forest people of the Guyanas and the Amazon basin.

◆ **Adophus Peter Elkin,** an Australian anthropologist who studied the indigenous medicine healers. He opposed the claim of some anthropologists and psychiatrists that shamans were mentally ill, describing them rather from his own acquaintance as "persons of special knowledge, self-assurance, and initiative."

◆ **Claude Lévi-Strauss,** the noted French anthropologist who observed shamans conducting curing sessions among the Cuna Indians in Panama. To him, the shaman was much like a psychoanalyst, except that while the psychoanalyst listens to the patient, the shaman speaks.

Loco Locals?

Meanwhile, as anthropologists began to investigate shamanism, some anthropologists and ethnopsychiatrists—psychiatrists or anthropologists with a psychiatric background who study ethnic groups—began to debate the mental health of shamans, since they were going into trance and thereby losing touch with everyday, mundane reality. Was going into an altered state a sign of insanity, they wondered? Some made this claim, including Howells, who thought that shamanism attracted "a certain psychological type: those who are less stable and more excitable than the average, but who have at the same time intelligence, ability, and … drive." But at least Howells found their shamanizing helped to give them social position and "psychiatric help," while helping to relieve tensions in the community.

Off the Path

Some anthropologists, psychiatrists, and psychologists who studied shamanism began to view their trances, spirit invocations, and otherworldly travel as symptoms of mental illness, such as schizophrenia and hysteria. It didn't matter if they never actually met shamans themselves—they drew their conclusions based on what they read about shamans!

Tuning In and Turning On: The 1950s to the 1970s

The next big sea change in learning about shamans came in the 1950s, when anthropologists increasingly became participants in shamanic activities and even journalists began to write about them.

In this period, many anthropologists began to conclude that shamans were a solid, well-grounded, well-respected group of people who were perfectly in touch with reality when they weren't shamanizing. Which made perfect sense. After all, why would someone in the community look to a shaman for wisdom or healing if that person didn't seem mentally sound and well-adjusted? So gradually, the tide was starting to turn, as anthropologists learned more about shamans and their practices and began to see them as a kind of professional group who had certain skills and knowledge, which they used to help and heal others in their community.

Then, in the 1960s, came the hippies, religious seekers, psychologists, and many others from the West who wanted to experience shamanism, adapt it to Western culture in various ways, and make it their own. For many, this route to enlightenment through shamanism came through hallucinogenic drugs—exemplified by Timothy Leary's message to the 60s generation: "Tune In, Turn On, Drop Out"—while others found ecstasy through shamanic meditation, chants, and dance.

In the process, the focus of shamanism for many people shifted from its traditional role in helping and healing others in the community to gaining insights about and healing oneself. Meanwhile, the research of anthropologists continued, providing both academics and this new generation of seekers with information on the practice of shamanism in still other areas of the world.

Bon Voyage

Francis Huxley went on to study the use of psychotropic drugs around the world, noting that the members of these native groups only use hallucinogens in a ritual setting to cure illnesses of the soul and body, for divination, to gain supernatural knowledge, and contact spirits—not for personal pleasure as in contemporary society (Huxley, 1985, 112–121).

For example, British anthropologist Francis Huxley became a participant in the 1950s, living with Urubu and Tembé people in the Brazilian Amazon. In his 1956 book, *Affable Savages: An Anthropologist Among the Urubu Indians of Brazil*, Huxley described how he participated in a big healing ceremony and tried some of the strong tobacco that the shamans smoked. As he describes it, everyone in the village came to the shaman's hut with their hammocks and hung them between the houseposts. Then, as the men, women, and children of the village stood or sat around the hut, each with a cigar of tobacco about 18 inches long, called a *tawari cigar*, the shaman began singing and beating time with a maraca.

These direct experiences by Howells and others helped to change anthropological thinking, since now they could better see the world as the shamans and indigenous people they studied did.

Though Huxley had trouble smoking the tobacco, and repeatedly coughed on the smoke, the others kept smoking and singing in a ceremony that went on until dawn. The shaman smoked five or six of these long cigars! The smoke from the cigar helped the shaman achieve an altered state of consciousness so he could summon his animal helper to help him cure the villagers who needed help (Narby & Huxley, 2001, 136–140).

Wise Ways

What was Wasson's experience with Maria Sabina like? Here's a brief excerpt from his article in *Life*.

> My friend Alan Richardson and I shared with a family of Indian friends a celebration of "holy communion" where "divine" mushrooms were first adored and then consumed. The Indians mingled Christian and pre-Christian elements in their religious practice … The rite was led by two women, mother and daughter, both of them curanederas, or shamans …

> Richardson and I were the first white men in recorded history to eat the divine mushrooms …

> At about 10:30 o'clock Eva Mendez cleaned the mushrooms of their grosser dirt and then, with prayers, passed Señora … broke a flower from the bouquet on the altar and used it to snuff out the flame of the only candle that was still burning. We were left in darkness and in darkness we remained until dawn …

> The visions … reached a plateau of intensity deep in the night, and they continued at that level until about 4 o'clock in the morning … They were in vivid color, always harmonious. They began with art motifs … Then they evolved into palaces with courts, arcades, gardens …

> From time to time the singing would stop, and then the Senora would fling forth spoken words … This was the mushroom speaking through her, God's words, as the Indians believe, answering the problems that had been posed by the participants. This was the Oracle." (Narby & Huxley, 2001, 141–147).

Seeking the Magic Mushroom

But the *really big* change came when R. Gordon Wasson, an American banker, wrote an article entitled "Seeking the Magic Mushroom" that appeared in *Life* magazine in May 1957. In it, he described his experiences in taking hallucinogenic mushrooms with a Mexican shaman named Maria Sabina, although he tried to disguise her identity by calling her "Eva Mendez." Whereas up until this time the research on shamans was read almost exclusively by anthropologists and other academics, now the several hundred thousand readers of *Life* magazine became aware of it. Suddenly, the world of shamans was opened up to a popular audience, and it triggered a wave of Western tourism to villages in Mexico by the rising hippie generation (Narby & Huxley, 2001, 141–147).

Maria Sabina, the well-known Mexican healer.

(Photograph by Bonnie Colodzon)

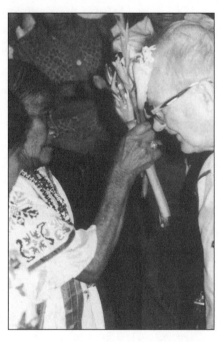

Marina Sabina conducting a healing ceremony, using a bunch of flowers to cleanse and provide healing energy to one of the participants in the ceremony.

(Photograph by Bonnie Colodzon)

An even bigger deluge of interest came in 1968 when UCLA anthropology student Carlos Castaneda published his account of studying with a Yaqui sorcerer named don Juan. While anthropologists generally make a clear distinction between the *shaman*, who uses his contacts with the spirit world to help and heal, and the *sorcerer* who uses this contact for personal aggrandizement and even harming others, Castaneda's work became part of the popular literature of shamanism.

Yet, while Carlos Castaneda's writings about don Juan became tremendously popular, many anthropologists and others questioned the integrity of his work, questioning whether he really did have all the personal experiences he claimed with don Juan.

A commonly held view is that Castaneda did engage in some real research, at least initially, but then may have drawn on other research to create a composite character and used many fictional devices. But, whether completely accurate or not, Castaneda created a compelling work that attracted millions of readers and led to a continuing outpouring of books about further conversations and adventures with don Juan. In 1998, he even published a book of energy exercises based on the teachings of Mexican shamans, called *Magical Passes*.

Despite any controversy about whether don Juan was really a shaman or a sorcerer or whether Carlos Castaneda actually studied with him or wrote a largely fictional work based on some research, Castaneda's book contributed to the growing popular interest in shamanism.

Through the 1960s and 1970s, anthropologists and others continued to explore the world of shamans even more deeply, increasingly as participants. For example, in 1974, anthropologist Barbara Myerhoff published *Peyote Hunt: The Sacred Journey to the Huichol Indians*, in which she described her experience in traveling with the Huichol Indians of Mexico across the desert to look for the peyote used in their ceremonies. Before the trip, she had ingested some peyote herself under the guidance of one Huichol shaman, and she experienced a growing euphoria, feelings of good will, and the disappearance of time and space. She found herself floating, and at one point, found herself impaled on the huge Tree of Life, also called the *axis mundi* or world pole, that connects the earth with the underworld and heaven. For her, it was an extremely significant vision, since this is the tree which shamans use to go on their magical flights—and the image she saw was "exactly the same as a Mayan glyph" which she saw several years later (Narby & Huxley, 2001, 154–157).

Though he didn't call it shamanism, Timothy Leary's call to "tune in, turn on, and drop out," played some part of this exploration of shamanism in getting people to look for other ways to explore

> **Off the Path**
>
> For a time, the UCLA anthropology department debated whether to give Castenada a degree, but ultimately did. Meanwhile, at anthropology meetings scholars debated whether Castaneda really was doing valid anthropology. One especially critical debunker, Richard de Mille, published two books on the topic *Castaneda's Journey* and *The Don Juan Papers: Further Castaneda Controversies*.

> **Shaman Says**
>
> **Esalen** was a major center for personal growth and spiritual learning that grew up in Big Sur, located on the coast of California about halfway between San Francisco and Los Angeles, in the late 1960s and flourished especially in the 1970s and 1980s. Many programs in transpersonal psychology, as well as shamanism, were held there.

altered states of consciousness. I participated in this early explosion of shamanic interest myself in California. Among other things, I went to a series of workshops at *Esalen* to explore altered states of consciousness, from hypnosis to dreaming. Alhough they weren't on the formal curriculum, many drugs once used by shamans were widely available—from psilocybin to mushrooms to peyote—along with LSD.

Some Western initiates also began bringing back what they learned from Indian shamans and developing this into a smorgasbord of teachings, such as Brant Secunda, who held "Dance of the Deer Workshops" to teach others about the ways of the Huichol shamans and their search for peyote. He became an apprentice of don José Matsuwa of Mexico for 12 years, during which time he learned the ancient teachings, was adopted by the group, and now works with don José Matsuwa's granddaughter, doña Josepha Medrano, to continue don José Matsuwa's vision. Among other activities, he leads groups on regular vision quests and pilgrimages to places of power to learn the Huichol way.

A Huichol yarn painting depicting several shamans calling on the various spirit helpers, including the deer and snake, to help them gain knowledge, understanding, and power in a healing ceremony.

At this point, however, medical practitioners were still quite skeptical of the healing powers of shamanism, and as shamanism became more widely known, local governments where traditional shamans practiced joined forces with the medical establishment and churches. They began to crack down on shamans, trying to put them out of business. The irony is that as the countries with traditional shamans sought to eliminate shamanism, the practice was growing increasingly popular in the West.

Shamanism Goes Global—From the 1980s to Today

Since the 1980s, shamanism has increasingly gone global, as traditional societies have become more integrated into mainstream society, and mainstream society has increasingly embraced traditional—and new variations of—shamanism. Furthermore, many anthropologists have turned to studying shamanic practices by ethnic healers living in cities, a healing practice which anthropologists today call *ethnomedicine*.

Shaman Says

Medicine as it is practiced today can be divided in three main categories:

- **Biomedicine** — the practice of ordinary, modern medicine based on a biological understanding of disease.
- **Ethnomedicine** — the term used to refer to the approach to treating disease based on the beliefs and practices of the members of a particular culture.
- **Folk medicine** — the term used by anthropologists and biomedical practitioners to refer to the treatments for illnesses as they are defined by the people in the community by local community practitioners, rather the treatment provided by the biomedical practitioners who are part of the medical mainstream and are using modern disease models of illness.

Shamans are typically involved in practicing ethnomedicine and folk medicine.

Many anthropologists began researching the work of the *curanderos,* or folk healers, throughout Latin America who conducted their healing ceremonies for individual patients or groups of clients. These practitioners typically used traditional herbs, sacred objects, tobacco, and trance journeys to gain the aid of spiritual helpers. Among the most well-known of these researchers were Donald Joralemon and Douglas Sharon, who profiled 14 healers in their book *Sorcery and Shamanism: Curanderos and Clients in Northern Peru.*

Some of these urban healers became quite famous as a result of these anthropological accounts. For instance, after Douglas Sharon profiled Eduardo Calderón Palomino, a Peruvian *curandero* and artist, Eduardo became quite famous. Sharon's profile started the process, and then came the journalists and TV interviews. Eduardo was even featured in a documentary movie.

Tourism Meets Anthropology

Researchers continue to study the practices of traditional shamans and introduce them to the world. They do so by writing about them, guiding groups of tourists to visit them, conducting workshops to teach their practices, or a combination of these activities.

In 1980, I went on one such tour to visit traditional shamans and healers in Ecuador, on a trip led by anthropologist Joan Halifax and an Adventure Travel guide. We went to visit four tribes, including the Cayapa, Colorado, Canelo, and Otavalo. The highlight of the trip was when we went to a traditional Cayapa healing ceremony. In the late afternoon, we gathered in a large hut, where people lay around on the floor or in hammocks. In the early evening, the shaman began singing, smoking tobacco, waving a cluster of branches around, and calling on the spirits from all over the area to come help him.

At some point in the evening, we were led upstairs to a large upper room, where we all had a chance to drink some of *ayuahuasca*. Although some people reported visions of jaguars and other animals, I mainly saw more intense colors and felt fairly groggy. Later, I was told that the shaman had traveled in his vision to neighboring valleys to gain the help of distant spirits and bring them back with them. Reportedly, most of the villagers who had come left in the morning feeling much better and very satisfied with the healing.

A Cayapa shaman performing a healing on a group of patients who are lying on the floor. He is waving a cluster of branches to cleanse them of evil spirits, and he asks his spirit helpers to help heal the people of whatever problems they have.

Examples of popular birds from the Oriente in Ecuador that were made in the villages where the shamans practiced, but the design for them was actually introduced by an American from Chicago.

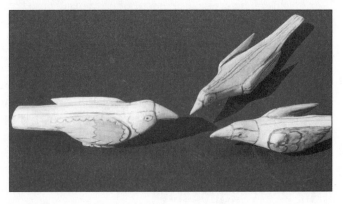

Although I felt privileged to be invited to see firsthand these traditional shamans, in some ways the globalization of shamanism was already changing it, packaging and promoting it for the Western mainstream. This realization really hit home after we traveled to the Oriente region of Ecuador, where I discovered some beautiful wood bird carvings that were made in the villages where the shamans we met lived. They looked like the birds the shamans called on as their animal helpers, and they were quite beautiful. However, soon after we left the village I learned the real story behind the bird carvings. A businessman from Chicago had become so enchanted by the area that he had decided to relocate there. He then set up a local factory to produce the birds for the tourists.

The New-Age Explosion

Another anthropologist who became a popularizer of shamanism, as well as a serious trainer of shamanic methods, in the 1980s and 1990s was Michael Harner. Harner originally studied the Jivaro and Conibo Indians in the Western Amazon in the 1950s. Then, in 1980, he published *The Way of the Shaman*, in which he not only described his own experiences in living with Indians and taking *ayahuasca* with them, but he described shamanic techniques in a way that anyone could practice them. His book was a mix of the techniques the shamans from these tribes and other groups used to work with power, achieve altered states of consciousness, and take shamanic journeys. He even discussed methods that readers could use to achieve altered states of consciousness without drugs.

Soon Harner was holding workshops on shamanism and set up a foundation to spread the teaching of his methods, designed for both novices who wanted to learn about shamanism and those interested in participating in an in-depth training program to learn about healing methods. His book and workshops contributed to the growing expansion of teaching such techniques in the West that contributed to the New Age explosion.

Another recent development has been the incorporation of traditional shamanic methods, including their use of medicinal herbs, into modern medical practice. Both modern and traditional healing systems actually often exist side by side, since patients may choose to go to local shamans for certain types of illnesses that they feel shamans can cure, and they go to biomedical practitioners for more serious illnesses. Or sometimes, shamans refer patients to biomedical doctors themselves, and in some hospitals and clinics, shamans have even been added to the staff. For instance, in *Drum and Stethoscope*, Julien Bastien describes this type of growing collaboration of shamans and medical personnel, noting that: "When shamans and doctors collaborate, a synergetic effect is produced which further promotes healing." (See Chapter 6 for more on using shamanism for healing.)

Off the Path

Although shamans are especially good at using culturally meaningful images, symbols, and rituals to help patients feel better and feel supported by family and community members, doctors are often better-equipped to treat the biomedical causes of disease.

The Downside of Popularity

Unfortunately, the dark side of this explosion of interest in shamanism is the corruption of traditional shamanism to appeal to Westerners seeking the shamanic experience. For instance, in 1994, American anthropologist and psychotherapist Marlene Dobkin de Rio wrote about the dangers of Mestizo men in the cities of Peru and Bolivia becoming instant traditional healers and offering American and European tourists a variety of hallucinogens, so they can have a mystical experience.

In some cases there have been psychological casualties resulting from these so-called "shamanic training" sessions by mostly middle-class men who have previously hawked other goods or services, but are now merchandising shamanism (Narby & Huxley, 2001, 277–278). It's a warning American anthropologist Eleanor Ott has raised as well, noting that:

> Today, many who dub themselves shamans no longer belong to a culture or community embedded in … a shamanic perspective, but rather come from the present generation of those primarily searching to find themselves. Thus, many of the new shamans are ill-equipped to engage in their practice of working with clients who come to them with a variety of physical, psychic, and spiritual ailments (Narby & Huxley, 2001, 280–281).

Many of these new "shamans" don't really have grounding in the traditional belief systems that are at the root of many shamanic practices. Also, many newly-minted shamans base their knowledge on what they have learned from others, such as anthropologists describing their own field work or people who have learned from these anthropologists or their students. And some new shamans have even gained their knowledge strictly from books, often drawing from this system or that to create a smorgasbord of techniques. The result is they may attempt to provide psychotherapy or heal mental, physical, or spiritual illnesses without really knowing what they are doing. They call themselves "shamans," but this is really only a veneer (Narby & Huxley, 2001, 284).

Questions have also been raised about the validity of the shamanic practices claimed by some popular writers. For instance, while Lynn Andrews has spent 20 years writing and holding workshops on her experiences with the Sisters of the Shields, who she claims are a group of traditional women healers from ethnic cultures around the world, many anthropologists and other professionals question the reality of these teachers. They think her books are really more popular fiction than fact—much as many have lobbed the same accusation at Carlos Castaneda.

Thus, while shamanism has increasingly moved into the mainstream and there is much to learn from traditional shamans and from modern shamans adapting traditional methods to the modern age, it is crucial to remain wary. Sure, it's fine to adapt shamanic methods for modern concerns and personal self-development. But be careful. This book will help show you how to navigate between authentic shamanism and its less authentic imitators.

The Least You Need to Know

- In the 1910s to the 1950s anthropologists began to look more closely at what shamans did in Siberia, South America, and other areas.

- Shamanism spread to the West in the 1950s and 1960s, when journalists, counselors, and others began visiting shamans around the world.

- In the late 1950s, anthropologists began to participate in shamanic rituals, and some even tried mind-altering drugs such as ayahuasca. As a result, they began to see that shamans were not mentally disturbed and that the people in the community looked to them for wisdom and healing.

- Since the 1980s, shamanism has increasingly gone global, as traditional societies have become more integrated into mainstream society and many individuals, from medical practitioners to New Agers seeking personal growth, have looked to shamanism for knowledge.

- A downside to the popularization of shamanism has been that many individuals with little training have claimed to be shamans or have created ersatz shamanic experiences for gullible tourists.

Chapter 4

Shamanism's Many Faces

In This Chapter

- ◆ The variety of shamanism
- ◆ The essence of shamanism despite the differences
- ◆ Traditional shamanism in Siberia
- ◆ Modern-day shamans in South and Central America

Once you get past the basic definition of shamanism—going into an altered state of consciousness to contact the spirits to help and heal others and, more recently, oneself—the forms of shamanism vary tremendously. Even the ways shamans relate to the spirits vary—from talking to them, going to other worlds to visit them, inviting the spirits to come to this world to visit, and in some cases, incorporating the spirits within oneself. It is like a huge buffet of different practices, and each time you come back to the buffet to make your selection, you'll find even more choices because shamanism keeps changing as society does. Shamanism is shaped by the personality of the shaman, too.

Variety Is the Spice of Shamanism

Shamanism differs from place to place in several different ways, including:

- ◆ **The shaman him or herself** In some cultures, the shamans are almost exclusively male, as in Siberia; in others, either gender can be a shaman.

♦ **Drugs** In the Amazon region from Ecuador to Peru, hallucinogenic drugs are a regular part of shamanizing; in Mesoamerica, the drug of choice of many shamans is tobacco; among many Native American groups peyote is popular; and in Siberia, many shamans don't use any drugs, although some use mushrooms.

Off the Path

Though drumming and drumming circles are often associated with shamans, drums are not universal. They never caught on in most of the South Pacific, for example.

♦ **Equipment** For some shamans, such as those in Siberia and Native Americans, the equipment is really simple—say, just a drum and rattle, and lots of singing, chanting, and dancing; in other regions, such as Peru, shamans use swords, knives, stones, ceramic figures, cups, and other objects laid out on or nearby an altar, called a mesa.

♦ **Dress** While some shamans may adopt a special type of dress, such as the leather cloaks hung with iron of the Siberian shaman, or the fur robes of some Indian shamans, others, such as shamans in cities in Peru and Ecuador, wear everyday casual clothes.

♦ **Travel** Here is lots of variation, both in where shamans go and how they get there—or if they go at all. Many shamans in South America follow the tree roots down under the ground to seek out animal helpers and other spirits; shamans in Siberia ride the wind to see the spirits in the mountains; and many healers in the Amazon basin of South America travel across the valleys or into the heavens. Finally, some shamans don't travel at all; instead, they invite the spirits to come to them.

♦ **Ritual** Some shamans generally work alone and see individual clients and their families; others do healings in groups; and still others may work with many other shamans, such as the !Kung where about half the men in the village dance and sing until they fall into a trance and begin shamanizing to help other members of the group.

♦ **Helper spirits** These spirits to whom shamans turn for help, spiritual education, and guidance, include Christian angels in the upper world and heavens, departed souls of ancestors and nature spirits in the middle world or earth, and power animals and animal helpers on the earth or underworld.

♦ **Healing or help** Shamans can do all sorts of things, from healing certain types of illnesses to solving certain types of problems, varying from individual problems like feeling angry, envious, or depressed to solving communal quandaries, drought, war, or famine. Some also forecast the weather and predict where game can be found.

Why All the Differences and What's the Real Deal

Shamanism varies so much because it reflects different cultural traditions and histories, including ancient traditions passed down from generation to generation and newer techniques developed in response to contemporary lifestyles and the needs of modern life.

Nevertheless, the essence of shamanism remains the same—going into an altered state of consciousness to contact spirits to help and heal—and this aspect is incorporated into each tradition. The important thing is to find a technique and tradition that works!

Whether or not shamanism is linked with a religious belief system, the emphasis is on shamanizing for practical ends—to help or heal. Shamans are essentially problem solvers, using the resources of the spirit world to solve different types of problems. That's why shamanism can be so helpful today, when you apply the techniques from it that work for you or whoever you try to help. To apply the techniques effectively, it helps to understand the roots of shamanism practice all over the world that contribute to its continuing power today.

From Siberia with Love

An ideal place to start a tour of the many forms of shamanism is in Siberia, since that is where the word "shamanism" comes from. The wilds of Siberia are among the few locations where traditional shamans are still practicing their craft today, although Siberian shamans suffered catastrophic losses as a result of persecution by the Russian Orthodox church and the Buddhists at the turn of the century and, later, by the Communists.

Unlike the shamanism that is practiced in most other places in the world, Siberian shamanism has been relatively untouched by the travels of Western tourists, mainly because its very cold in Siberia and far away even by plane or train. Usually the only travelers who visit Siberian shamans are anthropologists doing academic research.

> **Shaman Says**
>
> The word "shaman" is believed to come from the Tungus, a central Siberian tribe, which used the term "saman" or "hamman" to refer to a person who is "excited, moved, raised" or who had the ability to "know in an ecstatic manner" (Grim, 1983, 15).

Discovering the Shamans in Eastern Siberia

Many of the studies of Siberian shamans are centered in Eastern Siberia, so that's where we'll focus our tour of shamanism in Siberia. Here's a brief history of how shamanism developed there and how anthropologists and other researchers studied them.

In Eastern Siberia, shamanism developed in an environment of small rural villages centered around farming and/or reindeer herding. Here, the shaman was—and in some villages still is—a part of the village, and engaged in shamanizing on a part-time basis, besides primarily being a farmer or reindeer herder. However, the traditional practice largely died out by the mid-1900s. One reason was the conflict with the Lama Buddhists, who saw shamanism as a threat to their religion. The other major reason was the crackdown by the Communist government, which considered shamanism a form of medical quackery that interfered with its efforts to spread a state-sponsored medical system. Thus, most ethnographic studies of Siberian shamanism have been based on accounts from no-longer practicing elderly shaman or other informants describing their experiences of an earlier practice.

Off the Path

Despite the perception of Buddhists as gentle believers who seek to live in peace and do no harm to anyone, persecution of shamans by the Lama Buddhists has been well documented by scholars who have studied shamans in Siberia.

Wise Ways

Officials and doctors called Siberian shamans "practitioners of fraudulent medicine and perpetuators of outdated religious beliefs in a dawning age of science and logic" (Balzar, 1997: xiii).

According to researcher Majoroie Madelstam Balzer, the shamans were largely rooted out by the Soviets officials and doctors, who variously denounced them, confiscated their property, and persecuted them. Some shamans were even jailed or killed for their anti-Soviet activity. By the 1980s, most of the Siberian shamans had been discredited with their people and many of the most powerful shamans had died. Some parents even avoided telling their children that their ancestors had once been shamans.

With the end of the Soviet era and the changes in society making all religious faiths valid again, a more favorable attitude toward shamanism has emerged. Not only can the few remaining shamans practice again and teach new recruits, but scholars have shown a growing interest in recognizing how the traditional shamans helped to provide their communities with a mix of healing cures, psychotherapy, leadership, poetry, and entertainment.

Encounters with Old-Time Shamans

Typical of these ethnographic accounts of traditional shamanism is one by Vilmos Dioszegi, who describes two ethnographic research expeditions he went on in 1957 and 1958 in *Tracing Shamans in Siberia* (1960). Primarily, he traveled by long train rides through Siberia to cities with ethnographic museums and to the villages in Eastern Siberia. His goal was to collect the traditional shamans' accounts of their rituals, songs, and stories, and the clothing they wore.

Dioszegi was one of many mistaken researchers who saw shamanism as a dying or dead tradition, which had been stripped of its relevance by modern scientific and medical practice. Writing long before the revival of shamanism of today, he put his harsh judgment of shamanic death thus:

> Today ... there is no need for their healing activities anymore. Not only do they [the shamans] interfere unnecessarily with the work of the physicians but they often cause trouble and damage ...

The Communist party held the view that shamanism was certain to die out, too.

> Today, shamanism already belongs to the past. Due to the propagation of science it had to become extinct (Dioszegi, 1960, 10–11).

Even with the recent surge of interest, Siberian shamanism still exists much as it has in the past, where it is mainly practiced in small rural villages. It is very unlike the modern urban shamanism that is more characteristic of the cities, such as in Central and South America, where shamans have adapted traditional practices for their urban clients. Instead, among Eastern Siberian groups, like the Buryats, Yakuts, and Soyots, shamanism still reflects their traditional way of life as farmers and reindeer hunters, living close to nature.

Bair Rinchinov, a Buryat shaman in Russia.

(Courtesy Stanley Krippner)

Another contemporary shaman practicing in Russia today. Though practicing in an urban center, these modern shamans draw on some of the ancient Siberian influences in conducting their rituals.

(Courtesy Stanley Krippner)

What the Shamans in Eastern Siberia Believe and Wear

Eastern Siberian shamans believe that the cosmic order consists of three worlds: an upper world of higher spiritual beings, a lower or underworld of dark forces, and the middle world or earth. In the center of this cosmology is the sacred tree of life, which unites the three worlds. Its roots reach down into the underworld; its trunk is firmly in the middle world; and its branches rise up to the high gods of the tribe (Grim: 37–38).

The shaman's practices and clothing reflect the close link with nature, too. For example, the drum is fashioned from the trunk of a tree, and the shaman's ceremonial costume is made from animal hides and hung with iron discs and pendants. Especially important is the amagyat, a copper plate with a man's figure in the middle, which represents the shaman's ancestor-spirit, who helps the shaman see and hear into these other worlds. The figure is carved to look like a bird perched on a tree ready to fly to other worlds, and the bird skeleton of iron on the shaman's costume reinforces this bird symbolism. During trance, the shaman flies between the three worlds, much like the tree stretches from one world to another (Grim, 1983, 39).

An example of the traditional leather costume worn by the Siberian shaman. The hanging iron objects make noise as the shaman dances, contributing to the sound of drumming, chanting, and singing that helps the shaman journey in trance to meet the spirits.

Riding the Drum

The use of the drum is closely tied to the use of the horse or reindeer in Siberian tribal culture, in that the shaman views himself as taking a journey with the drum. As he beats it with his drumstick, he rides the sound as if he is riding a horse or traveling behind a running reindeer. Even the way the drum is constructed, using the skins of a horse or reindeer, contribute to this notion. As Dioszegi describes it:

The Soyots … call the different parts of the drum: ears, jaw-bones, upper rib and lower rib of the horse …. The two crossbeams supporting the drum from the inside are called breast strap and breaching stay …. The shaman's horse, namely the drum, was also equipped with reins, necessary for directing it …

The shamans said they could ride their drums like any saddle animal. If they had a drum, they were riding. When they were beating the drum with the drumstick, they were whipping their horse. Those who rode mounted upon their drums, could ride fast to faraway places (Dioszegi, 1960: 260–261).

A typical drum in Siberia, which is made of horse or reindeer skins and might be decorated with various images meaningful to the shaman. As the shaman beats rhythmically on the drum, he rides it like a horse or reindeer to the other world to meet the spirits.

Additionally, many of the hats the shamans wear are topped by antlers, reinforcing the association with the reindeer and its fast speed (such as among the Buryat), or with feathers and bird images, reinforcing the association with a flying bird (such as among the Soyots) (Dioszegi, 1960: 198, 215).

Going Through a Shamanic Initiation

The costume of the Siberian shaman is especially important to show everyone in the village that the person is a shaman and has gone through the required training or journey to become one. In many tribal groups, this training includes going through a trial by personal destruction and rebirth, based on the belief that the shaman must go through spiritual initiation. Among the Buryats and Yakuts, the people traditionally believed that a boy destined to become a shaman would go through a period of estrangement and visionary experiences, in addition to being trained by a shaman elder.

After many years, all this preparation eventually culminates in an ecstatic journey, in which the elder shaman introduces the new shaman to the various regions in the spiritual world. After this initiation of spiritual death and rebirth by the spirits, the initiate takes up the dress of the shaman, consisting primarily of his animal skin costume and the drum. The people believed these would give him the needed supernatural power to go to the upper and lower worlds to meet and deal with the spirits (Grim, 1983, 43).

CAUTION

Off the Path _____

In many shamanic traditions, it takes a lot of hard work to become a shaman and there are spiritual dangers. For example, traditional Siberian shamans commonly have to go through a trial in which they experience themselves being torn apart by the spirits and then are put back together again as a process of personal destruction and rebirth. The process is akin to the Christian notion of the long night of the soul or the Native American vision quest, where the initiate undergoes a period of deprivation and testing. Presumably at the end, the person comes out of the process stronger and now able to help and heal others. But for some the rigors might be too difficult, and they leave the shaman path.

Among these Siberian villagers, the individuals who became shamans engaged in the same lifestyle as other members of the village. Shamans received additional income for performing their rituals, perhaps in the form of an additional share of the fish catch. Besides shamanizing for immediate clan members and neighbors, the more popular shamans also helped patients who came to them for assistance from distant villages.

Communities usually viewed shamans as gifted individuals who were able to make contact with the spirits. While some shamans showed this propensity from childhood and many came from a family where a parent or close relative was already a shaman, others got the call a little later, generally in adolescence.

Rituals in Siberia

Equipped with their costume and drum, these Eastern Siberian shamans performed their rituals, using drumming, singing songs, and dancing to contact the spirits for various purposes. Most commonly, they did these rituals to heal sick people or livestock by expelling or appeasing the spirits causing illness. In addition, they were often asked to find a stray animal to accompany the soul of a deceased person to the other world, so it would not wander around the earth and scare the living. Sometimes, too, they might be asked to predict the future and help resolve domestic conflicts. Some even engaged in acts of sorcery, such as one shaman who performed a ritual to help a man get rid of an unwelcome wife, who later became sick and died (Alekseev, 1987: 78–83).

Rituals varied greatly depending on the purpose of the ceremony and were characterized by much improvisation. For example, the particular words in a song or chant could vary, with the contents improvised from session to session, though the intention was always to invoke and gain the help of the spirits to achieve the goal of the session (Dioszegi, 1960, 289).

Wise Ways

What were Siberian shamans' songs or chants like? Here's an excerpt from one of the long chants which Dioszegi recorded—this one from a traditional Soyot shaman, Ak Stephan:

> Obugeler, obugler
> Bay of Deriy Lake of Wild Ducks
> dwelt-in land mine born-in land mine
> the Great Taiga the Heart Taiga.
> I do climb it I do scale it
> spirit recluse spirit recluse
> my staff tingles the tender pine
> have you not seen Alan's mothers
> the ancestor's of our kam
> kuk-kuk-kuk-ku —
> Ancestors of Alan the kam
> wicked spirits recoil in fear
> those of the depths recoil in fear
> Tuvek's drum reaches the sun
> The drum of Alan the moon can hear ...

> (Dioszegi, 1960, 264)

To an outsider, the words don't make much sense; they may not even be in the speaker's usual language. But they express what the person is hearing and feeling as he or she communes with the spirit giving the message.

These sessions were usually done for the community as a whole, although they might be directed to healing or solving the problems of a particular person.

Regardless of this wide variation, the drum played a central role in every ceremony because of its powerful effect in creating the atmosphere for healing or divination through its repetitive rhythmic beat. The repetitive chanting and jangling of the pendants on the shaman's costume also contributed to the mood. The beat helped to guide the shaman, and sometimes the patient, into a trance state, and then, in this altered state, the shaman would call on the spirits for their assistance. With their help, he would use his vision to decide what to do to help the patient or resolve a problem. For instance, he might drive away the cause of an illness by scaring it or by sucking it out of the patient with his mouth and then spitting and blowing this illness away (Grim, 1983: 53).

From the Andes to the Amazon: Shamanism in Central and South America

Central and South American shamanism developed quite differently than its counterpart in Eastern Siberia. While at one time it existed in a rural village world, today it has become integrated into an urban environment, whether in Mexico, Ecuador, Peru, Guatemala, or other countries in Central or South America.

Many of the anthropologists studying shamans have worked in Peru, so that's where we'll focus our tour of this area—along the North Coast of Peru, which extends from Chicalyo in the north to Chimbote in the South. This region has become a thriving center of shamanic practice, with dozens of shamans working in the highlands and lowlands, catering to both local clients and a growing tourist trade of Westerners who want to visit shamans. While most practitioners are part-time shamans who have other urban occupations, such as being a factory worker, truck driver, small business owner, artist, or craftsman, an occasional shaman is able to turn shamanizing into a full-time practice.

Wise Ways
As in Eastern Siberia, shamanism in Peru went through a period of suppression, in this case by the Peruvian government, the Catholic Church, and medical doctors. In fact, the Catholic Church and government's persecution of the shamans began with the Spanish Conquest. The shamans responded by taking shamanism underground, keeping the practice alive until they reemerged in modern times.

Given this modern-day success, the ethnographic accounts of shamanism in Peru are more immediate and personal than the Siberian accounts from informants' recollections of past behavior.

Shamans in Peru are often well educated. While these modern-day shamans, called by various names, such as "curanderos" in Peru and in other parts of Latin America, have adapted to modern conditions, they have roots deep in the past. These roots date back to pre-Columbian times, when highly skilled magico-religious healers used herbs and ritual procedures to cure (Sharon, 1978: 2).

Why Peruvian Shamans Shamanize

To a great extent, the shamans in Peru use shamanizing for the same purposes as the Eastern Siberian shamans, most notably for healing, plus locating lost or stolen property, divining future events, countering witchcraft, and helping people overcome personal difficulties, such as problems in love. However, they also use shamanic practices to help with many problems that are more characteristic of a modern urban environment, such as helping clients gain success in personal projects and business, and helping them overcome problems with alcoholism and insanity (Sharon, 1978: 2–3).

Many patients also seek out healers because of the feelings of envy that arise in the more competitive urban environment, where some people have a low income or lack work and feel resentment toward others. Such feelings often lead the person to feel bewitched and get sick physically and spiritually (Sharon, 1978: 26–30). The shaman, in turn, helps to alleviate these symptoms through a healing ritual.

Unlike in Eastern Siberia, Peruvian healers typically use a more individualized approach to healing clients. They work with them as individuals or in small groups of patients, sometimes with family members in attendance. They don't put on a performance for a larger tribal community.

The Well-Blended Shaman

Modern Peruvian shamans are so successful largely because they have blended elements of popular Christianity with native shamanistic practices to address modern urban problems. Yet, even with many Catholic elements and the response to modern problems, the ritual is based on many traditional beliefs from pre-Columbian times, such as beliefs about the underworld, ancestors dwelling in sacred mountains, and deities of fertility. Also, almost all of the Northern Peruvian shamans travel to the two most sacred mountains at Chapari and Yanahuanga to look for magical herbs for their rituals. They collect them in a glass jar, called a "seguro" along with special perfumes to preserve them and use them during ritual to help divine and treat the patient's (Sharon: 34–36).

Shaman Says

A **curandero** is a spiritual healer or healing shaman, a term used in many parts of Latin America. This is also the term used commonly in the anthropological literature to describe healers in Mesoamerica, South America, and among Mexican Americans, whether they are shamans or practicing folk medicine techniques. In some communities, many of the healers are women, and they are generally called "curanderas."

The Power of Rituals, Drugs, and Power Objects

The rituals of the Peruvian shamans are also very different from those in Siberia. Whereas the Siberian rituals are more informal and based on lots of improvisation, focused around divining without the use of drugs, in Northern Peru, the shamans conduct very elaborate and formal rituals in which they use a hallucinogen made from the San Pedro cactus to put them in an altered state for contacting spirits.

The Peruvian healers also put on a relatively formal multipart performance that lasts about eight hours, and they use very elaborate curing altars, called *mesas* (Joralemon & Sharon, 1993: 4). While "mesa" is the same word that means "table" in Spanish, the shamans use this term to refer to their altars, and much is made of this term in describing ritual acts.

Peruvian shamans drink a liquid made from the San Pedro cactus and breathe in tobacco fumes during healing ceremonies. The San Pedro helps the shaman see visions, where he transcends ordinary limitations and travels into the upper and lower worlds. Once there, with the help of the spirits, he has a shamanic vision in which he recognizes and battles the sources of illness, witchcraft, and misfortune. He may also have to overcome ferocious animals, demons of diseases, and the sorcerers who direct them, as well as leap beyond the barriers of time, space, and matter to divine the past, present, and future. In effect, the shaman becomes like a Superman, propelled by the power of the San Pedro to gain this superhuman vision and strength in the supernatural world (Sharon, 1978: 37–38, 45).

They also use power objects and various utensils, such as swords for fighting against negative spirits. The shaman gradually accumulates these objects, which acquire special personal meanings for him over the years of practice, in various ways, such as by finding a stone in the mountains or getting it as a gift from another *curandero*. During the ritual, when the shaman drinks the San Pedro, he activates these objects by charging them with the power to help him see or heal. Such objects can range from sacred stones, such as the traditional "incaychus" stones shaped like alpacas, llamas, or sheep to assure fertility to Catholic artifacts, like images of saints, the holy mother Mary, and Jesus (Sharon, 1978: 52, 59–61). The shaman places them on the mesa according to a philosophy of healing and divination based on notions of good and evil.

The Importance of the Mesa

The mesas are of central importance. While the specific objects and their layout might vary from curandero to curandero, in general, they are divided into three sections. The left, or negative, is a section called the "banco ganadero" or "campo gandero" and is associated with evil for defensive work. The right, or positive section, is called the "banco curandero" or "campo justiciero" and is associated with good for offensive curing. The middle section, called the "campo medio," is where the healer is positioned, and is used for achieving a balance.

The mesas are conceptually divided again into four diagonals, called roads, which bisect each other to create four sections, called winds. The winds correspond to the four cardinal directions of the compass, and the roads correspond to four lines of a crucifix, which is placed in the center of the mesa.

Underlying this three-part division of the mesa into good and evil sections separated by a middle section is the shaman's belief that the opposing forces in the universe can be mediated and balanced, so they stand in a complementary relationship to each other. At the same time, this middle area provides a focus where the healer can concentrate his vision into the supernatural realms (Sharon, 1978: 62–64).

While the particular objects and how they are organized on a mesa vary from shaman to shaman, the basic belief system common to all has deep roots in an Andean cosmology inherited from the Incas before the coming of Christianity. According to this cosmology, the world of space and time is divided into three vertical planes—the underworld or inner world of the dead, the earth's surface, and the upper world, occupied by the Sun, moon, stars, and other deities (Sharon, 1978: 72–93).

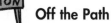

Off the Path

A mesa isn't just a table to the shamans in Peru, Ecuador, and other areas. Instead, it is an important and often elaborate space in which they put their ritual objects.

After the shaman takes several strong drinks of San Pedro liquor to facilitate the trance, he uses the large number of symbolic objects on the mesa to diagnose what is wrong with a patient and determine the appropriate treatment. While these objects reflect both Catholic and pre-Columbian influences, in general, the artifacts placed on the left side of the mesa and associated with the forces of evil and death tend to be pre-Hispanic ceramics and poisonous herbs. By contrast, the artifacts placed on the right and associated with the forces of positive energy and curing tend to be images of Catholic saints and curing herbs. The artifacts in the center field represent a reconciliation of these various oppositions, because they symbolize a balance or mediation between these opposite good and evil forces (Joralemon & Sharon, 1993: 6).

Conducting a Curing Ritual

Peruvian shamanic healing sessions take place at night and consist of two parts—a séance ceremony, which starts at around 9 or 10 at night, followed by a curing session. The first two- to three-hour period, which is held until midnight, is devoted to getting rid of negative or evil spirits and divining what is wrong with the patient or patients. From midnight until dawn, the shaman devotes himself to a long curing ceremony to treat each patient. Together, the two parts of the healing ritual enable the curandero to have a vision and manipulate the forces of the mesa to heal and solve the problems of each patient.

Typically, the ritual starts with an opening invocation, in which the shaman recognizes the four cardinal points, after which he sprays the mesa with perfumes and makes offerings to the lagoons and mountains.

The séance phase of the ceremony includes a mix of prayers, rituals, songs, whistling, and rattle shaking to a rhythmic beat. From time to time, the shaman and his assistants also drink some San Pedro cactus and black tobacco juice and pass it on to their patients and any friends or relatives attending the ceremony. Drinking the cactus and tobacco juice is intended to clear the mind and activate the fields of the mesa and the shaman's curing powers (Sharon, 1993: 101).

At midnight, the séance phase of the ceremony ends, and everyone drinks a cup of liquid made from the San Pedro cactus. During this next phase—the curing phase—the power built up from the séance is used to cure the patients. Among other things, the shaman breathes in more tobacco smoke and drinks some more San Pedro and uses a variety of cleansing and sucking procedures to get rid of negative influences, and engages in divination and diagnoses.

To receive a cure, each patient goes up to the mesa, while the healer chants a song in his name. Then, everyone is supposed to concentrate on the staffs and swords standing upright in the ground by the mesa, while the healer gives one of the swords to the patient to hold, as he chants, divines the nature of the problem, and describes what he sees to the patient to help the patient release any blockages causing his problem. During this process, the shaman might travel to the underworld or upper world or to distant places on earth with the help of his spirit helpers. Then, the shaman chants a final song for the patient, gives him a liquid to imbibe through the nose, rubs the patient with the staff, and sprays him with more perfume.

After all of the patients have come to the mesa, the shaman ends the session in the early morning with a final invocation to the four winds and roads, sprays more perfume, blows more tobacco to spread luck, and sprays each person with a mixture of water, lime powder, white cornmeal, white flowers, white sugar, and lime juice. Once the ceremony is over, the healer collects his artifacts, makes a sign of the cross where the mesa stood, and sprinkles the area with white cornmeal, thereby closing down the sacred space (Sharon, 1978: 105; Jorelemon & Sharon, 1993: 8–9).

The Common Ground Amidst All the Differences

The examples from Siberia and Peru show how varied this ancient practice can be. They vary in terms of whether the ritual is highly structured or improvisional; whether the shamans use many power objects or simply drum, chant, and dance; whether they essentially put on a performance or seek group participation; whether they wear a special costume or no costume; what the goals of the patient seeking help are; and in many other ways. You can explore even more differences in the next chapter, where you'll also learn more about the ties that bind the many varieties of shamanism together. In turn, knowing about all of the diversity can help you choose the best shamanic approaches for you.

The Least You Need to Know

- There is no one kind of shamanism—it is practiced in different ways around the world.
- Shamanism has survived in Russia and South America despite religious and political persecution.
- The term "shamanism" comes from Siberia, where shamans still practice many of the old ways.
- In Central and South America, many shamans now practice in the cities and perform elaborate and formal healing rituals.

Chapter 5

How Shamanism Can Help You

In This Chapter

- ◆ How ancient methods work
- ◆ Gaining the shamanic vision
- ◆ Applying the shamanic healing touch
- ◆ Using shamanic wisdom for guidance in daily life
- ◆ How to access the shaman in you

Just because shamanism is old, it doesn't mean that it isn't of value today. As a matter of fact, its ancient origins give it extra special value, as it has been improved over thousands of years and has been modified in response to changing cultures and conditions. Something that's still around after thousands of years has to be pretty good, right? Shamanism fulfils deep-seated spiritual needs and offers a form of help and healing that other arenas in society can't. Shamanism is also open ended, meaning that it can be changed to meet new circumstances, whereas religious systems generally emphasize following traditional practices, so they are more resistant to change.

Using Ancient Proven Methods

Here are a few of the ways that shamanism has provided help and healing where other methods haven't been able to help:

◆ Although medical doctors may be able to provide medicine to cure a disease, in many cases, a person may be suffering from an illness that has roots in feelings of personal distress or problems in relationships—or the disease may lead to such problems. Medical practitioners can't cure such problems, but very often, shamanism is just what the doctor ordered—or should have! And sometimes, a little self-help may contribute to the healing process, too, even if it just improves your outlook and helps strengthen your body and mind to better respond to an illness.

◆ In the case of emotional upsets and psychological disturbances, psychiatry, psychology, and other types of therapy might not always be helpful, because someone needs a more spiritually based, holistic, or community anchored type of help. Here, too, you may be able to gain an emotional boost on your own, using shamanic techniques.

◆ Although religious counselors may be able to help with advice and guidance, sometimes a shamanic counselor, using an altered state of consciousness to gain spiritual assistance, can offer deeper insights into the nature of the problem and what to do about it. Or you may be able to gain these insights directly for yourself. Also, a shamanic counselor may have more flexibility and openness to see things from the perspective of the individual seeking help, since religious counselors often have certain assumptions and beliefs about what to do, based on their religious system, so they may lack the flexibility offered by shamans who have a more pragmatic approach.

A growing number of medical practitioners and psychologists are using shamanic methods to help their patients and clients. And people whose roots are in these traditional cultures may still use or turn to the old practices today.

You, too, can draw on this ancient wisdom for help or healing. Turn back to the discussions of the different shamanic beliefs and practices described in previous chapters, and think about what sorts of ideas you might want to try and apply for yourself. As you encounter other shamanic practices in other cultures, think what approaches you might use from those traditions.

> **Wise Ways**
>
> Shamanism has always changed and adapted with the times, making it a practical spiritual and healing technique.

It's important to recognize the roots of these different methods and understand how they have been used in traditional practice, so you can fully and appropriately use this power. At the same time, it's fine to select those approaches that are best for you. After all, shamanism itself has adapted to changing social conditions and personal needs, while keeping its essence in using altered states of consciousness to seek spiritual assistance to help or heal.

When it comes to shamanism, change is fine, including using and adapting shamanism for your own personal needs and growth, although traditionally it has been used to heal and help others and used in a community context. But, hey, if shamanism is practiced in a culture that values individualism, independence, success and achievement, then shamanism can certainly be applied for those ends—including finding a job, gaining a promotion, and achieving personal success, whatever your goals!

The following examples from around the world illustrate how many people today still look to ancient methods for help and healing.

> **CAUTION**
>
> **Off the Path**
>
> Although the power of shamanism is neutral by itself, it can be applied to good or evil ends, like any form of religious and magical practice. It is critically important to use shamanism to achieve good, positive ends. Many people believe that if shamanism is used for negative ends, the negative energy will eventually turn against the person who used it.

How Native Americans Today Apply Old Traditions

Today many Native Americans still draw on the old traditions, and they have influenced many of the New Age practices, as well. There is no one Native American tradition—the forms of shamanism are extremely varied, given that there are hundreds of tribal groups in the United States alone and many more throughout the world, although popularly these different forms of shamanism are often lumped together.

Some Native American groups use peyote in their ceremonies, but others, such as the Lakota, do not. Different tribes call upon different spirits, including spirits of ancestors, plants, and animals. Some groups smoke a sacred pipe to call on the spirits; others do not. Some groups use energetic dancing and rattling by the shaman or members of the group, while others are more contemplative and prayerful in their approach. Finally, some groups of Native Americans use vision quests in their rituals, where they go off on their own to meditate and fast to achieve direct spiritual contact, but other groups do not.

Even though each Native American group incorporates unique elements into its shamanic rituals, they share some similarities, too, such as an emphasis on seeking balance and harmony in all things, having a deep respect for mother earth and all nature, and being humble in the presence of spirit.

An Indian smoking a sacred pipe in a ceremony—an approach used in many Native American tribes though not in others.

A medicine dancer from a Native American tribe performing a dance for a healing.

(Broderbund Clip Art)

Let's take a look at how one Native American shaman, Wallace Black Elk, has drawn on his own traditions for navigating the modern world.

Meet Wallace Black Elk

In *Black Elk: The Sacred Ways of a Lakota*, anthropologist William S. Lyons presents conversations with and stories by Wallace Black Elk, a Lakota shaman, who was guided by his spiritual elders to become a shaman. He was initiated in the ways of the *Chanunpa*—the Lakota word for the Sacred Pipe, used to reach out to the spirit world.

Black Elk began his training as a shaman in 1926 when he was five years old, rare for the Lakota, since usually, as in many cultures, shamans don't begin training until after puberty. But he had many Lakota teachers who began this early training, because they were afraid their shamanic tradition would be lost if they didn't act quickly to pass on their shamanic training to the next generation. So when Black Elk was five to nine years old, eleven shamans, which he refers to as "grandfathers" and "grandmothers," taught him the sacred ways, sometimes referred to as the "red road" or spiritual lifestyle (Lyons, 1990, xvii, 3–13).

Shaman Says _____

Chununpa is the Lakota word for the Sacred Pipe used to reach out to the spirit world; it is not a "peace pipe" as it is sometimes incorrectly called.

Among other things, Black Elk learned that: "We have a biological father and mother, but our real Father is *Tunkashila* [the Creator] and our real Mother is the Earth. They give birth and life to all the living, so we know we're all interrelated." He also came to understand that the spiritual power, which he experienced like a little tape recorder or color TV in his mind that was always on and came to him as wisdom given by the Creator and Grandmother the Earth (Lyons, 1990, 4).

When Black Elk was nine, he received his initiation by taking the sacred Chanunpa and going into the mountains, where he went before Tunkashila and Grandmother. As darkness descended, he felt the powers of the Four Winds come up, and he felt the mountain shaking, followed by the loud hooting of what sounded like an owl, though much deeper and louder. He felt it was the spirits coming to him, and he began to pray, doing so deeply from his heart, until he felt the spirit power finally inside him.

Once initiated, Black Elk found he could regularly communicate with the trees, animals and other spirits of nature, and he could use the power of the Four Winds and coyote to help and heal and counter negative forces. He found the coyote, a trickster figure in many Native American tribes and who is wily, clever, and good at getting out of difficulties, especially helpful. As Black Elk put it:

So you might say that I'm a scout for my people …

There are sicknesses and all kinds of death you have to maneuver around. But then there are the powers of the Four Winds. They come to your rescue … Then they make things good again. They never bring anything bad. They only bring health and help …

So like this coyote, it has the same power. If troubled times come, you call on this little coyote, and he'll maneuver you out from the danger. He also has sacred powers … So we have that power (Lyons, 14).

It is a spiritual power that has four parts: wisdom, knowledge, power and gift or love. Wear those four parts, and it will "beautify your mind and spirit."

Using Lakota Ways in Your Own Life

Among some of the basic teachings of the sacred Lakota way are these. As you read them, think about how you might apply them in you own life.

- ◆ When you start to study the Chanunpa, you will find it connects to everything. It "connects all life" (Lyons,1990,24).

- ◆ Everything has its own song. When you have spiritual knowledge, you will learn to hear those songs. For instance, the rocks and colors sing; the fire has a song; so do the earth, the water, the green leaves and grass. There are songs in all life forms— four-legged, two-legged, and even creeping-crawler creatures (Lyons, 1990, 34–34).

- ◆ The foundations of knowledge lie in the "fire, rock, water, and green" (Lyons, 1990, 36).

- ◆ Wisdom comes from Tunkashila or Grandfather; knowledge comes from Earth or Grandmother; and both the wisdom and knowledge are one (Lyons, 1990, 37).

- ◆ It is important to "walk in balance" and "live in harmony," although people today have lost that balance (Lyons, 1990, 39).

- ◆ When you hold the Chanunpa, you may experience bad words and thoughts blowing toward you; but they are like shadows, and if you connect yourself with such a thought, you will become lost or come back missing part of yourself. So don't connect yourself with bad words or thoughts, and don't say them since they will hurt someone (Lyons, 1990, 42–43).

> **Wise Ways**
>
> Living in balance and harmony is not only central to the Native American wisdom but to many other religious and spiritual traditions. For instance, the "way of the Tao" is based on finding balance, as is the notion of yin and yang that comes from the I Ching and Confucian philosophy.

Thus, Black Elk describes a life of continually being aware of spirit, going on regular vision quests to communicate with the spirits, participating in ceremonies, staying focused on the goals of health and help, and being continually aware of the spirits and the power they bring.

So does it work? Black Elk offers some examples of how well calling on the spirits has worked for him—even giving examples of how the spirits fixed his stove and TV and gave him advance warnings of events. He even used the spirits to heal people with life-threatening illnesses.

Gaining the Shamanic Vision

The story of Black Elk illustrates a few ways to use the traditional wisdom to gain a shamanic vision—through vision quests, sweat lodges, or prayer ceremonies to call on the spirits. Other groups use other ways, based on different beliefs and contacting different spiritual beings. Likewise, you can draw from these different approaches, the ones that will work best for you. Some of these other ways including using:

◆ Trance

◆ Dance

◆ Chanting

◆ Repetitive singing

◆ Hallucinogenic drugs, such as ayahuasca, peyote and mushrooms

◆ Deep meditation or contemplation

◆ Sensory deprivation

◆ Sensory overload

◆ And any of the above in various combinations

The key is to be prayerful, meditative, contemplative, or receptive to altered state of consciousness, so you are open to listening to the wisdom and knowledge of the spiritual beings, in whatever form they come to you.

Looking to Africa

Shamanic visions can also be gained by mixing trance and dance in a large community ceremony—the approach used by !Kung San in northwestern Botswana near the Kalahari desert in southern African. Anthropologist Melvin Konner, who lived among them in 1970, learned how the !Kung San gain the shamanic vision when he became an apprentice healer.

As he describes it, the !Kung used a group healing ceremony with dancing and chanting that triggered an ecstatic trance experience, so the individual becomes open to seeing and communicating with the spirits. In the ceremony, members of the village joined together in a healing circle of singers and dancers. About half of the men in the village danced, while the women sang, and the children and adolescents formed an outer circle of spectators (Konner, 1998, 174–175). Another researcher, Richard Katz, who reported on his studies of the !Kung in *Boiling Energy*, found that more than half of the men, and many of the women, danced as shamans.

> **Shaman Says**
>
> The !Kung are considered Africa's oldest survivors and last hunting-gatherers, having lived in Africa for about 40,000 years (Goodman, 1993, 38). About 10,000 remain today living in small village camps in the northernmost part of the Kalahari Desert in the area of modern Botswana and Namibia.

During this dance, the !Kung believe the dancer can access a healing power, called n/um which resides in their abdomen, stomach, or spine and is heated during the long repetitive dancing and singing, causing the dancer to fall into a trance. Then, once in this trance, the individual can use that healing power or energy to both heal and see.

- To heal, the healer can transfer his sweat and energy to others, protecting them with his energy, or he can pull out sickness from other people.

- To see, the individual takes a journey in which the soul leaves his body to meet with the spirits and gain insights that can be used to help and heal others (Konner, 1999, 173).

For instance, in one case a healer used a vision gained from a deep trance to help a young mother, who had a serious case of malaria. After the healer entered a deep trance and his soul left his body and traveled to the spirit world, he caught up with the woman's father, who was holding his daughter's soul. The healer persuaded the father to release her soul back to the world of the living. Soon after, she felt better, and within a few days her fever and chills were gone (Konner, 175–176).

The way Konner describes it, this trance state is a very powerful way to gain this spiritual vision and healing power.

> The trance and its power to heal are due in large part to the energy of the community …

> If the dancer is experienced, his soul can travel great distances, to the world of the spirits and gods, and communicate with them about the illnesses and problems of the people (Konner, 1998, 175).

Applying the Shamanic Healing Touch

Even while trance and altered states of consciousness to contact spirits is characteristic of most forms of shamanism, it is also possible to help and heal using what some anthropologists refer to as "symbolic shamanism." This is where the shaman is able to manipulate power symbolically and in a ritual, such as done by the Nahavo medicine men (Sandner, 1979).

Among the Navaho Indians, a tribe of over 100,000 members living in or around a reservation in northeastern Arizona or northwestern New Mexico, shamanism combines the function of priest and doctor. At the core of their system of healing is the notion that all should live in harmony, and that disharmony in nature and human relationships leads to disease and misfortune, so this evil needs to be controlled or balanced in order to restore harmony and goodness (Sandner, 1979).

In a typical Navaho healing ceremony, an individual patient goes to the medicine man for help, sets a date for a ceremony, and pays a fee, and then members of his family and sometimes members of the community attend the ceremony. To establish a diagnosis, the medicine man will often turn to a person who goes into trance, called a "hand trembler, stargazer, or diviner." Then, in trance, this person will determine the cause of the patient's problem and what to do about it.

Wise Ways
A hand trembler diagnoses a patient's problem by sitting beside a patient, going into trance, and letting his hand move freely. As the hand shakes, it may seem to point at a certain part of the patient's body, which may be viewed as the focus of his or her illness. While the diviner may go into an altered state of consciousness to diagnose the problem, he is not the active healer who conducts the healing ceremony, and this actual healer or medicine man does not go into an altered state or on a journey. Rather he relies on the power of the ceremony to affect the healing.

Then, however, the diagnosis is achieved, the medicine man goes to work, using prayers, chanting, and sand painting, sometimes combined with herbal remedies and sometimes simple medical procedures, such as bathing an injury with herbs.

After an initial purification, that involves fasting, sweating, and bathing, the ceremony may go for several days in which the healer sings a series of songs, drums, uses painted prayer sticks to invite the spirits to attend, and blesses sand paintings, which are made from colored rock and sand. These paintings feature a variety of images of supernatural animals, deities, and hero figures from the Navaho's long history, along with natural forces, such as the wind and stars.

During the ceremony, the patient sits on the sand painting, while the healer sings a series of songs and prayers. Through this process, the patient identifies with the evoked spirits and powers, who act to heal him of the illness or problem that led him to seek a healing.

A Navaho sand painting featuring spirits of the four directions enclosed in a sacred hoop. Although this is a small picture that goes on a wall, the actual paintings in a healing are several feet across, and the patient sits on one of them during the healing.

Wise Ways

A chant for transformation and recovery may go something like this:

> Happily I recover.
> Happily my interior becomes cool.
> Happily my eyes regain their power.
> Happily my head becomes cool.
> Happily my limbs regain their power.
> Happily I hear again.
> Happily for me the spell is taken off.
> Happily I may walk.
> Impervious to pain, I walk.
> Feeling light within, I walk.
> With lively feelings, I walk.

(Sandner, 1979)

Seeking Guidance in Daily Life

As these examples from traditional shamanism and modern-day shamanism illustrate, shamanism is used for many purposes—from solving everyday problems to healing. You can likewise use the contact developed with the spiritual forces or energies of nature for seeking guidance in daily life.

I have led a series of workshops on applied shamanism in which participants learned to do exactly that—and many participants described attending other shamanic sessions where they gained insights by using various techniques to enter an altered state of consciousness and contact spirits who took various forms.

For instance, when Beverly, a marketing professional, was thinking about changing to a new field, she consulted a counselor who used shamanic techniques to take her on a long journey in her mind. As Beverly relaxed on the floor, the counselor invited her to travel to a lower world to meet different power animals or teachers. There, she could choose one to work with who would give her the insights she needed. Eventually, Beverly found herself greeted by a large furry polar bear, who took her through a long tunnel into a cave where she saw herself in a new office in a new community. When she returned from her trip, Beverly realized it was time to not only change jobs but move, as well.

For Nancy, the uncertainty was whether to break up a current relationship, which seemed to be going nowhere, though her boyfriend kept assuring her he planned to divorce his wife. The timing just wasn't "quite right," he said. To decide what to do, Nancy sat in a large drumming circle, where people were chanting, shaking rattles, or beating drums. As the pounding rhythm continued, she felt herself slipping into an altered state where she felt very relaxed, peaceful, and clear. In this state, she asked herself the question—should she break up with the man she was seeing? When she saw only a blank screen in front of her, she felt she had her answer. He was no longer in her picture, and seeing this image gave her the strength to finally make the break and move on to something new.

In Herman's case, the problem was a loss of confidence, since he had experienced a great loss of income and clients during a recession. To make matters worse, due to his precarious financial situation a woman, whom he had fallen deeply in love with and wanted to marry, left him for a relationship with a man who was more successful and could give her a more secure and comfortable life. To gain insight into what to do, Herman listened to a tape of chanting and singing from a shamanic ceremony, leading him into a waking dream state as he lay on the floor. Then, he used this imagery to meditate on and explore his feelings about what to do. The exploration eventually led him to visualize himself in a small rural community where he could cut down his expenses, so he didn't have to do low-paying work he didn't like. Instead, he could use the time he saved to work on researching a subject that had long interested him, thereby devoting himself to what he felt was his life's work.

These people were all using various forms of shamanism to help them find answers to problems and questions in their lives and gain a new sense of certainty, direction, and self-assurance. While they might have used other, more conventional, modern methods of assistance, such as going to a career counselor, psychologist, psychotherapist, or member of the clergy, they turned to shamanic methods, like a growing number of people today, to gain the advice and support they needed. Likewise, you can do the same.

So what's your problem? What would you like guidance about in daily life?

To find out, get in a comfortable relaxed state, or use any of these other methods previously described—such as chanting, dancing, or singing. Then, ask yourself a series of questions about what you need help with in your life now. Ask the question in a very open-ended form and repeat it several times:

"What help do I need now?"

"What additional help do I need now?"

"Are there still other areas where I need help?"

But don't try to find solutions to your problems right now; instead, focus on identifying problem areas. Try to remain in a relaxed or meditative state, and let the answer come to you. Possibly you may see the images of a teacher or spiritual helper come to you along with the answer. Make note of what you see, since later you might want to look for this teacher or spiritual helper to gain assistance in looking for other answers. For now, just concentrate on the areas where you would like some help. Later, you can focus on getting advice on what to do.

Bon Voyage

When seeking guidance from the spirit world, it's important to remain open-minded and receptive.

Accessing the Shaman in You

The way to tap into these shamanic insights is to access your own inner shaman. Though it takes years and years of training to become a professional shaman who offers counseling and healing to others, you can still develop this intuitive, receptive, creative force within yourself that gives you ability to see and understand that lies at the heart of shamanism. You are, to quote Black Elk, seeking the essential quality of "awareness," along with courage, endurance, and patience.

You can work more with the various types of shamanic knowledge from different traditions that help you access this inner knowing. These methods range from chanting, singing, dancing, and drumming, to working with various types of teachers, power animals, and objects. Use your skills of visualization, meditation, and dreaming, too. The next sections of the book provide a guide to help you access this inner shaman, using shamanic journeying and other techniques to help you in this voyage of discovery to better help and heal yourself and others in everyday life.

The Least You Need to Know

- Although medical doctors, psychologists, and religious counselors can help with certain types of problems, in other cases, shamans can provide better assistance, as can using shamanic techniques yourself.

- Native American healers use a wide range of shamanic approaches that vary from tribe to tribe; however, a common emphasis is on seeking balance and harmony in all things, having a deep respect for mother earth and all nature, and being humble in the presence of spirit.

- Among some of the widely known groups of shamanic practitioners or traditions are the Lakota Way, described by Wallace Black Elk, the !Kung of the Kalahari Desert in Africa, and the Navahos, known for their sand paintings.

- You can learn from these different traditional and modern day shamanic traditions to contact with spiritual forces or the energies of nature to help you seek guidance in daily life or engage in self-healing.

Chapter 6

The Healing Shaman

In This Chapter

- ◆ Using shamanism to diagnose and treat illness
- ◆ Using plants and drugs to heal
- ◆ The path to becoming a healer
- ◆ The battle between doctors and shamans

One of the most common images shamanism calls to mind is that of the traditional "medicine man" or "medicine woman" who cures members of his or her community using medicinal plants, rituals, and by fighting off evil spirits. This chapter provides a brief overview of these and other shamanic healing practices. As you read it, please keep in mind that it isn't intended to teach you how to heal yourself or others of sickness or disease; rather, it's meant to show you how shamans who have gone through extensive training go about healing.

The Shamanic Approach to Illness

The methods shamans use for healing vary widely from culture to culture, but underlying them is a basic theory of illness. It differs from the mainstream Western medical model, which is based on ideas that diseases have physical causes and using medicines and surgery to kill disease-causing organisms and cut out diseased tissue. Although modern shamans generally recognize the value of Western medicine for certain types of diseased conditions they can't treat, they approach illness in a completely different way. Like medical doctors, shamans are also concerned with what causes disease, but they have a different theory of causation.

Shaman Says

Sorcery is the use of negative and destructive forces to harm others, such as by causing them to fall ill, experience bad fortune, or die. Sometimes the term **witchcraft** is used by the members of traditional societies and by traditional shamans to mean much the same thing as sorcery, though witchcraft has other meanings as well.

Shamans believe the major reasons for illness include the following (Vitebsky, 1995, 98–99):

◆ **Soul Loss**   Here the person may have lost his soul, inner essence, or vitality, which will be expressed as depression, anxiety, or physical symptoms. The problem could be a jealous neighbor engaging in sorcery, a family conflict, the loss of a loved one, a long chronic illness that won't go away, and so on. Whatever the reason, if the person's soul is lost, the shaman sends his own soul or spirit to the spiritual world to look for the lost soul, and in some cases, he may fight the spirits for it. If successful in finding or fighting for it, the shaman then brings back the soul.

◆ **Presence of a Foreign Object**   In this case, a person is suffering because some foreign object is in his body, such as a small insect or piece of bone. Or perhaps his suffering is due to some foreign spiritual essence, such as a magic dart, which has been directed at the patient by a sorcerer or hostile rival. Whatever the object, if the shaman diagnoses its presence, he or she then acts to remove it, such as by sucking it out. In some cases, this sucking may be used to remove an object that has an intangible, spiritual form, such as the magic dart or negative energy sent by a sorcerer or witch that has become like a tumor in the person's body. In other cases, the shaman will actually suck out and display a physical object, though some questions have been raised about the healers who do this, such as in the Philippines. The claim of skeptical observers is that these healers, sometimes called "psychic surgeons" use sleight of hand to seemingly pull an object out of a person's body, which they actually have in their hand. And then, the skeptics charge, they convince the patient it has come from his or her body. But whatever the case, the patients generally feel better, which is why they continue to go to such healers, though possibly their cure or improvement is based on their belief in the power of the healer's power and healing ability.

◆ **Breaking Taboos**   Here the problem is engaging in some kind of misbehavior that has led the patient to become ill or, even worse, for the community as a whole to experience problems, such as a failed harvest or a poor hunt in a traditional society. The particular behavior considered to be offending depends on what is considered taboo in a particular society: it is some action that offends the group's customs, norms, or morality. But whatever the wrong behavior, once it is determined as the cause, the treatment involves the wrongdoer(s) confessing what he or she has done and then engaging in some acts of atonement or promising to not engage in such acts in the future.

◆ **Conflicts and Poor Relations with Others**
While conflicts and poor relationships might lead to soul loss or sorcery from others who have become angry, jealous, or otherwise hostile, sometimes the problem is not deemed so serious. In that case, the patient's illness won't need such drastic measures as soul retrieval or foreign object extraction. Instead, the shaman might prescribe some simple steps for the patient to seek harmony or improved relationships, and perhaps he might use some other simple remedies, such as asking the patient to drink an herbal tea or follow a restricted or special diet for a limited period.

Shaman Says

Soul loss is a condition in which a person has lost his or her soul or vital force, usually characterized by a state of depression, anxiety, or loss of energy. Shamans retrieve the soul by journeying to the spirit realm, sometimes fighting with the spirit who has stolen the soul.

The shaman may pursue multiple strategies for healing based on different interpretations of the underlying cause of an illness, rather than mainly looking at the outer symptoms. This approach, in short, is based on having a very broad perspective for recognizing and treating illness, because, as Piers Vitebsky points out in his overview of shamanism around the world:

> The shamanic perception of well-being does not only encompass physical health in the medical sense, nor is it restricted to mental health in the psychiatric sense. It includes good nutrition, good friendship, prosperity, and successful business and warfare. All of these things depend on ideas of balance, flow and equilibrium in the environment, and on ideas of giving and withholding, love and anger, and motivation and intention among the spirits which animate this environment (Vitebsky, 1995, 99–100).

Shamanic Treatment Options

Though the basic notions of how to diagnose and treat the patient may be similar for different shamanic practices, the actual methods used couldn't be more different. They vary from culture to culture and from shaman to shaman, and are based on a mix of cultural traditions, the shaman's personal style, and differences in patients and their responses. There are also many different schools of shamanic practices in different regions, and modern medical practitioners and New Age healers, who use traditional healing techniques, have their own mix of methods, too.

Wise Ways

One major difference in approach among shamans is whether they treat people individually or as part of a group. The methods shamans use to first diagnose what's wrong with someone also vary dramatically, as do their treatments.

Thus, should you go to a shamanic healer as a patient or want to learn to use shamanic healing techniques as a practitioner or for self-healing, take some time to learn what methods the person is using. Find out about the person's reputation as a healer or teacher of these techniques. Look at his or her track record, and consider how this person's personality or approach fits your own personal style. There are many different valid methods of healing, and you want to choose what feels comfortable for you.

The Healers of Ecuador

I experienced a wide variety of techniques when I went with a group of people to visit healers and shamans in Ecuador. Some of the shamans we visited lived in remote jungle locations, while others lived in large cities.

Here our group is beginning to learn the methods of the shaman, who is holding a bundle of leaves and using it to cleanse and purify a patient.

When we met with the Canelo, then a fairly isolated group living deep in the jungles of eastern Ecuador, we saw the shaman, an older man, perhaps in his late 40s or 50s, use fairly simple natural techniques to treat local villagers one at a time.

He usually began his treatment by singing songs to call on the spirits. Then, he would take whatever action was necessary to cure the individual. For example, he used a bundle of leaves to cleanse a young girl; he bent over a young boy to suck a spirit causing a headache from his head, after which he cleansed the boy with his bundle of leaves; and he shook his bundle of leaves over a sick baby.

A Canelo shaman using a bundle of leaves to cleanse a young girl (left) and a baby (right) of hostile spirits or illness.

A Canelo shaman sucking a negative spirit or negative energy from the head of young boy.

When we went to visit another group, the Cayapa, in a larger village in eastern Ecuador, the shaman invited us to observe and participate in a large overnight healing ritual. In this case, a few dozen people from the local village and surrounding villages came to spend the night, bringing their sleeping bags or mattresses, and we brought our own sleeping bags, too. While many of the villagers had come to be healed, others were family members and friends who were there to offer their support.

People gathered to be healed in an all-night ceremony.

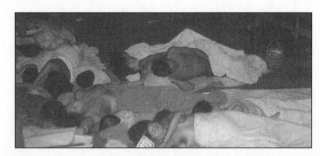

Wise Ways
Among the Pima, a tribe of Indians in southern Arizona and northern New Mexico, the shaman's role is primarily to accurately diagnose the nature and reasons for the patient's sickness and then turn that patient over to other practitioners for treatment. To this end, the shaman looks to benevolent spirits for their assistance and distinguishes between those conditions that can be treated and those that can't. For instance, certain conditions aren't treatable, either because the body's self-healing abilities will eventually overcome the problem, such as in the case of indigestion or a spider bite, or because any treatment will simply not work, say, because of a physical deformity (Krippner, August 1997).

As part of the ceremony, the people who came to be healed and the members of our group (some of whom did want to be healed of something) took a drink of the ayuahuasca mixture—a hallucinogen made from a jungle vine—that was passed around.

Then, after a few hours of healing songs, as people drank ayuahuasca and its effect of producing visions took hold, the shaman went to individual patients and engaged in various practices over them, depending on what he diagnosed. In some cases, he went on a shamanic journey to retrieve that person's soul; in other cases, he sought to suck out negative spiritual energy. The process continued until dawn, and those who weren't being healed watched, relax, sang, or went to sleep.

The third shaman we visited was a member of the Colorado Indians in western Ecuador by the coast. He practiced in his small house, which was located in an outlying area near the main town of Esmeraldas. He worked with a small altar of ritual objects placed on a bench in front of him, with a candle in a bottle at either end. He combined a mix of brushing and rubbing techniques, using a bundle of leaves or his hands, to draw negative energy from his patients.

A Colorado shaman uses brushing and rubbing techniques to treat a patient.

Finally, we saw yet another approach when we visited an Otavalan shaman who worked in a district of Quito, the capital of Ecuador, where he had a small house. In this case, the shaman, who dressed in an everyday suit with a shawl over his shoulders, used an elaborate mesa with ritual objects and tobacco juice as an important part of the healing ceremony.

The mesa of this Otavalan shaman includes a variety of objects used in the healing ritual, including special stones, eggs, candles, and a bottle of liquor.

While we were watching, the shaman treated a patient who came by himself and complained of problems with chest, back pains, and difficulty in breathing. After the shaman called on the spirits of the different directions to assist in his healing, he focused on the man's chest. At various points in the ceremony, he used a bundle of leaves for cleansing, held his hands around the man's torso and waist, drank liquor and smoked a cigar, and blew liquor and smoke at the patient to cleanse him of the negative spirits causing his pain. Afterward the patient left feeling much better.

Bon Voyage

Among the Navaho the emphasis is on viewing illness in terms of cosmic harmony, or the idea that that humans should be in rapport with every aspect of nature and with each other. Thus, when a person falls sick, the basic notion is that the person has fallen out of harmony in some way, and a healing is designed to restore this harmony (Krippner, August, 1997, 284).

Though we were in Ecuador as observers and not believers in the healing systems we observed, some people in our group still found the meetings with the shamans to be healing, particularly the overnight healing ceremony. It's hard to know if it was the shaman traveling to other spiritual realms, the ayahuasca most of us drank, gathering together as part of a community focused on healing, the long sleep-over, or something else. But afterward, several people in the group remarked they felt better and had more energy.

 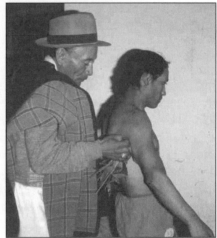

This series of photos illustrates various techniques the Otavalan shaman used in treating a patient, including drinking and blowing liquor and smoke, cleansing the patient, and holding him in the injured area to draw out negative energy.

How Does It Work?

These examples of successful shamanic healing can be repeated throughout the world, though the techniques the shamans use differ widely. As described in previous chapters, these can include drumming, chanting, singing, dancing, using assorted power objects, and using a mix of plants and drugs, which the shamans imbibe, and sometimes the patients do, too. In addition, the shaman will turn to different spirits, ranging from power animals and ancestor spirits to spirits of nature. In some cases, where shamanism is closely tied to a particular religion, such as Christianity, the shaman will call in the saints, deities, or prophets of that religion to help him heal. The particular mix of techniques include those passed down by tradition from shaman to shaman, often within families of shamans, and a shaman will add his or her personal style to the mix as well.

Wise Ways

Shamanism is effective for many patients because it treats the patient on a number of levels simultaneously and depends on many influences for healing. These include:

- The cause of illness (ie: is it a biological organism, response to a personal or family problem, or both)
- The seriousness of the symptoms
- The general health of the patient
- The particular treatment used (ie: ritual, chanting, herbs)
- The personality and charisma of the healer
- The beliefs of the patient in the effectiveness of the treatment
- The psychological support the patient gains from others (such as members of his family, friends, and neighbors)
- The interaction of these various factors

These healing techniques have endured, even with the coming of modern medical techniques, because they have proved effective in treating many types of illnesses. Their effectiveness raises an ongoing debate in the medical community about what contributes to healing—particular treatments; the expertise of the healer; the attitude and beliefs of the patient; the support of the patient's family, friends, and neighbors; or a combination of multiple factors. The fact is that healing depends on a mix of external factors, plus the participation of the patient in his or her own healing, so shamanism gains its effectiveness by working on multiple levels.

Wise Ways

Shamanic healing methods work effectively for treating many conditions. The methods take into consideration not only the patient's physical symptoms of illness or injury, but the patient's beliefs and psychological and social needs. Shamanism is a holistic approach to healing that treats the whole person and further treats the individual as a part of the community and natural world.

In turn, because illness is not solely due to particular physical causes, and the degree of healing depends on the patient's response as well as the treatment given, shamanism can contribute to healing, even when used in tandem with modern drugs and surgery. In fact, many modern shamanic healers know this, so they may refer some of their patients to medical practitioners as well as treat them with shamanic techniques. In this way, they adapt their approach to the needs of their patient and their beliefs about what they can heal through shamanic practices.

In general, these shamanic techniques usually prove effective in making the patient feel better and in helping to resolve any disruptions in the patient's relationships with others in the family or community that have contributed to the patient's illness. In turn, such improvements in a person's attitude and relationships play a key role in healing.

Is it the shamanic techniques themselves that do the healing? The belief and attitude of the patient? The support of community members? Probably the best answer is that these different factors combine together to help the healing process, much like a person who is treated by mainstream medicine will use a number of techniques—including taking medicine, bed rest, relaxing from work pressures, eating chicken soup, receiving get-well cards, and experiencing good wishes from others—to feel better.

Healing Plants and Drugs

The specific plants and drugs used by shamans vary from culture to culture and shaman to shaman. In fact, in some traditions, the use of plants and the many herbal remedies and drugs made from them is so extensive that there are specialists, such as herbalists, who prescribe or make these remedies, much like pharmacists in mainstream medicine.

Many of these remedies do, in fact, have specific physiological effects, as modern medical practitioners have been finding, such as when they have obtained tropical plants and have had them analyzed to discover their active healing properties. In other cases, the plants and drugs may open up doors to altered means of perception and to the spirit world, such as in the use of hallucinogens. Perhaps, too, a psychological or placebo effect may contribute to the healing process, regardless of any physiological or consciousness-altering effects, such as when you believe something will have an expected effect, and so it does. In any case, the specifics of what plants and drugs have what effects and why are so complex that this might be the basis for another book; in fact, there are dozens of such books for both the professional and general reader. So here, I'll just mention a few general ways in which the main types of plants and drugs are used.

Some of the most frequently used plants and drugs include the following:

- ◆ **Leaves used in bunches or bundles**   Typically these are large, flat leaves that are gathered together to form a medicine bundle or brush, which is used to cleanse or purify the patient and sweep away any evil or malevolent spirits. These bundles of leaves are commonly used by shamans in South and Central America, as well as in other areas.

- ◆ **Hallucinogens**   These are used by some shamans to change their consciousness, and sometimes patients take them, too. This changed consciousness enables them to open up the doors to perceiving and communicating with the spirits in the spiritual world or world of nonordinary reality.

The particular hallucinogens vary from culture to culture, but some of the most popular ones are:

- **Peyote**   used by many Native American groups, particularly in the American southwest, Mexico, and Central America; it comes from the peyote cactus and is taken in the form of a button or turned into mescalin.
- **Psilocybin**   obtained from the *psilocybe* mushroom in Mexico.
- **Ayuahuasca**   made from the *Baisteriopsis* or ayahuasca vine, often in combination with at least one other plant, and used primarily in South America.
- **Tobacco**   which is smoked and blown on the patient to purify and cleanse.
- **Liquor**   which is used much like tobacco, except it is drunk and then sprayed on the patient to purify and cleanse.

- **Plants used for symbolic purposes**   These plants or parts of plants are placed on an altar, held by the shaman, or given to the patient to hold. They may include dried or living leaves, flowers, bark, twigs, and the like. These plants are used because they are considered sacred, give off a healing energy, represent a particular saint or deity, or otherwise have symbolic meaning to the shaman or the patient.

- **Incense**   This is made from various types of plants that are burned for the healing properties of their smoke. Sometimes a patient will be asked to breathe in this smoke, or a shaman may breathe it in and blow it on the patient.

- **Herbal remedies**   Many types of plants are turned into salves, liquids, powders, and other medicinal remedies for the patient to eat or drink.

An **herbalist** is a healing practitioner who specializes in plants and their medicinal properties. Some shamans may also be herbalists, whereas others may refer patients to herbalists or work with them in treating the patient.

Depending on the culture, shaman's style, diagnosis of the patient's problems, and other factors, the shaman or a specialist practitioner, like an *herbalist*, will use different combinations of plants and drugs to help in treating the patient. Not all shamans will use them, such as shamans in the far north, like the Inuits of Alaska or shamans of Siberia, where there are few plants. However, in most areas, plants and drugs play a major part of the healing process, particularly in the botanically-rich tropical forests of Central and South America.

The Path to Becoming a Healing Shaman

So what makes a person a shaman? Who becomes a shaman and how?

Today that question is complicated by the changing role of the shaman and different definitions of who is a shaman, as this traditional practice has taken different paths in modern times. Many practitioners are primarily counselors or combine shamanism with a psychological or psychiatric practice, while others use healing, sometimes combining it with their work as medical professionals. And even those using shamanic techniques might not call themselves "shamans," in the traditional sense of being a priest, healer, or local wiseman or wisewoman.

For traditional shamans who engage in healing as the tribal, village, or community shaman for a region, there are certain patterns and paths to becoming a shaman. Even in groups where a large percentage of the population are considered to have shamanic power, such as in some groups in the Upper Amazon and among the !Kung in the Sahara Desert of Africa, where about half the males are regarded as shamans and participate in group rituals, some individuals will be considered more powerful shamans than others. Some of the key characteristics of these sole or more powerful shamans and how they are identified are as follows:

- Traditionally, a great many shamans have been males, because of the association of the shaman with power, though in some societies women have become shamans, such as among the Sora of India, where the woman gains her shamanic power by marrying an underworld spirit who represents her own brother (Vitebsky, 1995, 56).

- Sometimes an individual may appear to have the traits of a shaman at birth; at other times, these qualities become more noticeable as the child grows up, particularly in his teenage years.

- Often a child may come from a family where a parent or other close relative has been a shaman, and the parent or relative becomes a mentor, helping to train the child from an early age.

- In some traditions, people believe the shaman is chosen by the spirits and gets a powerful call to become a shaman, commonly in childhood or as a teenager. For example, in some areas, the person may have a dream or vision in which he sees a spirit who tells him to take on this role, much like a person drawn to becoming a Catholic priest or a Protestant minister might feel a call to serve.

- Commonly, the person who becomes a shaman will have certain personality traits that contribute to his or her ability to be successful as a shaman, such as being prone to dreaming, being more meditative and reflective, being something of a loner, and being able to go into trance and communicate with spirits.

♦ Once a person shows signs that he might make a good shaman, an older practicing shaman will often become like a teacher or mentor to that person, showing him the techniques of the shaman. So he becomes a kind of shaman's apprentice, learning the craft, and often serving as an assistant to a practicing shaman.

CAUTION

Off the Path _____

In some cases, a future shaman may go through a long period of struggle to evade a calling to become a shaman. As the person resists, he may experience warnings from the spirits that if he doesn't accept the calling, he will be injured or killed by them.

♦ In some traditions, a person may go through a period of great trials and tribulations, which is viewed as the spiritual journey the person must take to show he is able to deal with the dark spiritual forces he will encounter as a shaman and will have to battle to heal others.

In short, there are many paths to becoming a traditional healing shaman, which vary from culture to culture and individual to individual. Of course, once someone embarks on that path, he or she has to engage in rigorous training to practice and perfect the many skills required to heal and counsel others and to gain the confidence and trust of others in the community.

The Battle Between Doctors and Shamans

Unfortunately, as shamanism has moved into the modern world, shamans have proved much more receptive to working in cooperation or in tandem with doctors than doctors have been in working with shamans. In many areas of the world, shamans have been accused of being quacks and frauds by doctors, as well as by the state government, resulting in crackdowns on shamans, particularly in the 1970s through the mid-1990s, though this pressure has eased in recent years.

Wise Ways

A good example of the way shamans have been harassed by the medical community and the state comes from Peru, where the healers, called *curanderos*, have a marginal legal and social status. As a result, they have often been harassed by the local police to obtain protection payments, whereas the police don't seek such payments from licensed practitioners. Also, the church and local officials have sought to get repressive measures passed against the shamansm (Joralemon, 1999, 65).

For example, in *Drum and Stethoscope*, anthropologist Julien Bastien describes how many doctors discredit the ability of shamans to cure diseases. In their view, shamans can't affect the biological cause of diseases with their techniques. Although it's true that shamans can't directly deal with many underlying biological and biochemical malfunctions, it's also the case that doctors may not be able to effectively treat many illnesses that have other than biological or biochemical causes, such as stress, which can cause cardiovascular problems, liver diseases, and chronic pain. Furthermore, patients who go to both doctors and shamans for different types of illnesses may not even expect the shaman to be able to cure the underlying biological condition; rather, they see them as a major source of support during their suffering (Bastien, 1996, 76). Thus, it often works well when doctors and shamans work together, because they are treating different parts of the person that lead to illness. Or as Bastien puts it: "When shamans and doctors collaborate, a synergetic effect is produced which further promotes healing" (Bastien, 1996, 84).

Although there is still a lot of distrust of shamans by the medical community, an increasing number of medical practitioners, particularly in the United States and Europe, have begun to explore how shamanic practices, including herbal remedies, might be used to help patients. To some extent, this is due to the spread of New Age and alternative medical practices into the mainstream.

At the same time, other medical practitioners, who work with clients from ethnic communities where people go to shamans and other local healers, are becoming more sensitive to culturally based definitions of illness. To a great extent, this increasing sensitivity is due to the growing field of *medical anthropology* and the input of medical anthropologists working in local clinics and hospital. They have helped doctors, nurses, and other medical practitioners become more aware of the different beliefs and attitudes that patients have about illness. Once these practitioners understand their patients' cultural beliefs, they can better relate to their patients and use practices that will help them heal, including shamanic techniques.

Medical practitioners are also increasingly recognizing that shamans can play a role in treating patients, particularly in rural and ethnic communities, in ways the doctors often can't, especially when they work in a more impersonal clinical or hospital setting. As Julien Bastien notes in *Drum and Stethoscope*, some of the ways that shamans can treat patients include:

- Forming a close relationship or bond with patients, while showing their own power, knowledge, and authority.

- Cleansing the patient, which is a way of ritually announcing that the patient is now healthy and no longer sick—a technique especially effective when a patient has bodily symptoms due to feelings of depression or anxiety.

Shaman Says

Medical anthropology is a growing field within anthropology that looks at medical systems cross-culturally. **Ethnomedicine** is a medical approach that is based on recognizing that different cultures have different beliefs and practices related to the cause of disease, the method of diagnosis, and the appropriate treatments that should be prescribed based on determining its cause.

◆ Mending social relationships, which is one common reason that many patients go to shamans; they feel victimized, guilty, are jealous of a lover or ex-spouse, are upset because of an unrequited love, or have experienced a personal life crisis. In some cases, such patients attribute their misfortune to the use of sorcery by others who are hostile toward them. Shamanism can, in turn, deal with such feelings that are leading to physical illness.

◆ Healing a range of physical symptoms that express different feelings, which is especially useful in cultures where mental and emotional conditions are expressed through the body, a phenomena known as *somatization.*

◆ Inducing physiological changes, such as through meditation, prayer, trance, and dramatic performance, which have a healing effect.

Shaman Says

Somatization refers to the process of expressing a mental or emotional condition as a disturbed bodily function. It is especially common in nonindustrialized societies where people don't recognize mental illnesses or deal with psychological problems as medical conditions.

Thus, the potential of shamanism for healing today, as in the past, is great. Shamans offer techniques that are adaptable to different cultural traditions, based on the beliefs of the people in a culture. Today, shamanic healing is still practiced successfully in developing countries and ethnic communities in urban areas; and medical practitioners are discovering the value of shamanic practices as well, including the curative properties of some of the traditional plants. While shamans may not have the knowledge of physiology and biology that underlies much disease and forms the basis of the medical model of disease used by biomedical practitioners, their alternate model of illness can be effective for treating many conditions.

The Least You Need to Know

◆ Traditionally, a key role of the shaman has been to act as a healer, although much modern shamanism has embraced counseling and personal development.

◆ As healers, shamans use a number of techniques, including conducting healing rituals, using plants and natural remedies (or working with an herbalist to provide these), and prescribing activities for the patient to follow.

◆ Often doctors and other medical practitioners are wary of shamans and their methods, because these practitioners use a biomedical model of disease based on biological and physical causes.

◆ It can be effective for many patients when doctors and shamans collaborate together, since they can provide the patient with different types of needed treatments.

Part 2

Power, Shaman Style

Everybody talks about shamans' power and how their contact with the spirits or the spiritual world increases that power. What, exactly, is shamanic power and what do you have to do to get your hands on some? In this part you'll find out about these shamanic power sources and how to tap into them for yourself. You'll find out about power animals, power objects, power places, and a host of other *powerful* items and activities.

Virtually anything can be a source of power if it's meaningful to you. How? Read on to tap into these various forms of power to enhance your shamanic experience and more effectively achieve your desired results.

Working with Power Animals, Teachers, and Guides

In This Chapter

◆ Sources of power for seeing into other worlds

◆ How shamans use power animals

◆ Finding your own power animals

◆ The importance of teachers and guides

◆ Finding your own teachers and guides

As shamans conceptualize power, it's basically ability to know, see, and access the spiritual force or energy of the universe or the spirits they contact to achieve their goals. While any power can be put to negative as well as positive uses, shamans focus on using it for positive, helpful, healing ends. They also use their own positive power to counteract the harmful effects of negative power that might be used against them or others.

For shamans, the sources of power come in many different varieties. Think of them like tools in a shamanic tool kit, which the shaman can draw from to enhance whatever he or she is doing. Much like a doctor needs a stethoscope to listen to a patient's heartbeat or a medical technician needs an X-ray to see underneath the body's outer shell, the shaman needs tools to help him or her see into and gain access to other worlds. Yet, at the same time, the shaman remains solidly anchored in the everyday world of reality and in control of the process of entering and leaving nonordinary reality.

The Many Sources of Power

Some of the major sources of shamanic power are:

- **Power animals** These are the animals that shamans call on for assistance when they are seeking knowledge or attempting to do a healing. Such animals include birds, reptiles, fish, amphibians, and sometimes even mythical animals. Other terms for these are animals helpers and totem animals.

- **Teachers and guides** These are the beings who come to assist the shamans and may take many forms—from real live people to ancestors to angels to guardian spirits. Other common names are spiritual guides, spirit helpers, and allies.

- **Power objects** These items are considered to have a spiritual force or energy, which the shaman can use to create more power in a ritual. Another term for these is sacred objects.

- **Elements of nature** These are the major forces or ways of classifying nature. Commonly, the four elements are earth, air, fire, and water, which are the categories used by Native Americans and in the West. Other groups use five elements, such as in ancient China, where the major forces were water, metal, wood, air, and fire.

- **Power songs and chants** These are songs or combinations of words that express the purpose of the shaman in conducting a shamanic session. Songs are generally characterized by rhythm, meaningful words, and melody. A chant is a song that is repeated or a series of words or nonsense syllables that may have acquired meaning or simply act as a kind of rhythmic repetition, like drumming.

Off the Path

While it's important to understand how these different sources of power have been used traditionally for a deeper understanding of shamanism, your goal should be to understand, learn from, and then develop your own approaches and meanings for these various power sources. Many people from traditional cultures resent people simply taking over their heritage and traditions.

As you read about these different sources of power and ways to use them, think about which types of power you'd like to use yourself. Then, you can choose among them to create your own shamanic power tool kit and make these tools your own. This chapter focuses on using power animals and working with teachers and guides. The next will focus on other major sources of power.

Using Power Animals

Power animals are central to most shamanic traditions, including modern shamanism. Shamans look to animal allies for their power, which includes offering them protection and guardianship while the shaman engages in rituals. Also, animals may be sources of advice and information and guides for maneuvering around in different worlds.

How Shamans Have Traditionally Used Power Animals

The roots of power animals go very deep—back to the very origins of shamanism. Remember the cave of Les Trois Freres in Chapter 1? The male figure, often called the dancing sorcerer, is thought to be a shamanic drawing of a creature that is part-man, part animal. According to one interpretation of the drawing, every part of the humanlike creature's anatomy belongs to a different animal: He has the ears of a wolf, the antlers of a deer, the tail of a horse, and the paws of a bear. Another interpretation is that this is a Master of the Animals, who embodies the essence of all of these spirits at the same time (Vitebsky, 2001, 29).

The dancing sorcerer reflects the use of power animals, in that the shaman would presumably gain the different powers or abilities of the different animals by making them part of himself. (This has to be speculation, because we can't know exactly what these long-ago human ancestors were thinking back then.) However, there are many other examples of the way shamans closely identify with or connect with power animals to gain their power from more recent times. For example, there are many examples of shamans wearing animal masks, such as shown in the rock art from Siberia, dating back to about 3000 B.C.E.

A rock art image from about 3000 B.C.E. in which a shaman from Siberia is wearing the head of the bird. It appears that he has a drum behind him.

In many traditional cultures, shamans are closely identified with animals or become them in ritual. For instance, in the upper Amazon, shamans commonly turn into jaguars by using singing spells, putting on the skin or teeth of the jaguar, or taking hallucinogenic drugs. Among one group, the Desana, the shaman takes an especially large dose of snuff after spending months of fasting and chanting, then turns into a jaguar while the effects of the snuff last (Vitebsky, 2001, 29). And in the Pacific Northwest, the Kwakiutl and other

Indian groups don the masks and skins of animals, becoming wolves, bears, foxes, and other powerful animals of the Northwest coast as they dance. They decorate their totem poles in front of their houses with this animal imagery, and incorporate animal images in their art, too.

Animals are often incorporated into Native American art. Pictured are several animals drawn on an animal hide (left); an image of a bird from the Native Americans in the Southwest (middle); and a bird from the Kwakiutl Indians of the Northwest (top of next page).

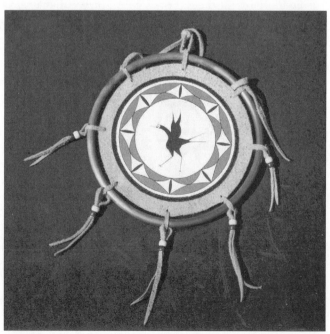

Power animals also provide the shaman with a form of transport to the other world, much like they might carry a person in real life. For instance, in Siberia, the shamans ride horses or reindeer, using the drum as a "windhorse" to call up this animal spirit. Other shamans use a bird to fly up into the sky or a fish, so they can swim and dive in the water (Vitebsky, 2001, 70). Even very small animals can play a part, such as when a shaman uses a mouse to help him get through very small openings.

Often these animal forms are represented by power objects, which are placed on an altar or carried with the shaman to give him power in doing a ritual. For instance, Eskimo shamans in Alaska kept carved wooden or ivory effigies of animals, such as an ermine or weasel, which they used as power objects. The shaman would take an effigy with him when he healed patients, and draw on its power, such as by directing it to bite the spirits attacking a patient (Vitebsky, 2001, 83).

The Power Animal Repertoire

What animals do shamans call on? Typically, animals that are native to an area: Shamans in Siberia use reindeer and horses, Indians of the Amazon call on jaguars, Eskimos seek out whales and seals, and Indians of the plains use the buffalo, coyote, and eagle. Whatever animals are familiar to you—or that you closely identify with and admire—can all be sources of power.

Think about the main characteristics of animals, and how those characteristics might help you. You want to think of that animal as having its own specialty, so it can offer you guidance in a particular area. Or if you identify with that animal, you can take on that animal's qualities. You can also call on several different animals for help in different areas. As Jose Stevens and Lena S. Stevens note in *Secrets of Shamanism*, "Each power animal has a specialty, so the shaman may need to consult with several if a problem has a variety of aspects to it" (Stevens & Stevens, 1988, 75). Here are the qualities often associated with some common animals, although the particular qualities vary for different groups and individuals:

- **Hawk**   the ability to see long distances
- **Eagle**   an ability to fly high and keen sight
- **Fox**   intelligence and cunning
- **Bear**   strength and power

- **Deer**   speed, gracefulness, and agility
- **Jaguar**   speed, stealth, and wisdom
- **Wolf**   aggressiveness and fierceness
- **Lion**   power and strength
- **Beaver**   industriousness, cleverness

Think about other animals and their associations for you. They may be the same as the associations held by traditional shamans; or you may have your personal associations you can use in your own shamanic practice.

Meeting Your Own Power Animal

How do you meet your own power animal? You can use various methods, including dancing until your animal appears, asking your dreams to provide you with a vision of your power animal, going on a vision quest, drumming and chanting to go on a journey to meet your power animal, or using mental imaging or visualization to take your journey. Animals are commonly thought to reside in the lower or middle world (though some tribes contact their power animals in the upper world and their ancestors in the lower world). So if you decide to find your power animal by journeying, the lower and middle worlds are good places to go.

Journeying to Find Your Power Animal

Are you ready to take a journey to meet your power animal? Like the other journeys in the book, you can use the following guided journey as general instruction for your journey by reading it beforehand, or you can read it into a tape recorder and play it back as you relax and take your journey.

Start by getting relaxed, and in a few minutes you'll be going on a journey into the lower world. First, focus on your breathing to get in this relaxed state. Notice your breath going in and out, in and out. You find yourself getting relaxed, but you are also staying alert and awake. Let your breathing go in and out; in and out; feeling very peaceful and relaxed, yet very aware as well.

Be aware of your purpose in going to the lower world. You are going to meet an animal, some sort of power animal. But don't try to meet that animal yet or decide what kind of animal you want to meet. Just let that happen when you go down there.

Find an opening to go down to this world. This opening could be someplace in the country, someplace in the city, someplace you're familiar with, someplace new. But it's some kind of opening going down to the ground.

Now see yourself there going to the opening. As you go in, you find yourself in a tunnel or some kind of tube, and you feel very comfortable and very safe. There's plenty of room to move around. See yourself, feel yourself, or experience yourself moving through this tunnel.

You are going down, down. Then, as you come to the bottom or end of this tunnel, you find it opens up into this lower world.

Now look around. Notice what you see, hear, feel.

You might notice the landscape. It could be a little bit like a cave in there, or it could open up on a landscape. Experience yourself moving around in this lower world, looking around, noticing what you see and feel, hearing sounds, and experiencing whatever happens.

> **Bon Voyage**
>
> A good way to get acquainted with your power animal is to act like it is just another friend you want to get to know. Take time to say hello and talk like you would be a friend. Ask your power animal about itself and tell your animal a little about yourself. After you've set the stage for a friendship, you can ask for help.

Now you can start going around to look for your animal. As you look, you may see different animals wandering around. One of these animals will stand out for you, come to you, or somehow seem drawn to you. Or if you don't see that animal at once, keep going on and pass by other places, other animals, until you feel drawn to one of them or notice one who seems drawn to you.

Then, go over to that animal or have it come to you.

Now meet it, get acquainted. Simply talk to it, make friends with it.

As you talk to or experience that animal, you may have the feeling that this animal represents a little part of you. You might notice the kinds of qualities that animal has, and as you do, you might be aware that these represent qualities of yourself which are part of you now.

One way that shamans strengthen their relationship with a special power animal is to make a painting, sculpture, or carving of it. The bear and coyote are particularly common power animals among many Native American groups. The bear is often seen as strong and powerful, while the coyote is commonly thought of as a wily, playful trickster figure who is often involved in difficult situations and scrapes, which he then gets out of.

You might also ask that animal if it has anything to tell you about itself, such as where it has been, what it does in the lower world, what it likes to do, or other questions. Then, listen to its response.

Now, as you get to know this animal, you feel this animal is there, ready to be helpful. You can come back and visit this animal again and call on it for the help or advice you need in the future. And the more you get to know this animal, the more help it will give you, and the more it will be a source of information and power for you.

If you want, follow this animal around and let it take you on a little journey, and you can explore a little more of this lower world and notice what's there. There's a path there you can follow. It could be straight or it might wander around. As you travel along it, you feel very safe taking this path, for this animal friend is with you. And you know this is just the beginning of your exploration of this world. Later, when you come back, you can meet this animal again, or you can meet other animals and explore even further. But for now, just keep walking around with your animal. As you do, you might be aware of the heat or coolness. You might be aware of the sounds around you. You might notice if there are any smells. Get a sense of this total environment you are in as you explore.

Bon Voyage

Anything can become your power animal—even a turtle, gorilla, or your family dog.

Now you are ready to go back. So you turn around, and your animal is starting to lead you back to where you first met it. On the way, your animal tells you that it will be there waiting for you the next time you come to see it. If you find this animal continues to be helpful, you can continue to visit it. But feel free to go back to meet other power animals who can be helpful to you later.

Wise Ways

After your journey, you can create a power object representing your animal. Create a sculpture, carving, or drawing as a reminder of your experience, and use it to draw on your animal's power.

Now, you are back where you first met. So you can say good-bye to your animal as you would to any friend.

Then, travel back along the same path, and you see yourself going back to the tunnel again. Now you are traveling through the tunnel back to the opening.

At the opening, step back out to where you began, and start counting backward from five to one. As you do, you will feel more and more awake and alert, and come back into the room. Five, four, more and more awake. Three, two, just about back. One, and you are back in the room.

The Meanings and Uses of Your Power Animal

Once you have met your power animal or animal helper, think about what it means and how it can help you. When you take these journeys to meet a power animal, you are likely to meet all types of creatures—everything from small playful creatures that are figures of fun to large aggressive animals that are symbols of power.

You may also meet more than one animal, and both can be your power animals, sometimes for different purposes. While some shamans do choose a particular power animal to work with, many shamans use a number of them. It depends on the cultural tradition the shaman comes from, and also the preference of a particular shaman.

> **Wise Ways**
>
> You can seek the assistance of different power animals for different purposes. If you need strength, seek the help of a strong power animal, such as a bear. Or if you face a problem that calls for wisdom, seek the assistance of a wise power animal, such as a fox or an owl.

What's important is choosing a power animal you feel a rapport with and is meaningful to you. While traditional associations with animals can help to provide initial guidelines, your own cultural and personal associations play a key role, too. That's because different people have different associations for different animals due to their own particular experiences.

After you meet your animal helpers, particularly the animal that you most closely identify with as your power animal, reflect on what this animal means to you. Think about how you relate to this animal, what traits you associate with it, and how it represents different aspects of yourself.

Drawing from Other's Experiences

Reading about other people's initial animal encounters can be useful for reflecting on your own experience. The following encounters were related by participants in a workshop that I taught on applying shamanic techniques in daily life. Notice how each person's power animals reflect different aspects of themselves or areas in which they needed some help at the time.

One very expressive and outgoing woman met a very playful little dog, who reflected this playful quality in herself. As she described it:

> I ended up in a place where there was a small pond with trees next to it. I entered by going into the water and went through the tunnel, and when I got to the end, I stepped into this place with the pond and the trees …

The animal I met there was a little dog with a really long nose. It was like a cartoon character. It seemed to be always smiling, but very wise. It was running around and leaping up and down, and I felt I could really relate to it, because I could feel the excitement, too. It had this spontaneous energy. It was very curious, eager to find out what's coming next, and it was very attentive. It seemed to be very independent, too …

I guess you could say those traits characterize me, too. Anyway, I liked this friendly little cartoon dog. He seemed so playful, so curious, so eager to help.

By contrast, another woman experienced a panther, who seemed very powerful and controlling. As she reported, she kept trying to direct it, but she found that the animal had its own mind about where it wanted to go, so she finally let go, and it had a more comfortable experience. But when she later tried to control the panther again, she found herself in a power struggle in which she kept losing her animal. As she described the journey:

I experienced a black animal. It was a panther, black, and dramatic. At first, it was trying to guide me, and I didn't think it was friendly at all. So I was concerned about where it was taking me, and when it looked like it was going over a ramp to Marin County (a county across the bridge from San Francisco), I thought, "No, that's not where I want to be." But then, I realized, I'm not supposed to control it. So I tried to let go of the control, and it felt very peaceful and much more relaxed. But then, I kept losing him, though then he came back. I think it's because I really wanted to stay in Marin, so I guess I should have followed him in the first place.

A third woman encountered two power animals, one a tiger, the other a panther, and she found they represented a balancing force, which helped to give her a sense of stability. As she reflected on her meeting with them, she realized she needed this balance and stability in her life right now, since she was going through a period of making choices. As she reported:

I had two power animals. When the journey started out, I came into a jungle, and the first animal that I met was a monkey. He jumped on me, but I knew it wasn't my power animal. The monkey was really friendly, and I had a good time with him. But it was more like he was a greeter, just showing me the way.

Then I met a tiger, and after that a black panther, who was full of power, began coming toward me. Soon they were both there in front of me, and they had very different qualities.

The tiger reminded me of the tiger I had been dreaming about in the last two weeks. I dreamt about him twice, and in both dreams, I slept with the tiger, and the tiger was very loving. We slept in each other's arms, like old friends. Now, here was this tiger again.

As for the panther, he reminded me of my sun sign, which is Scorpio. It's a very sharp, penetrating sign, which represents my very deep, cutting edge that's harsh and slices through things.

So it felt like the tiger and the panther were my two sides. I felt like the tiger was the soft part, the panther the hard part, and now I felt drawn to that soft part. So instead of just walking along with the tiger, I decided to go inside it. It felt very good and powerful being in there.

Then, I switched back and forth in between walking along between those two cats and being inside the tiger. It felt like I was experiencing the polarity of ying and yang, and finding that balance between them. When I went inside the tiger, I felt very grounded. I felt a wonderful, strong powerful feeling of both being inside and being the cat, and I felt this wonderful feeling of soft power, which was helping me come to terms with my female power by experiencing this warmth and nurturing, which I need right now.

So it's like this tiger was my soft feminine aspect, while the panther was my cutting and aggressive masculine side. I felt that having both of them walking side by side with me was showing me the two aspects of my power, which I'm trying to come to terms with, especially getting more in touch with my feminine side.

By contrast, another woman experienced the panther as a soft, cuddly creature who represented warmth and stability to her, which illustrates the importance of looking at the characteristics of the animal and the meanings which you perceive. It's also important to look to the animal to lead you, so you can better gain the power and qualities that the animal has to offer. Otherwise, if you try to direct and control your animal, that can be counterproductive.

> **CAUTION**
>
> ## Off the Path
>
> Your relationship with your power animal should be as unique as you are! Don't choose power animals based on other people's experiences, because then you won't get the useful information tailored to your own needs that comes from having your own personally chosen animal. Rather, the relationship should be based on your own goals and personality. Otherwise, it's like you are living someone else's life or following directives from your parents.

To Each His or Her Own

When you hear about others' encounters with power animals, you'll find they are each very individualistic, just as they are for different shamans. Even when you encounter the same animal as someone else, it will often have different personalities and characteristics reflecting your different backgrounds, experiences, personalities, and needs at the time.

For instance, the animal may be a part of yourself, which you have lost touch with and want to rediscover, though it may now be buried by other qualities. Say, for example, that you see a fox; you may have certain associations with it, such as thinking it is a very intelligent, clever creature, and maybe you need some help from such a creature now. Or if you see a deer, maybe you associate that with gentleness, which is a quality you want to develop. In other words, the creatures you see may have various meanings to you and various reasons for appearing. By reflecting on them later, you can seek to discover these meanings and reasons.

The ease with which you take this journey and meet your animal or other teachers will vary, too. People have different speeds at which they move around in the lower world and meet with their animals. Some people find an animal almost instantly; others take a long time traveling and like to spend more time with their animals. But whatever your speed initially, the process generally speeds up as you take these journeys more often, as will be discussed in Part 3.

Bon Voyage

Some examples of the many different types of teachers that shamans work with include:

- In Korea, novice shamans look to a living "spiritual mother," who help to coach them when they learn their songs and dances (Vitebsky, 2001, 67).

- Among the Wana of Indonesia, the shaman looks to spirit helpers to build and guide his canoe on a spiritual journey, in which he travels from his house through the roof and through the treetops into the clouds. Then, along the way, this spiritual crew discusses how to best navigate the canoe, the lost souls to look for, and the enemies to avoid (Vitebsky, 2001, 71–72).

- Among the Hopi of Arizona and New Mexico, the shaman might call on the spirits of the katchinas, the spirit beings of the surrounding sacred mountains, lakes, and canyons, who take on various human forms (Underhill, 1965, 207–210).

- Among the shamans of Central Asia and Khasakstan, where the Muslim religion is predominant, the shamans might appeal to Allah, various Muslim saints, and a variety of helping spirits, thought of as a kind of genie (Basilov, 1984, 39). In fact, these genies, also called djinns, are mentioned in the Koran, and represent a carryover of shamanism into Islam.

- And in his rituals, Peruvian shaman Eduardo Calderòn, who combined Christian influences with the ancient heritage of the Andes, would call on some of the Christian saints, as well as spirits of herbs and other of nature, as embodied in the many ritual objects collected on his mesa.

In short, shamans have traditionally called on all sorts of teachers as spiritual helpers in their rituals.

It is helpful to know about the vast range of possibilities when journeying to meet your power animal, so you can be prepared for this variety. The important thing is to be receptive and perceptive about whatever happens to you. This way you have your own informed and authentic experience, and don't end up incorporating someone else's symbols or meanings into your own experience, whether those symbols or meanings come from what you have read or from the reports of others you know.

Working with Teachers and Spiritual Guides

While many shamans look to animal helpers as teachers and guides, they also often turn to teachers and spiritual guides, and many seek help from both. It depends on the tradition, and you may find different types of teachers helpful for different purposes.

The major types of teachers and guides include the following:

- Angels, particularly for shamans working in a Christian tradition.
- Ancestor spirits, particularly in cultures that place a great emphasis on honoring the ancestors.
- Elders, particularly in groups that recognize the wisdom of the older members of the community.
- Cultural heroes, particularly in cultures that place a great importance on a tradition of myths and stories.
- Local deities, particularly in cultures that recognize many types of spiritual beings— from those that take on human form to spirits of nature.
- Well-known people and celebrities, a recent development in modern shamanism.
- Personal teachers, including friends, relatives, real-life teachers, business associates, and others—again, more common in modern-day shamanism.
- Aliens from outer space—and that's no joke! Some people have even joined together to form "calling circles" to invite these aliens to come to visit them.

You can call on many different types of teachers in your own shamanic practices. They can come from your own religious faith; from your own ancestors or elders in your community; or religious figures, deities, or culture figures from societies you feel an affinity with. Or if you wish, choose people you know and trust, everyday pop figures, or modern-day celebrities for advice or to help guide your shamanic journey.

What is most important is that you feel comfortable with your teacher and value his or her guidance and leadership. As in the case of power animals, in some cases you may want a continuing relationship with a particular teacher; if so, continue the relationship. You can also call on different teachers at different times for different purposes.

Meeting Your Teachers and Guides

Meeting your teachers is similar to meeting your power animal. You take a journey to look for a teacher, and travel in a very receptive state of mind, looking for the teacher who will come to you. Then, in the future, you can continue to work with that same teacher or take a journey to look for another teacher or teachers.

Whereas power animals are often associated with the lower world or middle world of Earth and nature, teachers are often associated with the upper and middle worlds. It helps to have a general idea of what to expect before you take your journey, so you know what to look for when you go to meet your teacher. In some traditions, teachers in the upper world are thought of as having greater power than the power animals in the lower world, so you might think of these teachers as very wise or powerful beings you can look up to.

> **Wise Ways**
>
> Perhaps another way to think of these animals and teachers is to look on the animals from the lower world as a metaphor for the physical level of yourself, while the teachers are a metaphor for your intellectual or spiritual level. However, this distinction reflects a more modern approach, since many native people do not see "spiritual" and "physical" as being separate realms of experience.

Making a Journey of It

When you take a shamanic journey to meet your teacher, as with meeting your power animal, don't go with any advance preconceptions of who your teacher might be. Rather, as you take your journey, simply start looking around for your teacher, be receptive, and let your teacher present him or herself to you.

Your teacher may appear in various forms—in human form, like an angel, or even a nonhuman form, such as a form of light or a glow or even some kind of mythical creature.

Your teacher may present him or herself to you in a number of ways, including:

♦ Telling you things in words or showing you things without saying anything.

♦ Giving you a vision of something.

♦ Leading you somewhere.

♦ Answering your questions telepathically.

♦ Validating or confirming your belief or opinion about something.

The key to a most productive, insightful journey is to realize that whatever happens is appropriate and it's all part of your answer.

Bon Voyage

Your teacher can be anyone—a spirit, ancestor, or even a celebrity.

The following exercise will introduce you to your teacher and let you ask your teacher what he or she wants to teach you now. As in the case of taking a journey to meet your power animal, you can read this guide to yourself and then use it as a general guide for taking a journey. Or read it aloud into a tape recorder; then play it back as you close your eyes, relax, and go on the journey.

You'll be going on a journey to meet your teacher. You'll be asking your teacher: "Do you have anything to tell me or teach me now?"

Start by getting relaxed, and focus on your breathing, going in and out, in and out. You are starting to feel more and more relaxed, but at the same time, you will stay alert and aware. Just concentrate on being relaxed, yet being alert.

When you are ready, find some kind of jumping-off or starting point, a place you can leave from to go to the upper world. It might be something like a tree or a ladder. It could be a mountain, a building, or any other high point, where you feel comfortable. See yourself there now.

Now see yourself going up. You feel very comfortable as you go higher. If you want to walk or climb that's fine, or if you want to fly up, do that. However, you travel, see yourself rising, rising.

Then, you may see some kind of membrane or cloud, and you move through it.

You are now in the upper world. Just look around. Notice what it looks like, how it feels. You may notice the surface under your feet. It may feel firm or spongy. Feel free to walk around.

As you walk, notice the colors around you, the forms, the textures. Get a sense of the total environment.

Now start looking for your teacher, and perhaps someone will appear. If someone appears, ask that person or being if he or she is your teacher. If so, ask your question: "Do you have anything to teach me or tell me now?" If not, go on and look for another teacher.

Don't be concerned if this person or being says they are not your teacher. Feel free to go on, moving along the path or up to another level. If you encounter someone else, ask them if they are your teacher. Keep asking "Do you have anything to teach me or to tell me?" until you find someone who responds positively. This person will be your teacher.

When you find your teacher listen to and observe him or her carefully. Be ready to follow your teacher and pay attention to wherever your teacher leads you. Everything that you observe or hear is part of the answer.

As you listen or observe your teacher teaching you, realize the wisdom of this teacher. Perhaps you might recognize that this wisdom is a part of you, just as this teacher may be a part of you. Or perhaps look on your teacher as a very wise being you can look up to.

Know, too, that you can come back to the source of this wisdom in the upper world, and you can meet with this teacher again or with another teacher in the future.

Let your teacher finish telling his or her message to you. Then, when you're ready, say thank you and tell your teacher good-bye.

Then, you can travel back along the same path. Just walk or travel along the surface of the upper world, back to the opening where you came in. Then, travel downward to whatever jumping-off point you used.

Now see yourself coming back to the surface of the earth and standing there again, as you were before when you entered.

Count backward from five to one, and you'll start to come back. Five, four, more and more awake. Three, two, almost back, and one. You are back in the room.

> **Wise Ways**
>
> Any type of teachers, wherever you meet them, in any kind of setting, can be a source of knowledge.

The Meanings and Uses of Your Teachers and Guides

The types of teachers you have and your experiences with them can be extremely varied, and you may find the teachers are not at all what you expect. In traditional shamanic practice, teachers and guides have typically been spiritual and religious figures, mythological beings, deities, saints, departed ancestors, and other culturally significant figures. They have usually been quite serious, sacred beings, who can bring wisdom or a healing ability to the shaman.

In today's modern secular age, your teachers and guides certainly can come from the ranks of such traditional figures. On the other hand, they might not. The teachers you meet may be very hip, contemporary figures or everyday people you know, not the wise old masters sometimes associated with this world of teachers and guides. Also, the setting where you meet could be a surprise as well, since it might turn out to be an ordinary room, not some kind of ethereal, otherworldly place.

How Others Met Their Teachers

The following experience illustrates how varied and personal these teachers can be, since the types of people or beings you can learn from is so various. They can even be popular outlaw figures, as one woman found. Here's how she described it:

I found myself on a cliff with the wind blowing through my hair. Then, I followed it into a place with a lot of colors—a lot of lavender, burgundies, and purples, and there was a very slick, smooth surface all the way around, like being in a big domed space. The first person I ran into looked like one of those old Hells Angels guys with a cap and a vest. He was standing there and he greeted me. Then, I went on, looking for this guy that I have had in my dreams, and I saw a woman who was him with white hair, and she looked familiar. She said: "Hello, hi, how are you doing? This is my place." It was very casual.

Then, I said or was thinking: "Is there anything you need to tell me?" All at once I began thinking about my dancing, and I got this image of silver birds and a sense of real bliss. Suddenly, I thought: "I'm going to get new dancing shoes, and I thought what a great idea, because I'll be able to get rid of the old ones, and I thought when I do this, I'll be able to get rid of a lot of self-consciousness and doubt.

In another case, a man met a Hugh Hefner-type businessman who was sitting on a bed, wearing a gilded bathrobe and lounging pajamas—not at all the type of person he would have picked for a teacher, since in reality he thought of Hefner as a lecherous comic figure. But then, the Hugh Hefner figure led him to a window, and as the man looked out, the figure gave him answers about what he should do with his ideas for inventing and marketing a new product, and he seemed to have all the information he needed.

As these examples of modern-day meetings with teachers suggest, you don't know what or who you'll encounter, so it's important not to have any preconceptions about who your teachers are going to be. Remain open to the wisdom and power of whomever you meet, even if they don't initially correspond to your images of what a wise or powerful teacher might look like.

It's fine if you do have someone you particularly want to see for help, much like traditional shamans have developed a personal connection with a teacher who repeatedly comes to help them. But generally, if you just leave your choice open and remain receptive, a teacher who will be especially helpful to you in your current situation will appear. Sometimes they might seem like very unusual or unlikely teachers. But if you ask, you will generally find they can help you with your needs and questions right now.

Off the Path

Don't reject images even if, at first, they seem irrelevant.

Off the Path

Be careful whom you tell your experiences to, since some people may not understand. Unfortunately, for some people, this kind of imagined conversation is akin to madness or delusional thinking. Only share learning and practicing shamanic techniques with people who you feel certain will be receptive to this kind of approach.

The Least You Need to Know

◆ The many sources of power include power animals, power objects, teachers and guides, the elements of nature, and power songs or chants.

◆ Shamans typically call on power animals that are native to the area; and commonly they go to the lower world or middle world to contact these animals.

◆ While it helps to have a general idea of the main characteristics or associations with different power animals, what's most important is that you are open and receptive to whatever animal or animals come to you to be your power animal.

◆ When you go to meet your power animal, regard it like meeting and getting to know a friend.

◆ Travel to the upper world to find spirit guides; when you find someone, ask them if they have anything to teach you.

Chapter 8

Using Power Objects and the Elements

In This Chapter

- Increasing your shamanic power
- The power and variety of power objects
- Choosing the right power objects for your needs
- The four elements of nature
- Using the four elements in your own life
- Visionary and healing plants

Because getting and using power is so central to shamanism, shamans use multiple power sources at the same time to maximize their power to help and heal. They pick and choose which sources of power to use in particular situations, and the more energy and power they need for a particular purpose, the more sources they will tap.

Multiplying Power Through Multiple Power Sources

You can think of the many sources of power available to you in shamanism in these ways:

♦ They are like a variety of light bulbs of different shapes, colors, and sizes, which you can choose from to illuminate a room. You might choose different lights for different purposes, and the more lights you use, the brighter the illumination.

♦ They are like tools in a toolkit, with different tools for different tasks. And for really big jobs, you may need to use multiple tools to get the job done.

♦ They are like a repertoire of skills you use on a job; and the more skills you have— and the more polished your skills—the faster and better you can do the job.

In fact, in some cases, several shamans will work together to call on power for a particular purpose, such as when Black Elk described a group healing for his brother-in-law, who had been seriously injured in a beating after an encounter on the road turned deadly. As his brother-in-law lay in the hospital, with possible brain damage, the shamans drew on several power sources: a power object, the Chanunpa, which was their sacred pipe and which they all smoked; power songs; plus prayers to the spirits. Black Elk's brother-in-law healed without brain damage, and Black Elk felt the ceremony played a key role in his brother-in-law's healing (Lyons, 1990, 108–110).

In the previous chapter, the focus was on accessing power through using power animals and calling on teachers and guides. Here the focus will be on the many other types of power that shamans can use. As you read about these power sources, think about which types you would like to use in your own shamanic practice. At different times, you will find different types of power helpful; and the more important or serious the situation, the more power sources you may want to use. For example, on a regular basis, you might call on your power animal, spiritual teacher, or guide for help. Or for special occasions, such as dealing with a serious problem or engaging in a healing for yourself or others, you might use additional sources of power, such as power objects, songs, dancing, prayers, or a ritual to call on the elements of nature. By using multiple sources of power, you strengthen your efforts and intensify your focus, so your efforts are more likely to be successful.

> **Shaman Says**
>
> A **power place** is a place that is considered especially powerful; often it is a place where very powerful or sacred spirits reside. A **sacred place** is considered especially spiritual and worthy of honor because of its associations with spiritual beings or sacred rituals and other activities.

For even more power, you can go to *power places* or *sacred places*, where a sense of spiritual power is especially strong. You can go there either in physical reality or via a shamanic journey, individually or as a group. (See Chapter 11 for more on power places.)

The Power of Power Objects

All sorts of things can become power objects, including natural, handcrafted, and manufactured ones. You can acquire objects that already are invested with power or you can charge and imbue the object with power yourself. Power objects often represent the elements of nature, which are themselves another type of power (the elements are discussed later in this chapter). For example, you might use a rock representing the earth, a candle representing fire, a cup representing water, or a carving of a bird representing air. Whatever you use, it should be something that you regard as powerful. While you may find it easiest to use a physical object, since you can touch and see it in front of you, once you develop your ability to visualize, you can imagine this power object and see yourself using it in your mind.

The number of objects you use can vary, too, from just a few objects to a great many. Traditionally, the shamans of Siberia only use a few very important power objects. Among these are the drum, made of animal skins; the whip, used to urge on the shamanic steed during the journey; and the staff made of iron or wood, which is often hung with bells or jingle cones, so it can be used as a rattle. They might sometimes use knives, swords, and other ritual weapons, such as a bow and arrow, spear, and ax, and some use a pipe (Sarangerel, 2001, 155–168). Many Native American groups use only a few key power objects such as the sacred pipe for smoking, a drum, and rattles.

By contrast, some traditions use several objects, such as the dozens of objects placed on the mesa or altar by the shamans of Peru, in addition to having swords and staffs nearby. The particular objects they choose have both personal and cultural meanings.

There is also great variation in what objects are used where. For instance, take the drum and rattle, which are central to shamanism in some areas, but not in others. In Siberia, the home of traditional shamanism, the drum is the "instrument of shamanism" as Piers Vitebsky, who surveyed shamanism around the world calls it. In North America both the drum and rattle are used. But in

Bon Voyage

You can use visualizations of your power objects to stand for the physical object and imagine yourself working with them, but generally, shamans select particular physical objects to use in their practice.

Wise Ways

The famous Peruvian shaman Eduardo Calderón used dozens of power objects, which he divided into those associated with forces of evil, those associated with forces of good, and those associated with a balance of powers. He collected his objects over the years, and they reflected a mixture of Christian and Indian influences (Sharon, 1978, 62–64).

South America few shamans use a drum, while the rattle is very important, both because it is a symbol of the world tree and because it helps to induce an altered state through its rhythmic shaking sound.

Bon Voyage

Rattles often symbolize the world tree for South American shamans. The rattle's handle symbolizes the tree, while the hollow gourd of the rattle is associated with the cosmos, and the seeds or pebbles inside the rattle represent the spirits and souls of ancestors. When a shaman shakes the rattle, he activates these spirits, who then come to help in the shamanic ceremony (Vitebsky, 2001, 49).

The use of masks, hats, and headdresses vary, too, from ordinary street clothes to very elaborate costumes. Even individual shamans may vary in what they wear under different circumstances. For example, in some traditions, such as Siberia, the shamans wear hats to keep their head covered while working with the spirits. If they are doing everyday shamanism, Siberian shamans commonly use a regular hat, which is a traditional Mongolian or Siberian-style hat with a rounded or pointed top that is decorated with fur and bells or jingle cones for shamanic work. But for more advanced work, where they merge with the spirits, they put on a special kind of hat, a feathered headdress, much like those worn by some Native American shamans. (Sarangerel, 2001, 160–161).

In other areas, masks are popular, such as among some Native American groups in the Pacific Northwest and among many peoples in Africa. The use of masks often creates a kind of shamanic theater, where the shaman takes on or merges with another spirit, such as a bear or other animal, deity, or ancestor spirit (Vitebsky, 2001, 120–121.)

Art pieces, too, can be objects of power, although they might not have originally been created as art, such as the Navaho sand painting used in a healing ceremony. In the traditional ceremony, the sand painting is trampled and discarded after the ceremony ends. Many of these paintings are now turned into wall hangings, where they can be a focus for meditation and journeying, much like an Indian *mandala*, a design in which the shapes and colors radiate out from the center, like the bull's eye of a target for directing one's focus. Another example is the gods eye woven by some Native American groups in the Southwest—an image which has become especially popular in tourists shops.

Many figurines of saints, deities, ancestors, and other beings can be objects of power, too. These can be made from many types of materials, from stone, wood, and ivory to ceramic, tile, or yarn; and they can be handcrafted or manufactured; purchased or handmade; new or old. What's important is that they have meaning and power for a particular person.

A god's eye, which is characterized by a central point and radiating spokes (there are usually eight of them), with an image that is divided into four sections representing the four directions.

A human figure like those used by the Cayapa shamans in Ecuador. These figures represent ancestor or other spirits, and the shamans place them on the altar during a healing ceremony.

In an actual healing ceremony, the shaman would place figures such as these on his altar and focus on them when calling on his ancestor or other spirits to join in the ceremony and bring their wisdom and assistance in helping and healing the patients.

Choosing Your Own Power Objects

Given this vast diversity, how do you choose a power object or objects for yourself? If you are working within a particular tradition of shamanism, then select from among the types of objects used in that tradition. Otherwise, select objects that have a positive feeling and symbolic meaning for you.

Because many power objects come from nature—such as rocks, stones, feathers, dried leaves, pinecones, shells, and pieces of driftwood—a good place to start is by taking a walk in nature, where you can look for objects in your environment. On your walk, just pick up objects because it feels good to do so—don't worry about why you're picking them up. Later, after you've had a chance to reflect on your found object, you can ask yourself what they mean to you. If you continue to feel a kinship with them, you can use one or more of them as a power object.

Still another way to obtain these objects is to make them yourself. For example, you can make prayer sticks by gathering sticks of wood and attaching feathers and create gods eyes by wrapping yarn around crossed sticks. Or you can combine a collection of small found objects, such as feathers, small stones, and twigs, into a small sculpture. Once you've constructed the object, the next step is to charge it with power and meaning (which will be discussed later in this chapter).

You can even buy ordinary objects in local stores, even in a department store. But then, you still have to charge an object you buy with power, after you acquire it.

However you obtain your power objects, to keep them even more powerful, it is usually best to keep them in a special place or use them only for your shamanic practice. Otherwise, they will start to seem like mundane, ordinary objects again.

An example of a collection of objects from various sources that might be used as personal power objects. For one person, they might be purely decorative objects; but for another, they could become power objects used in their shamanic practice.

As for constructing your own mesa or altar, if you are working with a tradition that pro-vides special guidelines on how to design and work with an altar and power objects, go with that. Otherwise, just put whatever objects are meaningful for you wherever you like and use them as a focus. The point is there are multiple ways to create an altar and use these objects—so use what feels good for you.

Still another consideration in choosing or creating your own power object is using them to represent other sources of power. For instance, once you choose a power animal, consider getting or mak-ing arts or crafts objects that represent this ani-mal, such as making a sculpture of a jaguar or creating a prayer stick with feathers from a bird. If you are calling on the spirits of one of the ele-ments, such as earth, use an object from the earth to represent the element, such as a rock or box in which you have collected some earth. If you are using healing plants, perhaps use a dried leaf of that plant on your altar. If you have gone to a place that you consider a sacred place or power spot, take an object from that place to keep a bit of that place with you as a reminder.

> **Wise Ways**
>
> Keeping power objects charged is like using a rechargeable bat-tery. You have to charge it ini-tially; then, if you use it regularly, it will keep recharging itself. But if you don't use it for awhile, the charge will run down and you'll have to recharge it. Plus, if you keep it in a protected place, it will be less likely to become damaged or mishandled by oth-ers, mixing in their everyday and possibly negative energy with the positive, special quality of these objects.

A Potpourri of Power Objects

Following is a list of objects you can use for power objects. Pick those categories that appeal to you and use that list as a guide for the objects you might get.

- Natural objects such as rocks, leaves, shells, crystals, feathers
- Objects representing your power animal, such as paintings or sculptures
- Objects representing your spiritual teachers or guides, such as a picture or something that person gave you as a special gift
- Figurines of saints, angels, or deities
- Staffs, swords, knives, or daggers
- Hats and headdresses
- Art objects such as sand paintings, yarn paintings, gods eyes
- Decorative objects or beads
- Noise-making objects like drums, rattles, bells, or didgeridoos
- Anything else you can think of that might be a power object for you

After you get each object, take some quiet time to reflect on its meaning. Also, imagine you are charging it with your personal power, so you can draw on that power when you engage in shamanic practices, such as conducting a ritual or going on a shamanic journey.

You can charge objects with power by conducting a charging ritual or visualize that object being charged with energy or power. These charging rituals can be fairly elaborate in different traditions, and involve such things as a preliminary purification ceremony, chants, songs, and dancing as the shaman holds the object or uses it as a focus. For example, if you were charging a staff as a power object, you might lay it on an altar surrounded by different representations of the four elements, such as a candle for fire, cup of water for water, rock for earth, and feather for air. Then, you might lift it up and hold it to the four directions as you chant about how it is gaining the energy of that direction. Or more simply, you can simply hold that object and focus on it in a quiet place, and imagine you are charging it with your personal energy. Shamans from different traditions use different approaches to charging objects, and so can you.

Understanding the Four Elements and Directions

The four elements—earth, air, fire, and water—are another central concept in many shamanic systems, particularly in the West and among Native Americans. Often they are associated with the four directions (or four winds used in some shamanic systems, such as by many shamans in Peru), and with the four seasons of the year.

Popular associations with these four elements common in Western and Native American systems have also become part of everyday culture, such as when you think of a person who is very stable, reliable, and practical as "down to earth" and "grounded," a person who is the opposite—unstable, uncertain, and unrealistic—as "spacey," a "space case," or an "airhead." Or to take two other examples of opposite characteristics: you might consider a person who is very aggressive and quick to anger as "fiery" or a "firebrand," while you might associate someone who is very calm, cool, collected, and quiet with water images, such as in the expression: "still water runs deep." In shamanism, you work with these elements and their associations even more deeply.

The basic associations with the elements include:

Bon Voyage

Specific links between elements, directions, and seasons may differ from region to region, just as the seasons change depending on where you live.

- ◆ **Earth** associated with the ground, geologic formations, rocks, and the things directly growing on it, including the grass, bushes, and trees (which is why some Native Americans, such as the Lakota, use the term "green" to refer to this element).

- ◆ **Air** associated with winds, from light breezes to whirlwinds, tornadoes and cyclones; with clouds; with birds; and with the notion of flight generally;

- ◆ **Fire** associated with flames, smoke, the heat from a fire, lightning, and the idea of energy.

- ◆ **Water** associated with bodies of water, like lakes, streams, ponds, rivers, oceans, and waterfalls, and with the different ways that water falls to the earth, such as rain, snow, and hail.

The Four Directions

Shamans often associate the four elements with the four cardinal directions and four seasons. Associations can vary from tradition to tradition. The following are common in the northern hemisphere, according to Tom Cowan, who has practiced shamanism for several years.

- ◆ **Earth** associated with the North and winter, since these are "dark, dense, in their own way impenetrable" (Cowan, 71).

- ◆ **Air** associated with the East and spring, since the light of dawn begins in the East.

- ◆ **Fire** associated with the South and summer, because these are associated with heat and warmth.

- ◆ **Water** associated with the West and fall, since water "runs downward into the earth, like the setting sun" (Cowen, 71).

Then, too, in various systems, there are color associations with the elements, as well as with the directions and seasons. Most notably, these are: black, brown, or green with earth; white or yellow with air; red or orange with fire, and blue with water.

Sometimes certain animals are linked to these elements, directions, and seasons. For instance, in parts of North America heavy animals, like the bear, are linked with earth and north; flying animals, like the eagle, with the air and east; aggressive or cunning animals, such as the coyote, with the fire and south; and animals that live in the water, such as fish, with water and the West.

Very often these elements are viewed as having different personalities or spirits associated with them in different cultures. Earth is classically seen as the "Mother," "Great Mother," or "Grandmother," because of Earth's nurturing qualities and its association with fertility and birth, since things grow from the earth. Conversely, the sky is traditionally seen as the "Father," "Great Father," or "Grandfather," because the sky, heavens, and movement of the stars through the sky are associated with great power and with the rule of law. By contrast, fire, because of its power to destroy, as well as offer warmth, is often associated with figures of evil or wrath; while water, due to its usually calm nature, is associated with figures that bring comfort and healing.

Working with the Four Elements in Your Own Life

You can work with the elements in your own life in various ways. One way to incorporate the elements into your life is to collect objects that you associate with the different elements and use them like power objects:

- ◆ The objects associated with earth are obviously the easiest to get, since you can pick up almost anything, such as rocks, stones, soil, animal bones, dried leaves, crystals.

- ◆ For air, look for things like feathers or incense or herbs since their scent is transported by air.

- ◆ In the case of fire, you can look for objects associated with the spirit of fire, such a crystal that can focus the sun's rays, wooden objects burned by fire, or candle wax. Alternatively, you can burn a candle or light a small fire in a fireplace or burner.

- ◆ For water objects, look for objects from the beach or the bed of a creek or stream, such as a seashell or pebble, or fill a small bottle or other container with water— preferably from a natural body of water. Don't just turn on the tap.

A good way to use these elements is to reflect on the different elements of nature and think about how you express the characteristics you associate with these elements. Another approach is to think about how you might use these elements in a present-day situation.

Reflecting on the Elements

It might take some practice to learn how to reflect on the elements and the items you've chosen to represent them. So, in this section, I'll walk you through the process.

Start by choosing an element to focus on first. If you have an object that represents that element, place it in front of you and use that as a focus.

As you think about that element or look at the object representing it, think about the qualities of that element. Sense and feel those qualities in yourself. Close your eyes and imagine you have become that element, and see yourself being and moving as that element.

After you have done this exercise with one element, release the spirit of that element. Then, repeat this exercise with a second element. After that, do it with a third element, and finally with the last element.

Afterward, reflect on the differences you noted as you thought about the different elements. How did your feelings differ as you became each element? Which element did you most strongly identify with? Which did you least identify with? These differences you observe will indicate your primary or strongest personality traits and your areas of greatest weakness. Later, you can work with these elements to further develop those where you are the weakest or tone down those that are too strong for you.

You can use your associations with the elements to focus on acquiring those traits you want to further develop. For instance:

♦ If you want to become more aggressive, say to get a better job or promotion, you might

Shaman Says

A ritual is any series of actions that are performed repeatedly for a particular purpose. So even setting your clock regularly before you go to bed is a kind of ritual. However, as the word is used here, a ritual performed by a shaman is essentially more or less complex series of activities to help or heal. And a **ceremony** is a generally a more elaborate or longer ritual, often involving more than one person.

concentrate on feeling the energy of fire spreading through you, and use that image when you go out for a job.

◆ If you feel you need to relax and calm down more, you might concentrate on feeling the flowing and cooling quality of water spreading over you and soothing you.

◆ If you want to feel more stable and solid after a period of turmoil in your life, you might concentrate on earth images to become more grounded.

◆ Finally, if you feel you need to be less serious, lighten up, and have more fun, try focusing on air imagery and feel yourself rising up on the currents of the air, so you feel lighter and freer.

By concentrating on these images and reminding yourself of them as you go through your everyday life, you will become more like the qualities you focus on.

You can also engage in rituals focused around particular elements, so you connect to them even more deeply on a spiritual level.

Putting the Elements to Work for You

When I worked with a shamanic group called the Order of the Divine Flame, or ODF, we engaged in a series of exercises to show our ability to connect with and influence the elements.

We had already learned to use a power object—in this case a long staff, and we had learned to focus our energy and intention through it. Now the goal was to influence the energies of the four elements in some way. We took a series of field trips into the surrounding woods, mountains, or seashore at night to do so. In the case of the earth energy, the exercise involved first seeing some of this energy take form, such as a dark humanoid-like mass or flashes of light. Then, we were asked to direct this form to move it, so that others in the group could also see this movement. In the case of air, the goal was to direct our energy to change the pattern of the wind, to make it rise up or die down on command. The water exercise involved going to the ocean and causing energy to rise up and take form out of the water, so it could be seen on the horizon by other group members. Finally, the fire exercise involved directing the flames in a campfire, barbecue pit, or candle to rise up, die down, or move left or right on command.

Did these things really happen? Or did members of the group just imagine this? I'm not really sure what was real and what was imagination; however, we all felt a sense of power and connection with the elements that helped to make us feel an increased sense of energy, confidence, and control over ourselves and what we could do. Likewise, what matters for you is that you fully believe you can work with the elements yourself, so you have power to see them and use them for your own purposes.

Green Power!

Working with plants might be considered by some to be an aspect of working with the elements of earth. For example, Black Elk describes the "green" as one of the four basic elements that form everything in existence (though he uses "rock" instead of "air" in his system).

But working with plants involves a deep knowledge of the particular plant properties and how they can be used to heal or give visionary experiences. It is a subject that goes far beyond the introduction to shamanism in this book. Even many shamans think of herbalists as having a specialized form of knowledge, and a vast library of books has been written on this subject. However, just by way of introduction, here are basics in how you can get to know plants and work with them.

Shamans typically distinguish plants based on their uses:

 ◆ **Healing plants**   These have healing properties in their leaves, roots, or bark, which you can access by chewing them, swallowing them, boiling them as a tea, using them as a salve, burning them to release beneficial odors, or otherwise using them for healing purposes. These include plants that offer herbal remedies, like St. John's Wort, sage, ginseng, and chamomile.

 ◆ **Visionary plants**   These have hallucinogenic properties, such as ayahuasca, peyote, datura, and psychedelic mushrooms. Since the use of such plants is illegal in most countries, apart from their use by indigenous peoples who have used them traditionally, their use is not recommended here, though you can make your own choices about whether to use them.

 ◆ **Magical plants**   These are viewed as symbolizing various illnesses and, when used on sick patients, can help to cure the patient.

 ◆ **Ordinary plants**   These include all other plants that don't have specific healing, visionary, or magical properties. They can be valuable for being generally healing or good for the spirits, such as when you put plants in your room to create a restful, soothing atmosphere or provide more oxygen, or when you send flowers to someone in the hospital to cheer them up. Of course, the function of some plants might simply be to look beautiful!

A pot of ayuahasca, which is being brewed to make a hallucinogen that a shaman and his patients will drink at a healing ceremony. The vines have been cut up and are being boiled to make the brew.

Apart from learning the specific healing or visionary properties of plants, you can work with them in a more general way to contact the plant spirits and relate to them. Generally, to do so, you need to spend more time with them than in creating a relationship with a power animal or teacher. The reason you need this extra time is because these are stationary, slowly growing beings, so it takes more time to tune into them, as noted by Jose and Lena Stevens in their *Secrets of Shamanism* book. That's why shamans who work with plants often sit for hours with a particular plant, "sensing it, talking with it, listening to it, and just being with it." Then, eventually, they may hear the plant talking to them and telling them how they might use the plant's properties.

Likewise, you might try to connect with plants around you—in your house or when you go out in nature.

Communing with Plants

Want to connect with and learn from a plant yourself? Here's an exercise you can use.

Go into your yard, park, or other place where you feel comfortable. You can also use a plant growing in your house or a greenhouse, but it's best to find a plant in nature.

Then, sit comfortably in front of the plant and look at it closely.

Next, close your eyes, and see or sense the plant in your mind's eye.

Imagine how you would feel if you were that plant.

Finally, ask that plant for a message. Ask the plant: "What do you have to tell me? What advice do you have to give?"

Then, listen for the answer.

You can also ask the plant a question, much as you might ask a question of a power animal, guide, or teacher.

Finally, thank the plant for its assistance and open your eyes.

Later, you can repeat this exercise with this same plant to get to know this plant even better, or try it with other plants. You may find that different types of plants have different types of wisdom to tell you—and you may feel differently as you experience yourself communing with different plants. Note that this exercise is designed to use your power of visualization to have these experiences with plants, not to actually ingest visionary plants which, depending on the plant, is illegal in the United States.

In sum, think of using power objects and the elements as a way to supplement your ability to work with your power animals, teachers, and guides and enhance your personal power generally. They are a way of essentially magnifying your own skills and characteristics, so you can see, know, and do more. They are like the magnifying glass that focuses the sun's rays; like the wind that stirs the embers to start a fire. You can use any number of objects in many different ways, just like different shamans in different shamanic traditions. Likewise, whether you use the four classical elements of the Western and Native American tradition, or use other systems of elements, you can work with the qualities and associations with those elements to increase your power, too.

The Least You Need to Know

♦ Because gaining and using power is so central to the practice of shamanism, shamans use many different sources of power to increase their own power.

♦ Among the many types of power objects are natural objects, such as rocks, leaves, and shells; objects representing your power animal, spiritual teachers, or guides; figurines of saints, angels, or deities, and staffs, swords, and knives.

♦ The four major elements are used in many traditions as sources of power.

♦ Plants can be used for power, too.

Chapter 9

The Power of Singing, Prayer, and Dance

In This Chapter

- ◆ Power songs, chants, and prayers
- ◆ Creating your own songs, chants, and prayers
- ◆ Dancing to raise power
- ◆ Dancing to raise your consciousness
- ◆ Dancing to contact power animals

Songs, chants, and prayers can be very powerful, especially when combined with the use of repetition, drumming, incense, and other elements used in a shamanic ceremony or ritual. Together, they help to build an atmosphere that draws everyone into the experience and focuses the energy of the shaman and other participants toward the goal of the event. In some cases, the words of a song, chant, or prayer may be directed toward the focus of the ceremony, such as sending prayers to heal someone who is ill or sending a song to ask a spirit for help in learning information, finding a lost object, or repairing a broken relationship.

Songs, Chants, and Prayers

Songs, chants, and prayers can be distinguished as follows:

◆ **Songs** These express thoughts and feelings in a series of words and sounds that are turned into verses or statements combined with rhythm and melody. In songs, the emphasis is on expressing ideas and emotions.

◆ **Chants** These are more repetitive, with the emphasis on repeating a few words or sounds again and again. In chants, the recurring sound and rhythm helps to produce a trancelike effect or carries the shaman on a journey between the worlds of ordinary and nonordinary reality.

◆ **Prayer** It is the expression of thoughts of hope, supplication, or thanks conveyed in a song or chant, or expressed internally in one's thoughts. The purpose is to appeal to a higher power, and the prayer can be expressed in various ways: in a song, chant, statement, or just prayerful thoughts.

The Power of Songs, Chants, and Prayers

Sometimes shamans use the same song, chant, or prayer with little variation from ceremony to ceremony; other times shamans create new songs, chants, or prayers before or during a ceremony in response to the situation. Uses vary from culture to culture and shaman to shaman, so don't hesitate to do what's most comfortable for you.

Given the many different traditions and approaches to shamanism, the varied circumstances in which it is used, and the variation in personality and style among shamans, it is only to be expected that songs, chants, and prayers vary greatly, too. They differ in style and content, in the use of rhythm and melody, and in whether they are used by an individual shaman working alone or in a group. In some cases, only the shaman sings, chants, or says the prayers; in other cases, participants sing, chant, and pray, too; and sometimes, the ceremony includes a mixture of the shaman's solo performance for the spirits and the participants expressing themselves, too.

CAUTION **Off the Path**

Using chants, songs, and prayers can seem a lot like a service held in many Christian churches. The difference is that the shaman, and perhaps the participants, are stepping into or contacting another world. They use them to send their focused, directed energy between worlds to contact the spirits, so these songs, chants, and prayers are, perhaps, more intense than in a formal church service conducted by a minister or priest.

Chants, songs, and prayers can take many forms, including imitations of animal sounds, repetition of words or sounds, or poetry.

Listening to Different Voices

As you read the following songs, chants, and prayers from different parts of the world, think about how you might use them as inspiration to create your own chants, songs, and prayers.

For example, in their shamanic ceremonies, the Tuvan shamans improvise verses of their songs, and often imitate the sounds of local animals, such as the raven, magpie, crow, wolf, stag, and bear. Frequently, they use onomatopoeic words and a form of throat singing to produce these deep powerful sounds. Sometimes these songs or chants are addressed to their helper spirits; sometimes to members of the audience. While these chants are designed to call on the spirits' help for a particular problem, they also contribute to the energy and atmosphere of the occasion (Kenin-Lopsan, 1997, 132–133).

Here, for example, a shaman is calling on his wolf spirit to come and help, yet not appear too ferocious to scare the participants. Also, he uses some seemingly senseless words, and this repetition produce an intoxicating effect on the participants (Kenin-Lopsan, 1997, 133).

> Your mouth, oo-ooi,
> Do not open, oo-ooi,
> Your fangs, ooi-ooi
> Do not show, ooi-ooi.

And here's an example of a shaman exalting his helper spirit, a raven, appealing to it to come and help him (Kenin-Lopsan, 1997, 137-138).

> He flies swiftly ...
> The flute sounds piercingly ....
> He ascends to the zenith,
> Such thou art, my slender, my black raven.
> You are carried easily through the air,
> My black raven, hungry raven!
> You are my black scout, you are my white scout!
> I beg you to come to me tonight ...
> Descend from the skies,
> Drop on my head with a dance.

CAUTION — Off the Path

Repetitive chanting is usually an enjoyable, positive experience that promotes expanded awareness and insight. However, if it starts to unleash any negative thoughts or feelings, stop the process because it might be putting you in touch with some deeper knowledge you may not be able to handle without professional guidance. Also, if you have any history of epilepsy, don't engage in repetitive chanting, as it could trigger an epileptic fit.

Songs or chants might also be directed to the spirits of a particular place, such as in the following chant by a Peruvian shaman, which is directed to the forest:

Spirits of the forest
revealed to us by honi xuma
bring us knowledge of the realm
assist us in the guidance of our people
give us the stealth of the boat
penetrating sight of the hawk and the owl
acute hearing of the deer
brute endurance of the tapir
grace and strength of the jaguar
knowledge and tranquility of the moon
kindred spirits, guide our way.

(Lamb, 1974, 88)

Still other chants might be used to produce a particular result, such as this chant sung in a ceremony of the Ojibway Indians. It is sung by an officer of their *Mide Society*, which uses knowledge of herbs and plant medicine for healing, during their eight-day *midewiwin ceremony*. As this officer, called the Bowman, sings the chant, he picks up a medicine bundle made from weasel skin that contains shells symbolizing the strength that the great spirit, the Kitshi Manitou, has given to them in the ceremony. As he sings:

Here it is,
The weasel skin.
Through it I shoot the white shells.
It never fails.
The shell goes toward them.
And they fall.

(Grim, 1983, 156–167)

The energy of the weasel skins is aimed like a gun at initiates to the society, to give them vital healing energy (Grim, 1983, 166).

A song or chant might also be used to offer a blessing, such as this blessing in the Navaho Emergence Myth (Cowan, 1996, 60, citing Sander, 1979, vii).

Then go on as one who has long life,
Go with blessing before you,
Go with blessing behind you,
Go with blessing below you,
Go with blessing above you,
Go with blessing around you,

Go with blessing in your speech,
Go with happiness and long life,
Go mysteriously.

As these examples illustrate, songs, chants, and prayers come in many forms and are used for many purposes. They can be drawn from long traditions or improvised on the spot. They can both express ideas about what the shaman hopes to achieve in the ceremony, appeal directly to the spirits or describe them, and contribute to the overall mood of the event that helps to send the shaman into an altered state of consciousness so he or she can better contact and communicate with the spirits.

Shaman Says

A **Mide Society** is a group among the Ojibway Indians that is focused around gaining knowledge of herbs and plant medicine. Their key ceremony, in which new shamans are initiated, is called a **midewiwin ceremony**. It takes place over an eight-day period and involves trance, cosmological stories, sacred chants, and herbal lore.

Using Your Own Power Songs, Chants, and Prayers

You can adapt or create your own songs, chants, and prayers for various purposes.

If you are already working in a particular shamanic tradition, that can be a good place to start. Feel free to adapt the words, phrases, sounds, rhythms, and melodies to your own style and to the purpose of a shamanic ceremony. There may be group songs, chants, or prayers you can learn, which can help to create a community spirit, as well as focusing the group energy for a particular purpose.

Alternatively, you can adapt or develop your own personal songs, chants, and prayers, to use on your own. Or combine a mix of traditional and personal elements in your songs, chants, and prayers. Don't worry about mixing and matching from various sources and traditions. What's most important is that you invest whatever you create with your own personal energy. This way, you invest this energy into however you express your hopes, desires, requests, or commands.

To give your songs, chants, or prayers even more power, combine them with visualization, performance, dance, power objects, or other sources of shamanic power. For example, you might:

◆ Dance your song, chant, or prayer (more on this later in the chapter).

◆ Hold a power object and focus on as you sing, chant, or pray; perhaps even offer that object with the energy of your words to the spirit—such as offering a feather in a ceremony to call on a bird helper.

- Create a mask and sing, chant, or pray as you focus on it or wear it to invest the mask with that power of your songs, chants, or prayers Then, later, when you put on the mask, sense that power you have invested in it to help you feel even more power when you sing, chant, pray or dance in the future, while wearing that mask.

- Look at a visual image, sculpture, or ceramic figure of your power animal or teacher and direct your song, chant, or prayer to that image or object.

- Bring together a group of people you are working with in your shamanic practice and take turns sharing your songs, chants, or prayers with each other; then join together in expressing them.

Do It Yourself!

Following are tips for developing your own songs, chants, or prayers. If you prefer, take some quiet time alone to reflect on what you want to say and write out your thoughts or recite them aloud into a tape recorder. Or if you respond to the spontaneity of the moment, improvise during a personal or group ceremony and tape record what happens, so you can later transcribe and capture what you have expressed.

Start by getting very relaxed. If you are writing, try using automatic writing. To do so, simply write as you think, so the words flow without your trying to edit them. You can use this process with a computer, too. To direct your thoughts to a particular spiritual helper, you can put up an image of that power animal, teacher, or guide to help you focus; or picture that helper in your mind's eye. Perhaps use some repetitive music or drumming to help you stay focused and in the mood. You can play the music or drum yourself or put on a tape and listen to that in the background. Then, when you are ready to begin, focus on your purpose or goal, so you have a general idea of what you want to say. Here are some tips on what to say:

> **Shaman Says**
>
> When you write by simply letting the words flow—without doing any editing—you are engaging in **automatic writing**.

- **Developing Your Own Songs**   Think about the purpose of your song and who it is for. Decide if you want to express a hope, wish, desire, need, or command, and ask yourself what you want to say. To help yourself get started, try using a song already written on this theme. Then, with this song as a jumping off point, let your imagination go. Put the ideas in your own words. Let the words and emotions come from your own heart. Try to think of visual images and actions to make your song come alive. Then, try singing your song, adding rhythm and melody to give it even more power.

People using singing and chanting along with drumming in a shamanic ceremony. After the group uses singing, chanting, and drumming to raise their energy, they direct it to a particular purpose, in this case healing one of the group members.

♦ **Developing Your Own Chants**   As in developing a song, think about the purpose of your chant, who it is for, and whether you want to express a hope, wish, desire, need, or command. You might start with an already written chant on a chosen theme. Then focus on a few words or short phrases to convey what you want to say, since you will be repeating them over and over to create your chant. Just write down the first words or phrases that come to you, as you focus on the purpose and audience for your chant. They can even be sounds or nonsensical words. Then link these words, phrases, and sounds together. As you do this or after completing your chant, experience it by saying aloud what you have written, repeating it with increasing intensity and energy, and you will feel the power of the chant building, reinforcing the purpose of your chant.

◆ **Developing Your Own Prayers**   Again, start by thinking of the purpose of your prayer and to whom you want to direct it, remembering that a prayer is the expression of a hope, wish, desire, need, or expression of thanks—never a command. So approach the process of writing a prayer in a spirit of humility, where you are making a request to the spirits or a particular spiritual being or saying thanks for past help. If you have found a previously written prayer inspirational, start with that. Then develop your own prayer, letting the ideas and words express your deeply felt hopes, wishes, desires, needs, or offer of thanks. After you finish your prayer, try reciting it, repeating it with a deep humility, that characterizes the expression of prayer.

Dancing Your Way to Power

Dance is another very important source of power in many shamanic traditions. It can be used to celebrate, promote a sense of community in a group ceremony, contribute to an altered state of consciousness, and raise energy and power. It can also be used to open up access to a particular spirit or group of spirits, such as when shamans use it to dance a spirit or power animal.

Like songs, chants, prayers, and rituals (see Chapter 10 for more on shamanic rituals), dances can range from highly spontaneous and improvised occasions to very structured, orderly affairs, where the shaman and other participants have to learn a series of steps. Often, whether highly improvised or very structured, dances are combined with songs, chants, and prayers. When improvised, often anyone and everyone can participate in the dance, promoting wide group participation, while dances with specified steps commonly require extensive training, turning the shamanic ceremony into more of a performance by the shaman for the group. Or sometimes a ceremony can be a mix of both, with steps with a certain meaning or symbolism performed by the shaman; but at other times participants can join right in however they want.

Dancing is tremendously powerful in helping to speed up the receptive state, either by raising the energy or by leading the shaman and other dancers to feel a kind of exhaustion that leads to trance. It can also help lead to the sense of merging with the spirits, particularly when combined with masks. In *The Way of the Shaman*, Michael Harner describes how dancing, accompanied by drumming, was a very common method—even more common than using hallucinogenic drugs—in traditional societies for a person to metamorphosise into a bird or other animal.

Dancing Your Way to a New Consciousness

You can also use the power of dance to change your own consciousness or contact and merge with your own power animal. You can use it by itself or with other consciousness-altering techniques, such as visualization, singing, and chanting.

First, let's look at simply changing your state of consciousness in preparation for a shamanic journey.

In general, any type of long, repetitive dancing—especially to a recurring rhythmic beat—will lead to an altered, trancelike state of consciousness.

Dancing in a natural setting can further contribute to the use of dancing to create an altered state of consciousness.

If you want to use dance to alter your state of consciousness for any type of shamanic activity, here are some tips on how to do this, either on your own or in a group.

♦ Use a drum or put on a tape with rhythmic drumming sounds or music. The kind of house music used in a rave is ideal for this purpose.

♦ Dim the lights or do this in a setting with low illumination.

♦ Focus on where you want to go in this trancelike state. Think of this process as more like going somewhere as a traveler, visiting to see what's there, rather than trying to contact any particular spiritual being or power animal. For example, take a trip to visit the lower world, upper world, or somewhere else in the middle world or earth.

♦ Now, as you or others drum or the tape plays—or both—let yourself go. Move, sway, and dance to the music or beat. Experience the rhythm going through you, and as it does, project your consciousness to this other world.

◆ Imagine that your consciousness or awareness is going out on the beat of the music or sound to wherever you want to send it.

◆ Keep focusing on sending out your consciousness or extending your awareness, and keep moving. Don't try to control your movement; just let the rhythm move your body wherever it wants. At the same time, release your consciousness to journey where it wants. The idea is to remain in this very receptive state.

◆ If your consciousness starts to go someplace where you feel uncomfortable, pull it back and direct it somewhere else. This process is designed to create a comfortable, trancelike state, where your consciousness or spirit travels to view other worlds; not to engage in any kind of personal therapy. So while you are receptive, continue to stay in control of the process and rein in your consciousness, as if you are riding a horse while you dance.

◆ Keep the experience going as long as you feel energetic and enthused by your journey or, if you prefer, set a time limit such as 15 minutes to an hour and use a gentle signal to pull you back, such as a timer with soft bell-like sounds.

Such dancing can be a very powerful consciousness-changing tool, and you can combine it with other methods that follow or lead-up to the dancing to enhance the dance experience or draw on it for insights afterward. For example, before you start dancing, take some time to meditate or put on a mask or costume to make you more receptive. Or after you dance, have a notebook or tape recorder handy, so you can write down or record your experience and reflect on as you do this or later. Or if you are doing this in a group, after the dance, join together in a circle and use this as a period of reflection or sharing to think about what happened and how you can use the experience. An advantage of working with a group and sharing your experiences is that this keeps you and the other group members from becoming too self-centered in working with these experiences.

Dancing Your Animal

You can also use dancing to contact and identify with your power animal, called variously "dancing your animal" or "dancing for a power animal." The idea here is to focus the altered state on looking for and inviting your animal to appear in your consciousness and then meld with you. Or if you have already met your power animal, use this altered state to invite your animal back and get to know it even better. As you continue this process, you will find you evoke your animal more quickly and you will more quickly and intensely blend with it to become that animal. Much as in hypnosis, which varies greatly in the depth and intensity of the hypnotic state for different people, the more you dance to go into the trancelike state, the more effectively and efficiently you will do so.

Michael Harner adapted the technique of dancing an animal from the practice of traditional shamans as part of his teaching of core shamanism, and it is described in his book *The Way of the Shaman*. I experienced it myself in one of his workshops at Esalen in the early 1980s, and it has since been developed and used by many others, including Tom Cowan, who describes using the following key steps in his book on *Shamanism: A Spiritual Practice for Daily Life*. Cowan suggests using a rattle to provide the rhythm, although you might substitute listening to the sounds of drumming on a tape or dance as someone else drums.

1. Begin with a starting dance in which you start rattling quickly and strongly as you face each of the four directions. You can keep your eyes open, closed, or partly closed as you prefer. First face the east, and then turn clockwise, so you next face the south, west, and north. Take about a minute for each direction. As you face each direction, call on the animal spirits that you associate with each direction.

2. After you have finished calling the spirits from each of the four directions, raise your rattle above you and acknowledge the spirits of the sky and the heavens above the sky. Next, bend down and shake your rattle toward the earth to recognize the spirits associated with everything that grows from the earth and fertility.

3. Keep rattling with your eyes closed or partly closed and start dancing. Don't worry about how you do this. Just let yourself go and be open to the experience. Any kinds of movements, steps, or patterns are fine. Your goal is to open yourself up to the spirit of the animal you are dancing, so it will enter into you and move your body. The animal that does so will be your power animal—or one of them.

4. With the goal of contacting your animal in mind, start swaying in place or walking in a slow circle. If you are doing this by a fire or a candle, circle around your fire or in front of your candle. As you move, call on the animal spirits and ask the animal that is your power animal or helping animal to move into your body. The amount of time needed will vary, depending on how receptive you are and whether you have done this before. Just be patient, and continue to sway and walk while you shake your rattle. Eventually, you will sense that a particular animal has come near you or has even entered your body. Once this happens, you will feel your body move on its own and you don't have to think about dancing, since your animal spirit is now dancing through you.

5. In some cases, you may simply keep walking or swaying, feeling this animal in you. In other cases, you may find you are imitating the movements of the animal as you dance. In either case, let the spirit of the animal guide you and move your body. Keep dancing like this for awhile, as you continue to experience the animal within you, which will help to reinforce your connection with that animal.

6. Finally, when you feel ready to stop, do so. A good way to conclude, as Cowan notes, is to "welcome the animal into your life, asking it to leave some of its spirit or energy in your body" (Cowan, 1996, 33).

Combining Dance and Other Consciousness-Raising Techniques

These techniques for using dance to alter your consciousness or dance your animal can be very powerful, whether you use them alone or in combination with other trance-producing techniques, from meditation to sensory overload to sensory deprivation.

However you use them, the idea is to use these bodily movements to move you into the other world, just as you might use singing, chants, and prayers to move you there.

So consider using multiple techniques in combination as a way to increase the intensity of your journey into other realms. It's like driving a car. The more energy you add to your gas, the harder you step on the gas peddle, and the more firmly you hold the wheel, the greater your focus and power, and the faster and straighter your journey will be to your destination.

The Least You Need to Know

♦ Songs, chants, and prayers can be a very powerful addition to a shamanic ritual or ceremony, especially when combined with the use of repetition, drumming, incense, or other ritual or ceremonial activities.

♦ You can draw on the songs, chants, prayers from different shamanic traditions or develop your own, or do a combination of both.

♦ To give your songs, chants, or prayers even more power, combine them with visualization, performance, dance, power objects, or other sources of shamanic power.

♦ Dancing, whether done alone or in a group, can help the dancer become more receptive.

♦ You can dance your power animal to call on and connect more closely with this animal and get to know it better.

Chapter 10

The Power of Ritual

In This Chapter

- How shamanic rituals vary around the world
- Using rituals to celebrate seasons
- Celebrating rites of passage and your own shamanic rituals
- Participating in rituals with others

Rituals in shamanism can be as varied as journeying, smoking a sacred pipe, or dancing an animal. One more purpose is to help achieve a particular objective, like a ritual to seek a healing or to obtain information to solve a problem. Also, rituals are used for other purposes, such as to honor the seasons, celebrate rites of passage, and bring together participants in a group devoted to shamanic practice to reaffirm their bonds with each other.

A ritual is any series of actions that are performed repeatedly for a particular purpose. So even setting your clock regularly before you go to bed is a kind of ritual. However, as the word is used here, a ritual performed by a shaman is essentially more or less complex series of activities to help or heal.

These many types of rituals help to make shamanism a part of everyday life and contribute to creating a shamanic community of others on the shamanic path. In traditional cultures, such ceremonies have been used to mark the various times of the year and occasion of importance, such as the first fruits and the solstices and equinoxes, and the shaman has often played a part in leading such ceremonies. Then, as larger, more developed societies emerged with more specialized roles, the priest often came to lead such events. Even so, the shaman often continued to lead these ceremonies for smaller community or family groups within these larger societies.

The Many Types of Rituals

The many ways in which you can perform rituals in shamanism include the following:

◆ Rituals to heal, whether for others or for oneself.

◆ Rituals to gain information and solve problems for yourself or others.

◆ Rituals to honor and celebrate the seasons, sometimes referred to as the *Wheel of the Year*, since the year travels through a repeated series of four seasons, which is like the turning of a wheel with four spokes, one for each season.

◆ Rituals to recognize, honor, and work with the elements of nature.

◆ Rituals to travel through the upper, lower, and middle worlds.

◆ Rituals to meet and work with your power animals.

◆ Rituals to strengthen your relationship with your teachers and guides.

◆ Rituals to honor and celebrate your levels of learning in shamanism, sometimes regarded as degrees of knowledge in a particular shamanic system.

◆ Rituals for getting together with others to celebrate as a shamanic community.

Such shamanic rituals have many parallels with rituals in other areas of life. We have many cultural rituals, from those that mark the seasons to those celebrating life's passages. Religious groups have their own rituals, such as days of atonement, remembrance, forgiveness, high holiness, and celebration, in Christianity, Judaism, and Islam. There may also be days to throw off old roles and try on new ones, if just for a time, such as Mardi Gras or Halloween, when you can "be" someone else. All our major institutions have their own rituals, too, such as school graduations, corporate picnics, and holiday parties.

So it is with shamanism, though the difference is that the rituals may involve going into an altered state of consciousness for some purpose. Or they may be designed to honor particular symbols, events, occasions, individuals, elements in nature, animals, and traditions that have a special meaning in shamanism. Then, too, rituals may serve as a reminder or reinforcement for the individual on the shaman path, or they may bring together a group of people in a celebration of shamanism, so they can support and reinforce each other.

Often a reason for a growing interest in shamanism and its many rituals today is because modern Western societies don't have a strong tradition of spiritual rituals. Rather, rituals are generally secularized, such as emphasizing gift-giving during Christmas and celebrating Halloween as a gala costume party. Thus, for many, such rituals lack a sense of deeper feeling and meaning.

Although elements of ritual will overlap with a discussion of other aspects of shamanism, like the drumming, dancing, chanting, and singing used in various rituals, ritual is so important to shamanism that it merits its own chapter to show its many uses and how you can create your own.

The Pervasiveness of Ritual in Everyday Life

Like everything else in shamanism, rituals vary tremendously around the world from simple rituals performed by an individual to elaborate ceremonies that go on for days and involve the whole community, such as the four to eight day Sun Dance ceremonies for many Plains Indian groups, such as the Arapaho, Cheyenne, Crow, Sioux, Ojibwa, and Blackfoot tribes.

Rituals can become like an anchor for everyday life. The day-to-day moments to acknowledge nature, recognize the spiritual qualities of plants and animals, and think about ways to raise one's energy for the coming day can be like little rituals in a continuum of ritual activity, which ranges from simple rituals to grand community ceremonies. Such shamanic practitioners live in a world of spiritual power where all of time, space, thought, and action is connected.

Wallace Black Elk expresses this notion when he speaks of wearing spiritual power like a cloak:

> The spiritual power I wear is much more beautiful and much greater. We call it wisdom, knowledge, power, and gift of love. There are these four parts to that spiritual power. So I wear those. When you wear that power it will beautify your mind and spirit. You become beautiful. Everything that Tunkashila creates is beautiful (Lyons, 1996, 17).

> **Wise Ways**
>
> Even the simplest acts may be considered rituals, because shamans often think of themselves as living in a world of spirits and spiritual power in which everything is interconnected. So every act, even the very smallest, might be seen as an act that has some impact on the spiritual world.

In short, recognize that virtually anything can become a ritual when you start practicing shamanism, since every thought, every act, has some influence both on you, on those you interact with, and to a greater or lesser degree on the world. It is like a long causal chain stretching back to a series of individual acts, whereby developing shamanic powers increases your ability to have an effect on the world, as you gain the help of various spiritual energies and powers.

Bon Voyage

Tom Cowan emphasizes the pervasive nature of shamanism in *Shamanism: As a Spiritual Practice for Daily Life*. He writes:

"A spiritual practitioner commits himself or herself to performing these activities with dedicated regularity: some practices will be done daily, others weekly, monthly, or seasonally, and a few practices only on special occasions when the practitioner feels ready or called upon to do them. What is important for a practice is the commitment to pursue a spiritual path and walk it faithfully, incorporating some elements of it into one's life on a regular, if not daily, basis." (Cowan, 2001, 17)

Shamanic Rituals Around the World

It is interesting to compare the wide range of ritual styles around the world. In many ways, they reflect a personality footprint for a culture—and you might think about how you are drawn to different styles of rituals based on your own personal and lifestyle preferences.

Some of the ways in which rituals might differ include:

◆ The purpose of the ritual, also referred to as the goal or object of a ritual.

◆ The length of the ritual—from short to long, and whether it's limited to a particular time-period.

◆ The timing of the ritual—during the day, at night, or at any time, because the particular timing doesn't matter.

◆ How often a ritual is performed—daily, weekly, monthly, seasonally, or occasionally.

◆ Whether the ritual is performed by an individual alone or with one or more assistants.

◆ Whether the ritual is more like a performance for others or includes others as participants.

◆ Whether the ritual is more spontaneous or structured.

◆ Whether the ritual is more meditative or more forceful and dramatic.

◆ Whether the ritual includes dancing and what type.

◆ Whether the ritual includes singing, chanting, or prayers—and whether they are already learned or are improvised.

◆ Whether ... well, you fill in the rest. What other differences do you notice when you look at different rituals put on by different groups?

Take healing rituals. At the one extreme, these rituals can be very simple and spontaneous, such as the traditional Siberian ritual. The shaman appears before the gathered members of the community with the few essential items of the shamanic ritual, such as his leather costume, drum, and rattle, and begins the two-part ceremony. In each part, the shaman largely improvises, guided by his feelings and the sense of the spirit's energy flowing through him. The words of the songs and chants, the particular songs and chants chosen, the steps of the dance, all are improvised in a high-energy performance, which involves the participants, too, as they sing and chant at times along with the shaman. In fact, this highly spontaneous, improvisational style seems to be well matched to the few implements used in the healing ceremony.

> **Wise Ways**
>
> Even just imagining something can become a kind of spiritual act when you focus your energy and intention on achieving it.

Healing rituals can take many forms, including this spontaneous, in which the participants are raising their hands to send the man healing energy.

By contrast, there is the extremely formalized and structured ceremony of the healers along the coast of northern Peru. Not only do they have a vast number of objects with different symbolic meanings on their mesas, or altars, but they have a very structured, ritual form. Though it is also divided into two parts, each phase is highly structured, just like the mesa and beliefs about the cosmology that underlie this structure.

> **Bon Voyage**
>
> As you read about the many different kinds of rituals, ask yourself which ones you are most drawn to. Consider using these rituals to help you achieve your goals.

Ritual altars can be prepared in different ways, depending on what tradition you are working with or whether you are using your own personal combination of meaningful objects.

Rituals differ not only in how informal/formal, improvised/planned, and spontaneous/ structured they are, but also in their purposes and themes. For instance, among the Navaho, who emphasize the importance of walking in beauty and living in harmony, the beautiful sand painting that is the centerpiece of their healing ceremony reflects an emphasis on beauty and harmony. It presents a very calm, ordered image of balance, with images of the spirits of the four directions. As the patient sits on the sand painting during the healing, the imagery and accompanying chants link him symbolically with the history and myths of the Navaho people. As anthropologist Donald F. Sandner writes: "He has a place in the unity of the whole. Harmony is restored" (Sandner, 1979, 136).

Ritually Celebrating the Seasons

Because connecting with nature and spirits of nature and animals is so important to shamanism, rituals to celebrate the changing seasons are very important in many shamanic traditions. You'll find many of these rituals are commonly practiced if you are working with a particular shamanic tradition or shamanic community. If you are working by yourself, you can create your own. Here are some general guidelines on seasonal rituals.

Rituals to Celebrate the Seasons or Yearly Cycles

These seasonal rituals that mark key changes in the yearly cycle are especially important in some shamanic traditions—including modern shamanism.

Amber Wolfe describes the importance of seasons to shamanism in her book, *In the Shadow of the Shaman: Connecting with Self, Nature and Spirit.* Wolfe incorporates wisdom from Native American, Wiccan, and other nature-based traditions into her understanding of season rituals.

Wolfe says that nature is made up of "many smaller cycles or wheels," and by connecting with them, we can enhance our shamanic practice whatever our particular path. It is a way of even more intensely linking to the spiritual world on a regular basis, thereby promoting our ability to journey there and work with the spirits of this world.

Paying attention to the seasons makes you more aware of the spirits and spiritual energies associated with those seasons. Also, these recurring festivals and rituals become a way of reaffirming your own commitment to shamanic practice, as well as linking you to others who are similarly celebrating yearly seasonal changes. The major ceremonies center around the solar cycles, although some individuals also mark the lunar cycles—the new moon, waxing moon, full moon, waning moon, and dark of the moon—and time certain practices to these cycles. For instance, they might begin new projects during a new moon and engage in meditating and burning goals on paper to release them to spirit (Wolfe, 1989, 192–199).

> **Shaman Says** ___
>
> Rituals to honor the seasons are often linked to various pagan religions, such as Celtic and Wiccan groups, but nonpagans also perform rituals to recognize and honor the seasons, including many Native American groups.

Honoring the Sun

Solar cycles, which are celebrated by many pagan and other groups that have been influenced by shamanism, are marked by four major divisions: the *winter solstice, spring equinox, summer solstice,* and *fall equinox,* plus four other major seasonal holidays along the way. These are *Candlemas* or the festival of Bridget around February 1; *Beltane,* also called May Day, around May 1; *Lammas,* also called August Eve around August 1; and *Samhain,* also called Halloween, on October 31. Among some modern pagan groups, including practitioners of Wicca and Celtic traditions, these are referred to as *the four quarters* and *cross-quarters*, and they are marked as a time for community celebrations (Wolfe, 1989, 213).

Different traditions have different associations with these different seasonal turning points along the Wheel of the Year. However, starting with the winter solstice, here are some things you might consider recognizing and celebrating, which reflect a blend of Native American, Wiccan, and ancient and modern shamanism:

- **Winter solstice** (December 21–22)   Use this time to celebrate the birth of the sun and the returning light to the earth. Some of the plants associated with this time are evergreen, mistletoe, and oak, since they are associated with growth or strength. Animal associations include deer, owls, and eagles, associated with vision and high flying. This is considered an especially good time for journeying, vision quests, and doing healings because, because of the associations with new beginnings and growth.

- **Candlemas** (February 1)   Since the light and energy is growing stronger, this is a good time to celebrate the returning growing season and creativity. Some plant associations here are the crocus, which first appears during cold weather, and camellias, which grow during the winter. Some animal associations are any hibernating animals, such as bears. This is considered a good time for personal hibernation, listening to music, writing, art, and inner journeys.

- **Spring equinox** (March 21–22)   Since this is a time when the sun and earth are in balance, this is a good time to think about how your own personal qualities are in balance, such as your receptive/active and masculine/feminine qualities. Some plant associations are any new spring flowers or green leaves. Animal associations include gentle animals or baby animals, like lambs, chickens, and baby birds. It's a good time for doing light, gentle, and even fanciful ceremonies yourself.

- **Beltane** (May 1)   This has traditionally been a time of celebrating growth and fertility, such as the May Day celebrations highlighting fun and joy. The plant associations that express this joyful exuberance include wildflowers and lilies. As for animals, hawks, deer, and rabbits are good associations with this period, since they represent energy and fertility. It's a good time for having joyous celebrations yourself, including picnics and weddings.

- **Summer solstice** (June 21–22)   Since this is the height of summer, it's a good time to celebrate growth and prosperity, and to relax and enjoy what you have achieved. The plant associations here include roses and other blooming plants that reflect the "full-blooming energies of summer." Some of the animal associations include peacocks, a symbol of fulfillment; jaguars, associated with the deep energy of the earth; and doves, which are associated with peace and harmony. It's considered a good time for healing circles and self-healing, as well as having outdoor ceremonies. It's also ideal for all sorts of shamanic journeys, especially to the upper world, because the energy of the sun is at its height.

♦ **Lammas** (August 1)   Since this is a time when harvests are beginning and prepara-tions are being made for the fall, it's a good time to think about what you have har-vested or achieved at this point. The plant associations for this time include corn, a symbol of the harvest, plus other products of the earth, like wheat and barley, as well as the first falling leaves of fall. The animal associations of this time include strong animals, such as buffalo, bears, and wolves. It's also a good time, according to Wolfe, for "spiritual housecleaning" when you find ways to balance your mind, body, and spirit, such as by taking time for self-healing and meditation.

♦ **Fall Equinox** (September 21–22)   The traditional associations here are with thanksgiving and harvest. Some of the plants associated with this time include nut-bearing trees that symbolize harvests and herbs like sage and sweetgrass that are used for purification. The animals associated with this time include squirrels, which hoard up nuts for the winter. Think of this as a time for getting together in groups to prepare and plan for coming winter activities and to think about balance and healing for both yourself and the world generally.

♦ **Samhain.**   This falls on the same date as Halloween, developed from the earlier pagan celebration to mark the cross-quarters on this date (October 31). Since this is considered the time when the connection between the spirit and everyday world is the closest, this is a good time to communicate with the spiritual world, including the spirits of those who have passed on. It is a good time to celebrate the last har-vests and prepare for winter. Some of the plant associations with this time include harvest vegetables like pumpkins. The animal associations for this time are generally "shadowy or night animals," such as black cats, ravens, owls, and night hawks. This is also considered a good time to do deep, introspective shamanic journeys, includ-ing personal vision quests in which you look deep within, including at your own shadow side and chase away any of these negative spiritual energies.

Use these and any other celebration and rituals in whatever way feels best for you, either mixing different traditions or taking one approach to shamanism and developing it as deeply as you can. There is no one right way, no one size that fits all.

Developing Your Own Seasonal Rituals

You can use these associations to develop themes for your own shamanic practices and journeying at these different times of year. But consider them just suggestive, since you may have your own associations with these times. Or you may prefer to do some more spontaneous journeying and let the spirits you meet guide you into deciding how to appropriately recognize and celebrate the different seasons. The key is to become aware of the changing seasons in nature and relate more closely to them, thereby deepening your own shamanic practice and the way it can help you and others.

There are a number of approaches you might use to recognize and celebrate the seasons, such as these suggested by Tom Cowan in his book *Shamanism: As a Spiritual Practice for Daily Life*, which represents a mix of shamanism and modern pagan practices, with a particularly strong Celtic influence. As Cowan notes, many individuals and drumming groups like to participate in shamanic journeying during these turning points on the Wheel of the Year, often in conjunction with a seasonal ceremony that honors the changes in nature at these times. Some of the ways to take these journeys, as he suggests, include these:

♦ Journey to the spirit of the season, and ask this spirit to help you understand or experience the changes that are occurring. In doing so, you may travel deep into the earth, water, or air to more deeply experience the energies of these changes in nature.

♦ Ask your power animals or the spirits of the seasons to give you a task to do in the spiritual world to contribute to these changes in nature. As Cowan describes it: "By doing the task you put your own spirit energy into the season and help the Wheel turn" (Cowan, 1996, 201). Then, while doing the task or afterward, dance and celebrate the season change before you conclude your journey and return to everyday reality.

♦ Ask your power animals or the spirits what kind of work or ritual you or your shamanic group might perform in everyday reality at this time of year. Such work might range from something quite ordinary, such as going on a walk or starting a garden. Or it may involve putting on a special ritual or ceremony.

Celebrating Rites of Passage and Other Personal Rituals

Still another area for ritual is in marking and in celebrating a variety of rites of passage through life, including gaining different degrees of shamanic knowledge. Essentially a *rite of passage* is one that marks a person's shift from one stage of life to another, such as moving from infancy to childhood, from childhood to adolescence or adulthood, from single adulthood to marriage, or from middle age to senior or elder status.

Some stages are widely celebrated through ceremonies to mark a transition from one stage to another, such as the birth of children, the change from child to adult, marriage, the shift from adult to being an elder, and death. There are also many personal transitions, from birthdays to starting a new job to a promotion.

Given the connections of shamanism with natural rhythms and cycles, like the passage of time through the year, there are deep associations with these life changes. Shamanic practitioners—both traditional and modern—think of them as changes with a spiritual significance. So they may look to spiritual helpers or ancestor spirits to assist or be present at such occasions.

To take one of many examples, among the Hopi, once a year, a *wiiwuchuim* ceremony is held in which the dead are believed to come to visit and the young men who have reached the age of puberty are initiated into manhood. They are taken to the kiva, an underground or partly underground room, where they sit on blankets as they learn the sacred knowledge of the tribe, such as the story of Emergence. They may see ancestor spirits, too. Like many initiations, their experience represents a kind of death to one stage of life and a rebirth into another. Then, after this initiation, they can perform the Soyal ceremony, which begins the ceremonial year, when the seed corn is blessed during the winter solstice in the hopes it will bring a good harvest in the coming year (Underhill, 1965, 208–215).

You can celebrate your own rites of passage as well as create other personal rituals for experiences that are important for you. When you do so, take some time to reflect on the meanings of these events to you. Perhaps create a little—or maybe even a big—celebration to mark this transition from one stage of life or experience to another. Invite your spiritual guides, teachers, and power animals to join you in the celebration. If you are participating in shamanic practices with others, invite them or create a ceremony of recognition and celebration with them.

While many rites of passage may often be celebrated in a very ordinary way, such as when you go to a party at work to celebrate your new job or promotion, what makes them a part of a shamanic practice is celebrating them in a special way. You go beyond the usual recognitions given to such events and transitions to turn them into a ritual or ceremony, where you see these as spiritual celebrations and invite the spirits to celebrate and acknowledge these changes in life, too.

> **Shaman Says**
>
> A wiiwuchuim ceremony is the annual ceremony of the Hopi in which the young men who have reached the age of puberty are initiated into manhood. A **Soyal ceremony** is the ceremony which begins the ceremonial year, when the seed corn is blessed during the winter solstice in the hopes it will bring a good harvest. It is led by the Soyal chief and priests.

> **Bon Voyage**
>
> Rites of passage and personal rituals can be used to mark all sorts of occasions, such as family events like births and marriages, personal achievements like graduations or promotions, and relationship transitions, from anniversaries and engagements to break-ups and divorces.

Celebrating Rituals with Others

If you are part of a shamanic group or know others who know about and support your shamanic practice, it is ideal to include them in your rituals and celebrations. You will also find many groups to join where you can participate in such activities, such as those listed in the resource section of the Appendix C.

Otherwise, it is a good idea to keep your participation in these rituals more private and personal. It is often better not to tell people who are not involved in shamanism about your activities, because many people who are not familiar with these practices, or worse, skeptical about them, can prove to be a real downer when you tell them about your activities. They can interfere with these rituals while they are being performed or create lingering bad feelings later that can undermine your shamanic practice. Don't avoid inviting people you feel comfortable with, just exercise caution.

But by all means, find others who share, encourage, or support your shamanic path and with whom you can share rituals!

The Least You Need to Know

- ◆ Shamanic rituals are used for a variety of purposes: to heal, to gain information and solve problems, to honor and celebrate the seasons, to recognize and work with the elements of nature, to travel through the upper, middle, and lower worlds; and to meet and improve your relationship with your power animals, teachers, and guides.

- ◆ Rituals vary tremendously around the world and from shamanic tradition to tradition in the way they are conducted; they range from simple rituals performed by an individual to elaborate ceremonies that can go on for days for special occasions.

- ◆ You can use rituals as an anchor in your everyday life, such as by taking time to acknowledge nature, recognize the spiritual qualities of plants and animals, and think about ways to raise your energy for the coming day's activities.

- ◆ While some practitioners use lunar rituals to recognize the different phases of the moon, the solar rituals marking the turning points of the year are the most common.

- ◆ Other major rituals to celebrate include rites of passage, to mark moving from one phase of life to another, and personal rituals marking events that are important to you.

The Power of Place

In This Chapter

- ◆ Why some places are so powerful
- ◆ The types of powerful places
- ◆ Techniques for discovering places of power
- ◆ Using places of power for rituals and journeying

Given shamanism's close connection with nature and natural forces, it makes sense that places are an extremely important part of shamanic practice. Shamans are very attuned to their environment and the setting in which they conduct a shamanic ritual or contact spiritual beings. They want a setting that will be conducive or add to the power of whatever they are doing. Conversely, they want to avoid places that are considered to have negative forces or energies associated with them, since that will detract from the effectiveness of a ritual or journey.

Commonly, places of power are called *power spots* or *sacred places*. The first term emphasizes the power qualities or physical characteristics of the place that makes it so powerful, while the second emphasizes the spiritual qualities that make it revered and honored, as well as powerful, in a religious sense. But the terms are often used interchangeably. So call it what you want, these are locations that are considered to have power.

The Importance of Powerful Places

People have long associated certain places with great power. Prehistoric hunters and gatherers associated power with high mountains, lakes, and streams where game was especially abundant, tall or unusual rock formations, or spots where geysers poured out energy from the earth. Caves, too, often were considered places of power.

Over time, all sorts of mythic and symbolic associations developed with these places of power.

The Many Types of Places of Power

There are all sorts of power places. They can be natural or human made, visible or invisible. Some power places get their energy from the ground. Other places gain their association with power because they stand out in some way, such as very high mountains, cliffs, unusual rock formations, waterfalls, geysers, or large body of waters.

You may be familiar with places in your own area that have associations with power. In Northern California where I live, Mount Shasta and Mount Tamalpais are considered strong power spots, and they attract many groups that perform rituals or have celebrations there, drawn by the power.

Some examples of power spots that have drawn groups in the Mount Tamalpais area of Northern California—often beautiful spots by the mountain or ocean. Sometimes these sites of power are indicated or consecrated by some kind of image or ritual to start a gathering, such as the skull.

Others power places are built environments, and often the site chosen is already considered to be a natural center of power, such as the stone circle at Stonehenge in England. It was built, according to many archaeologists, as an ancient observatory to mark the movements of the stars and solstices. Then, given its traditional associations, it later became a place where twentieth-century Druids and witches came to conduct their seasonal rites, before it was turned into a tourist attraction in recent years, closed off to religious activities. Still other examples of power places include the great pyramids and temples in Central and South America and Egypt. And then there are the large heads on Easter Island that archaeologists believe were built by the native peoples who used to live there.

Often a tradition of honor and reverence will develop around these power places, and people may look to them because they have special healing or empowering qualities, such as Lourdes in France, known for its healing springs. Another well-known spot is the Ganges River in India, where people bathe to purify themselves of their sins and begin life anew as part of a Hindu religious festival, the Kumbh Mela, or Great Sacred Jug Ceremony.

Although many of these power spots are easily observed, other places may be less obvious, since they are underground sources of energy. For example, they may lie below the ground in caves and natural springs. But even so, those attuned to these forces may feel the energy.

Shamans sometimes locate the power that resides within the earth by talking to their spiritual helpers or to the spirits of the rocks, trees, and other landforms.

Shamans might also sense the kind of events and emotional charge that has built up in a place over time. If a murder, battle, or series of problems has occurred in that location, the negative energy associated with those occurrences can lead the place to become negatively charged itself. Conversely, if a place has been used for uplifting activities or has been spiritually cleansed, it may be positively charged. Shamans or others who are sensitive to these energies can pick up on such qualities and positive and negative charges.

A good example of how different types of events can change the feeling of a place is the way people respond to a house where something bad has happened, such as a murder or suicide. Not only are people more reluctant to live there, so property rates can go down and the place can be harder to sell, but sometimes people believe that the spirit of the person who died there can hang around as a ghost. Then, too, whether or not a person knows the story of what happened, a person who is sensitive might feel the negative energy that pervades the place and have odd or queasy feelings when in the area.

By contrast, when positive events are associated with a place, such as annual celebrations and festivals, people may simply feel good when they go there. They may feel uplifted, inspired, and feel a sense of joy.

While anyone may feel such positive and negative sensations associated with a place, someone trained to be more aware will feel these sensations even more strongly.

You can experience these differences when you go to different places. As you walk or drive through an area, pay attention to how you feel. Notice how you may feel differently in one place as compared to another. You can do this wherever you are—in the city, in an office, in a house, in a park, or as you walk through the woods or by a lake.

Initially, you may not be sure exactly what these feelings or sensations are. But as you keep paying attention, you will notice some differences in the way you feel and start making connections between the different places that lead you to feel different sensations.

We often aren't aware of these differences in feelings today, since modern society encourages action and speed rather than reflection and awareness. But these sensations and feelings, if you pay attention to them, have deep roots in the development of human society. They are ancient survival mechanisms that helped people determine if they were in a secure place or a place of potential danger, at risk from predators or other dangerous hazards.

Finding Places of Power

Apart from just getting a general sense of the power or positive and negative energies of a place, you can use various spiritual techniques to tune into the power of a place.

Tuning Into Feng Shui

The ancient Chinese art of *Feng Shui*, which is based on determining the natural forces associated with a place, is an invaluable way to gauge a place's energy—essentially the positive or negative feelings or vibrations associated with a place. For example, it can be used as a guide to determine where to build a house, how to build it, and in what direction it should face (Cowan, 1996, 134). The Feng Shui practitioner will walk around before a house is built, just sensing the energies, and then will consult with the client or architect with advice on how to build. Or after a house is built, a Feng Shui practitioner might come through it and provide suggestions on

Bon Voyage

Some of the sensations to look to for help in identifying positive and negative places include feeling relaxed or tense; happy or sad; alert or tired; energized or drained; comfortable or uncomfortable; trusting or wary.

Shaman Says

Feng Shui is an ancient Chinese technique that involves determining the natural positive or negative forces associated with a place and using these as a guide as to where to build a house, how to build it, and what direction it should face.

where a resident or prospective buyer might experience problems with negative energy and how to change the house or décor to correct these problems. For instance, if your bathroom faces the front door as you open it—not a good placement according to Feng Shui theory—the practitioner might advise you to relocate the bathroom, or barring that, tell you to keep the door closed or do some positive healing ceremony to overcome the negative charge.

A Dose of Dowsing

Another of these techniques for sensing and working with the energies of a place is *dowsing*. Dowsers use dowsing rods to pick up the energies of the earth and sense how intense they are. As they walk over an area, the rod vibrates more intensely when they come near or cross over an area of greater energy. While professional dowsers use this technique to locate geological formations and mineral deposits, such as to find gas or oil wells, practitioners of shamanism may use it to sense negative and positive energies and locate power spots.

Power spots can amplify your own thoughts and feelings. Thus, they may be especially good locations for going on a shamanic journey or doing a ritual, because it will make it even more powerful. One downside of this amplification effect is that a power spot may make you feel more negative if you are already feeling scared, angry, tired, or have other negative feelings. But if you are in a place associated with strong positive energy, such as a retreat center or place of healing, the positive energy will generally overcome your negative feelings with its inspirational or healing energy. An example of the strength of this positive power is when people suffering from an illness or injury go to a holy shrine like Lourdes.

Shaman Says

Dowsing is the technique for sensing and working with the energies of a place by using a stick or metal rod, called a **dowsing rod,** to pick up the various positive and negative energies of the earth and sense their power.

You can use dowsing to locate such power spots. Certainly, people familiar with an area might tell you where these power spots, which is a good way to begin your dowsing in an especially powerful area. Then, you can use dowsing, as well as visualizing and sensing, to locate particular spots in these areas that feel more powerful for you.

Want to learn to dowse for power spots yourself? You'll need at least one other person to help you do this or a way to get feedback about what's really there after you have dowsed to test your success in locating a power spot. If you do this with another person, try taking turns, so you each get the experience of dowsing.

Bon Voyage

Consider using some of the objects for dowsing:

◆ A traditional dowsing rod, which consists of a thin branch of a tree, with a fork at the end.

◆ A wire hanger, which you bend into two even sections, to create two handles; then you use the tip to dowse.

◆ A long staff, charged with power, as a power object for dowsing.

Here are the main steps to follow:

1. Obtain or make your dowsing rod. If you are using a wire hanger, strip off any paper and cut off the two curved ends. Then, straighten out the hanger, locate the middle point, and bend it in two. If the bend of the hanger is not quite even, cut off one of the ends, so they are equal. Then, pull them apart slightly, so you can hold the ends, while the bend at the end becomes the tip of your dowsing rod. Alternatively, if you have a long staff that you consider a power object, such as a walking stick or cane, use that.

2. Select a place to dowse. Either choose a place that has some underground water streams you don't know about, (such as a natural stream or network of underground pipes with water) or ask your partner to hide some power objects. These might be rocks, stones, ceramic figures or other objects, which your partner uses as a focus and charges with energy, or some naturally occurring object regarded as a power object, such as a large crystal. Any type of underground water works because it is considered to have a higher level of energy or power than earth or rock.

3. Now start at one end of the area and start dowsing for energy spots. Keep your eyes open or closed as you prefer. Wear a blindfold if that helps you concentrate and stay focused. Hold out your dowsing rod firmly, but not tightly, allowing some looseness, so it can vibrate slightly up and down or from left to right.

4. Now walk slowly, with awareness, letting the rod guide you along. Feel yourself being drawn by it, and pay attention to any vibrations or movements. Let them guide you. If you experience any sudden or sharp dips or pulls, that is a sign of power and energy. Let yourself be drawn by any tugs. If the rod starts to move more strongly in any direction, that indicates you are getting closer. As you move and the sensation becomes slower or weaker, that is an indication you are moving away from this focus of power, so you should move back to where the sensation was the strongest.

5. Once you have located this area of a power surge, stop, and look around you. If you are using a blindfold, pull it down. Notice where you are.

6. Then, if there is more than one power spot in the area, you can continue on to locate other spots.

When you first start dowsing, you may not get a hit—locate a power object or source of water—right away. But you'll find you become more and more sensitive as you continue to practice, and you will generally get more and more hits.

Finding Power Spots Through Visualization

The second way to identify power spots—at least the ones that feel more powerful for you—is by visualizing and sensing what places in an area have more power. This process is much like what you would do in a large room, where you feel drawn to a particular seat or location that just feels like the right place to go. But now you are using your abilities to visualize or sense in an area, usually in a natural setting, where you might want to go to feel extra power, when you do a shamanic ritual or go on a shamanic journey.

Wise Ways

Anthropologist James A. Swan, author of *The Power of Place: Sacred Ground in Natural and Human Environments*, has spent a lot of time speaking with Native Americans in developing a guide to sacred spaces. Among the places he has listed as places of power or sacred sites are:

- Burial grounds
- Places for purification and healing, such as sacred waters, where people go to fast, meditate, and conduct ceremonies
- Sites which are a location for special plants or animals
- Quarries that contain especially powerful stones or gems
- Places where people have gone for vision questing or dreaming
- Sites associated with myths and legends
- Locations of temples and shrines, which may be on already sacred sites or become sacred due to the building and ceremonies there
- Places for pilgrimages and spiritual renewal
- Historical sites that have acquired special meanings for a particular group of people
- Sunrise sites, where people go to honor the rising sun at major turning points of the year, such as quarters (solstices and equinoxes) or cross-quarters days (periods between the solstices and equinoxes)

Try going to different types of sites and experiment with various exercises for getting to know better the energies there.

You can also do a more directed form of visualization, as described by Jose and Lena Stevens in *Secrets of Shamanism*. Using this technique, you visualize the spirit body of the earth body—essentially an aura of energy around it—and sense for pockets of increased energy—places where the intensity of that energy feels or appears stronger. As you do this visualization, look for those energy pockets that you feel drawn to and most comfortable around. It's best to choose a place where you have a lot of room, such as a large park or place in the country. Then, sit down, close your eyes, and initially visualize your own spirit body—or energy field around you—and then visualize the energy field of the earth around you. In other words, visualize pulses of energy emanating from and surrounding both you and the earth.

Next, ask your spiritual helper or just ask generally to be guided to the nearest power site. You might recognize this by seeing a brighter energy in a certain area, or you could experience a sudden urge to move in a particular direction. However this feeling comes to you, trust that impulse and go there.

Then, the Stevens suggest using a self-validation process when you get to the spot, in which you sit down and repeat the exercise. If you feel you want to stay where you are, do so. Or if you see a brighter energy or are drawn to another spot, change your location. According to the Stevens, "not all power spots agree with everyone," and you want to be sure you have an affinity for that place. Once you find a power place that's right for you, then choose that as your power spot.

Finally, the Stevens suggest one further step to fully bond with a power spot. Close your eyes and notice the qualities of the spot. Sense what is different about this spot for you from surrounding areas, and ask how you can benefit from being here. After you have spent as much time as you want doing this, ask the earth if you can continue to use the spot. Usually, you will experience a yes as a feeling of peace or fulfillment, leading you to sense that the earth is giving you its continued permission. What is important is that you have the sense that this is a place that is comfortable and welcoming for you now and in the future. Finally, thank the power spot and the earth for giving you a good experience and inviting you back. Then, you are ready to leave, having selected and affirmed the spot for your future activities there.

Using Power Places for Rituals and Journeying

Once you have located a power place, you can take some time to get to know it, thereby putting you in closer touch with the energies or spirits of the place. This will make it even more powerful and meaningful for you, and contribute to the power and the intensity of your journeying there. You can also ask the spirits you encounter at this place for help and guidance.

Making observations and tuning into your feelings and perceptions are part of the process of getting to know the power and spiritual energies of a place. To better experience the energy vibrations, which represent spiritual energies, try using the unfocused seeing technique discussed in Chapter 1. Another way to experience these energies is to close your eyes to focus on what you are experiencing from your other senses. Then, listen, notice the temperature, sense the smells, and otherwise fully feel the energies and power emanating from where you are. By doing so, you will become more sensitive to this place, make it more fully your own, and become more in touch with its power and special characteristics.

> **Bon Voyage**
>
> Besides going to local areas to find power spots, you can travel to other areas or even around the world to look for power spots that have become well-known. There are even groups that sponsor trips to such power sites. You'll find some of these listed in the Appendix C.

You can use the energy of a power place to add power to any rituals and journeying you do there. In fact, in the future, you don't even have to actually go there. You can call up an image of the place in your mind's eye and go there in your imagination. Or instead of going there, you can visualize that you are drawing the energy of the place to you to use for your rituals or journeying, wherever you are.

Asking Your Power Animal for Assistance

Still another way to get to know the spirits of a place is suggested by Tom Cowan in *Shamanism: A Spiritual Practice for Daily Life*. His approach is to ask your power animal (if you have already developed a relationship with one) or to send out your consciousness to the spirit of the place in order to start a dialogue with it or to merge with it so you can learn from it. Often this spirit may be one that dominates the region, such as the spirit of a particularly large tree or rock formation. Or the spirit could be a larger spirit that represents the whole area, such as the spirit of a valley or mountain. Still other types of spirits might be strongly associated with a place, such as the spirits within the roots of a tree or in a creek bed.

Cowan also suggests using a small drum or rattle to call the spirits. As you sit in the power spot you have selected and feel ready, send your consciousness to draw that spirit into a conversation or draw it into yourself, so you can ask it questions and learn from it more about the place where you are.

When you have finished communicating with the spirit, thank it, and withdraw your consciousness back into yourself.

The Least You Need to Know

◆ Power places are places associated with energy, such as high mountains, tall and unusual rock formations, geysers, caves, and places of great beauty; even human made places can become power places. Essentially, they are sites that stand out in some way and have a special majesty or mystery about them.

◆ Often power places, because of their energy, become areas where groups are attracted to perform rituals or have celebrations.

◆ While many power places are easily observed, some are less obvious, since they are underground sources of energy, such as natural springs or water flowing through networks of pipes.

◆ You can use dowsing and visualization to locate power places.

Pack Your Bags, We're Going on a Journey!

Journeying is the heart of shamanism. You can take a shamanic journey for personal and professional development, problem solving, conflict resolution, making decisions, setting goals, and otherwise achieving success. You can also journey to heal your own psyche and recover from deep psychological wounds, when you use these techniques with a trained counselor or shamanic practitioner. Also, you can apply these techniques for helping and healing others, though you need a trained teacher to guide you.

So, get ready to go on the three major types of journeys—to the lower, upper, and middle worlds. Also, should you want to look within yourself more deeply, you can learn how some psychologists today are incorporating the journey with other in-depth psyche-probing techniques.

Fasten your seatbelts for an exciting ride!

12

Spiritual Travel: The Shamanic Journey

In This Chapter

◆ The many styles of shamanic journeying

◆ Modern approaches to journeying

◆ Using different techniques to enhance your journey

◆ The safety of journeying

◆ Different purposes for journeying

Shamans use many different techniques to contact, travel, or journey to other worlds. They might use drumming, chanting, or rattling—techniques which have a long heritage in the Siberian, Native American, and Central and South American Indian traditions. Other techniques include meditation, dancing, hallucinogenic drugs, breathing in repeated infusions of tobacco, smoking a sacred pipe, vision questing, and a variety of forms of sensory overload or deprivation. All of the techniques are meant to trigger a shift into an alternate or altered state of consciousness, ranging from a state of light hypnosis to deep trance.

Whatever method you use, a key to journeying is developing the ability to see and project your consciousness. Another way to think of this process is to imagine that you are extending your awareness outward. Through this process you can see spirits or spiritual energies, communicate with the spiritual beings you see, and experience yourself traveling in spiritual realms.

While shamans who engage in this process do believe they are actually contacting spirits, another way to think of this process is that you are traveling to another world that exists symbolically in your imagination. Then, you can experience traveling to this other world much like a traveler going on guided fantasy you direct yourself, so you can journey safely where you want and you can travel light for a short trip; you don't have to venture deeply for an extended stay. In this case, you are essentially looking within your consciousness or using your imagination to think about things in a more visual and symbolic way. It does not really matter whether this journey is to real or symbolic worlds for you, as long as you use these techniques in a way that is comfortable for you to accomplish your goals in taking the journey.

You can use journeying for day-to-day problem solving, goal planning, decision-making, brainstorming, or even just to have fun or learn about other worlds. You also can engage in deeper psychological or healing work on your journeys, although if you do so, work with a trained professional or ask for their guidance in how to use these exercises.

Journeying is the essence of shamanism, and in this chapter, you'll find out why. So fasten your seatbelt, and get ready to explore the fascinating world of shamanic journeys!

The Many Ways to Take a Shamanic Journey

Just like you can walk, crawl, run, jump, bike, or take a car, train, or plane to get somewhere, you can use a variety of different methods for going on a shamanic journey.

Whatever means of travel you take, you have to learn to do three key things:

♦ See into nonordinary reality.

♦ Project your consciousness.

♦ Be open and receptive, but conscious and in control of your state of consciousness.

Shaman Says

An **altered state of consciousness** is any state that differs from the ordinary state of consciousness you are in when you engage in everyday activities. When you are sleeping, meditating, and journeying, you are in an altered state of consciousness.

You'll want to use a method that will help you do all three things and, at the same time, remain in complete control. For example, you should be able to slow down the process if you feel you are losing control. Once you know what you are doing and feel comfortable with your technique, you can open up the spiritual throttle, so to speak.

Different ways in which some traditional shamans from Ecuador alter their states of consciousness and/or contact other worlds. The Canelo shaman (upper left) is calling on the spirits by beating on a pan. The Otavalan shaman (upper right) is drinking some liquor to help him get in an altered state of conscious. The Cayapa shaman (bottom) is waving a branch of leaves to call in the spirits and gain their assistance to purify and cleanse the patients around him.

Taking a Shamanic Journey the Modern Way

Many modern practitioners have developed a style of journeying based on using drumming and rattling, such as using the system called *core shamanism*. This approach was originally developed by Michael Harner in 1980 and is promoted through his Foundation of Shamanic Studies, which does extensive trainings and gives its teachers and counselors, who have completed its program, a certificate as a Certified Shamanic Counselor. In core shamanism, certain key elements have been drawn from traditional, indigenous shamanism around the world and developed into a modern-day spiritual practice (Cowan, 1996, Preface).

> **Shaman Says**
>
> A shamanic **drumming circle** is a group of people who get together to participate in drumming, usually to induce a shamanic journey for one or more participants in the group.

Like many other modern approaches to shamanism, core shamanism doesn't involve any particular religious beliefs, so it can be combined with other religious systems. However, core shamanism is based on animism—the belief that all things in the world have a spiritual essence or spirit, including all animals, plants, landforms, bodies of water, elements, etc. In order to see and communicate with the spirits, you need to believe they exist or at least view them as symbolic representations of the natural forces or energies that exist in nature.

Wise Ways

According to the Foundation for Shamanic Studies' website, **core shamanism** is "the universal and near-universal basic methods of the shaman to enter nonordinary reality for problem solving and healing." In this approach, the emphasis is going on the "classic shamanic journey," in which participants use drumming and other techniques to experience "the shamanic state of consciousness" and awaken their "dormant spiritual abilities, including connections with Nature." Harner adapted this system by drawing on major key elements from traditional indigenous shamans around the world to create a system for the modern practice of shamanism.

The Visual Basics of Shamanism

Although many people find that drumming and rattling helps them get into the altered state necessary for a journey, others—myself included—find the noise distracting. If you're more of a visual person, you can use creative visualization, guided fantasy, or mental imaging to help you see and get into an altered consciousness state. It's an approach you can easily do anywhere, anytime, and you can do it alone or with others.

Because visualization, also called mental imagery, is my preferred approach, the guided journeys I'll be describing use visualization or mental imagery, though feel free to use your own drumming and rattling if you prefer. Though I use the terms "visualization" or "mental imagery," these also include using your thoughts or self-talk to guide you, if you have trouble seeing things in your mind eye.

Let Me Count the Ways

You can easily combine visualization with other techniques, such as meditation, crystals, and magical rituals, if you want. You can visualize as you dance, chant, beat a drum, shake a rattle, or engage in any of the other means of going on a shamanic journey.

CAUTION Off the Path

Aside from the legal obstacles of using controlled substances for journeying, you may not have control over the drugged state, and it may be hard to tell what visions are coming from the drugs and what are coming from you. Also, when you use drugs, you can't stop the experience at any time you want, as you can when you use your mental powers alone to move you into an altered state. When you use guided meditation, creative visualization, or any other nondrug techniques, you can readily stop the journey and return to the everyday world if there's something you don't want to see there or if you feel it's time to come back. Thus, for a number of practical reasons, it's generally better to avoid using drugs when going on a journey, because you have more control.

You can journey alone or in a group. For some, journeying in a group is especially powerful, particularly when it is combined with other shamanic practices and ceremonies. Others prefer to work with a partner or alone. Feel free to do your journeying in different settings and situations, with different people or on your own. For different people, different systems may be more or less conducive to journeying to the other world.

Different systems may also be more appropriate to use at different times. For example, often it is easier to use visualization than a method requiring other equipment or making noise, such as rattling or chanting. You may not have a rattle around or you may be unable to chant where you are, since you might disturb your neighbors or housemates, or the people you work with may consider any shamanic practice peculiar. By contrast, if you can use a visualization to get into an altered state, you can readily use this wherever and whenever you want, and you don't have to explain what you are doing to neighbors or others.

Whatever approach you use, you can learn the basic journeying process very quickly—in a matter of minutes or hours, depending on how quickly you respond, though learning to deepen and more firmly direct and apply this state takes longer. Also, the journeying process takes no special psychic ability, because it's a matter of letting your imagination and the power of intuition free to explore and take you into an altered state and other world. While some people may be better at mastering this ability, everyone can learn and apply the journeying process.

But Is It Safe?

Sometimes people wonder about the safety of going on a journey—they are concerned about opening up doors to past memories and buried feelings, much as they might experience in deep hypnosis. They may also be concerned about working to develop shamanic mastery, since traditional shamans have commonly gone through a period of great struggle with spiritual forces, similar to experiencing a dark night of the soul or going through a death-rebirth experience.

Another reason you should have little concern about using the process is that you can control your own shamanic journeying experiences by setting your purpose in advance and focusing on using the journey for general self-improvement, not in-depth therapeutic or healing work, where you should work with a trained professional. Then, in addition to following these guidelines, you can also control the depth of your altered consciousness experience as long as you don't use drugs.

You can also learn to trigger an end to a journey if you encounter anything upsetting to you, so you come back to ordinary reality right away. Additionally, if you encounter any unfriendly or negative spirits on your journey, there are ways to deal with them apart from simply leaving, such as using various spiritual protections, like visualizing a white light around you or calling on your spiritual helper to send those negative forces away.

> **Wise Ways**
>
> Though many traditional shamans have gone through a period of extreme suffering and hardship to gain shamanic powers, it is not a requirement for becoming a shaman. Many people can attain shamanic powers without any suffering at all.

Because you are normally in full control of where you go on your journey, for what purpose, how deep you go, and when you return, shamanic journeying is generally very safe, and you can usually develop powerful shamanic abilities without encountering any difficulties.

The Power of Purpose in Journeying

Although it doesn't matter what method you use to go on your shamanic journeys, it is very important to know your purpose. A key to having a productive journey is beginning it with a clear purpose or intent. Otherwise, you will just drift around and may experience a blankness or lack of imagery.

Knowing What You Want to Ask

Before you go on your journey, make sure you have a clear goal in mind. This goal can take a number of forms:

- ◆ You have a question or a few questions for which you want to find the answers.
- ◆ You want to meet your power animals or teachers.
- ◆ You hope to discover what objects might have power for you, so you can acquire or make them later.
- ◆ You want to resolve a problem or conflict situation.
- ◆ You seek advice to feel more energy or improve a physical condition.
- ◆ You want to help another person deal with a psychological issue.
- ◆ You want to heal yourself or another person from a physical condition.

Balancing Your Purpose with Being Receptive

While it is crucial to start with a clear purpose or intent initially, once you assert this, let go and be receptive to whatever happens. Consciously express your purpose by that part of you that remains in control and in charge of the journeying process. But having stated that purpose, you let your unconscious, intuitive part go, so you can relax, enjoy the journey, observe, and learn what you seek to learn on your journey.

Bon Voyage

Balancing these two sides of your perception in journeying reflects this emphasis on balance in many philosophical, religious, and psychological systems. The ideal is to use moderation in all things (Confucianism), walk in harmony and balance (Native American), follow the way of the Tao (Taoism), and generally seek a middle way.

When on a shamanic journey, you might think of yourself as a traveler, explorer, or observer—or perhaps even the captain of a shamanic ship. You are at the rudder and steering as you travel the shamanic seas, and you can observe and communicate with whatever you see as your shamanic vessel goes by.

Looking for Help, Information, or Power

Among the many reasons for journeying is to seek various types of help, information, or power from the spiritual beings that you encounter on your journey as guides, mentors, friends, or others you can talk to. The answers may come in the form of a verbal message or vision, or these beings may lead or direct you to a place or to meet other spiritual beings where you can obtain the information, sources of help, or power you need.

Off the Path _____

Generally, any spiritual beings you meet on these journeys will remain separate and apart from you, so you will not be taken over or possessed by them. That's because you are not taking your trip as a channel or medium. Instead, one part of you is staying in control, so you are seeking to balance being both receptive and asserting control. However, if you do find you are losing control or feel too much negative energy coming at you for you to handle, slow down and stop the process.

When you go on these trips, you can seek help or information to help yourself or help others. While many people today use journeying primarily to gain assistance or knowledge for themselves (whereas the traditional role of the shaman was to use shamanic techniques to help others), many people still do use these tools to help others. Shamanic techniques are particularly good in problem-solving and trouble-shooting for other people, because you can go on the journey as a completely objective, neutral observer, who has no advance agenda about what you would like to find (which can sometimes interfere with one's objectivity on a personal trip). This helper role can also be very useful for aiding another person seeking advice, because it's like you are a second person who can provide that person with your insights (see Chapter 20 for more on partnered journeys). Then, too, those with special training can use shamanic techniques in the role of a therapist (see Chapter 17 for more on this).

Some Reasons to Go On a Personal Journey

The reasons for taking a personal journey are as many as the questions you might want to ask. Some of the most common reasons include the following:

- You want to ask a question about a problem in your own life, which you haven't been able to resolve by coming up with an answer consciously, such as how to deal with a relationship or a career decision. But you might be able to resolve it through a shamanic journey, where you meet some power animals, teachers, or other guides who will give you answers about what to do.

- You want to relax or get a charge of power.

- You are seeking support for whatever you are doing, so you feel more confident and assured. By contacting your spiritual helpers and gaining their support or endorsement, it's like having a cheering squad or group of advisors on your team.

♦ You want to open up or keep the path open to this altered state of conscious or other spiritual world, so when you need help or information, you can better use the journeying process to get it. The way to keep the path open is to take a journey from time to time, so this feels like a famil-iar, comfortable approach to use when you need assistance.

♦ You want to get reacquainted with some of the spiritual guides or helpers you have con-tacted on previous trips. Going on an occa-sional journey can help you keep up these contacts, much like reconnecting with a friend or relative you haven't seen in awhile. By reestablishing these friendships and investing them with more energy, these guides and helpers will be more present and better able to help you when you really need them.

> **Wise Ways**
>
> So what are your reasons for tak-ing a shamanic journey? What kind of help would you like to get from your spiritual helpers or guides? How else might you find shaman journeying helpful for you or others you know? Start brainstorming and make a list of all of your reasons and ways you might use a journey.

Self-Help and Journeying

Certainly, there are other ways to get personal answers, relax, and gain power, and there are many other sources of help. For instance, I sometimes use automatic writing, where I simply ask a question and write out whatever answers come from my unconscious mind. Or I use a creative visualization technique, such as imagining the situation is occurring on a screen in front of me, as I watch it unfold, and like a director, think of different possible resolutions and choose what I feel is the best approach.

But the shamanic journey is a powerful addition to a repertoire of techniques for getting help for yourself or others, because it involves going into a deeper state of unconscious-ness to gain these insights and power. It also involves seeking additional sources of insights from another level of reality, whether you see this as a symbolic projection of a spiritual world or one that really exists beyond the ordinary realm of consciousness. Either way you conceive of this other world, these spiritual beings or forces can be powerful tools for gaining great insights and mobilizing your energies to help yourself or others.

The shamanic journey is an important part of your spiritual toolkit, which you can take with you and use wherever you want. While this toolkit derives from a traditional world of shamans that hardly exists anymore, it is extremely adaptable and can be applied in new modern situations. These have existed so long because they have provided deep sources of wisdom and healing. You can apply them in the modern world to deal with modern problems.

The Least You Need to Know

♦ While many modern practitioners use drumming and rattling to go on their journeys, you can also use visualization or mental imagery to take you on your journey.

♦ If at anytime you feel uncomfortable or threatened while on a journey, you can stop the journey by simply opening your eyes.

♦ When you go on a journey, it's important to have a goal and start with a question or few questions you want to ask.

♦ You can combine journeying with other self-help techniques.

All Aboard! Taking a Journey

In This Chapter

- Picking your destinations
- Taking a lower world journey
- Taking an upper world journey
- Taking a middle world journey
- Journeying and other states of consciousness

Shamanic journeying is like traveling with a map of the world in your mind. You can travel to popular destinations, such as the *lower world*, *upper world*, and *middle world*, or you can also travel off the beaten track by exploring other universes and galaxies, even traveling back in time and traveling into the future.

So get out your map of the spiritual world (hint: it's in your mind), and get ready to take a journey.

Taking a Lower World Journey

Newcomers to modern-day shamanic groups and workshops typically visit the lower world on their first shamanic journey, since this is where you can go to meet your power animal (although traditionally these animals are located in either the middle or lower world).

Whatever your reason for visiting the lower world, you typically travel through a hole in the earth or go down through a natural form, like a cave, to get to it. The underworld landscape is typically filled with tunnels and caves. In many traditions the lower world has been associated with the earth and Mother Earth, including Native American, Central and South American, and various Pagan and Wiccan traditions. Sometimes the earth is called Grandmother, such as when Wallace Black Elk talks about the female aspect of the Creator associated with Earth, birth, and knowledge (Lyons, 1996, 188). Or people may have other names for the earth as a deity or goddess, such as the Shuar of the Upper Amazon, who call their goddess of the earth, plants, and gardens, Nùnkui. They see her as the "protector of women" and believe she resides in the earth during the day, where she heals the soil and works with roots. Then, she rises above the ground at night to "dance with the plants, animals, and people," as described by John Perkins, an environmentalist who visited the Shuar and took part in their sacred ayahuasca ceremonies with them (Perkins, 1994, 132).

> **Shaman Says**
>
> The **middle world** typically corresponds to the everyday natural world. The **lower world** is underground and is usually associated with power animals and evil spirits and thought of as dangerous or mysterious. The **upper world,** which exists in the air and in the clouds, is frequently associated with spiritual teachers, guardian angels, and the most powerful helpers.

> **Wise Ways**
>
> Traditionally, the lower world has had two types of associations: the Earth Mother and demonic powers.

The lower world is also associated with negative or demonic powers. For example, Dante's *Inferno* highlights going down through evil, infernal realms. In Greek mythology, Persephone travels to the underworld and becomes the wife of Hades, the lord of this world. And many traditional peoples, such as the classic Maya, have viewed the underworld as the place of frightening, dangerous monsters and demons. Not only did they see the king of the underworld as a twin deity named One/Seven Death, but they had many other demons with names like Blood Gatherer, Skull Scepter, and Stab Master, according to Maya scholar Douglas Gillette. They created images on their paintings, carvings, and ceramics, representing different forms of death, such as skeletons with burst bellies and skulls with hacked-away faces.

The main associations with the lower world are:

- Underground geological features, like caves and tunnels
- Power animals
- Associations with Mother Earth
- Birth, nurturing, support
- Warmth, protection

- ◆ The feminine, female principles
- ◆ The underworld
- ◆ Demons, dangerous and mysterious creatures
- ◆ Death
- ◆ Darkness, night
- ◆ Knowledge, including of secrets
- ◆ The past

In modern shamanism, however, the lower world has largely been stripped of any deathly and demonic associations, while the associations with the Earth Mother or goddess have become more widely accepted. In modern shamanism, journeying to the lower world does not mean you are going to a place that is negative, inferior, or evil. Rather, the term "lower" is used in a geographic sense to indicate going lower or underground, where you can contact many different types of spiritual helpers, particularly power animals.

When you take a shamanic journey into the lower world to meet an animal and other helpers to seek power, insights, and information, view your journey in a positive light. See your lower world journey as one to gain nurturing from Mother Earth and as a place to seek wisdom from your power animal or other beings you meet there. In turn, your own beliefs in the helpful, supportive qualities of this lower world will help to create this helpful, supportive environment you seek on your journeys there.

Taking an Upper World Journey

In contrast to the lower world of dark demons and the Earth Mother, the upper world is more generally associated with the higher spirits and Sky Father, which may take various forms. For instance, the Western Judeo-Christian tradition has its angels, heavens, and heavenly Father, while other traditions use other terms such as Father, First Father, Grandfather, First Lord, and First Jaguar (Gillette, 1996, 92–101).

While some may feel there should be no distinction in which is higher or more spiritual— the spirits of the lower world or the upper world, these common distinctions are made in many traditions, particularly in the West, with its Judeo-Christian influences. But you can certainly regard the spirits of each world as having equal spiritual qualities, as you prefer.

The upper world is often associated with rules and laws, the place where the universe is ordered, so it becomes a place of wisdom and inspiration, rather than support and nurturing. Traditionally, it is associated with the male principle and light, in contrast to the female principle and darkness associated with the earth.

But here, too, many modern shamanic traditions drop many of the more religious associations, so the term "upper" is often simply used in a geographic sense to indicate going higher or into the sky or above the clouds, where you can contact many different types of spiritual helpers associated with wisdom, such as teachers and guardian spirits.

The main associations with the upper world are:

- Places in the sky, like clouds, winds, stars, the moon, and planets
- Teachers, spiritual guides, angels
- Associations with the Sky Father
- Rules, law, direction
- Strength, guidance
- The masculine, male principles
- The overworld, heaven
- Enlightened, beatific, ethereal beings
- Eternal life
- Light, day
- Wisdom, enlightenment
- Future

On an upper world journey, you typically go up into the air through a jumping-off point like a high mountain or tall tree. Then, once up in the air or clouds, you will seek your helpers and teachers. Though the term "upper world," like "lower world," is designed to refer to a geographical place, not to imply something better or superior, commonly shamans find their most powerful helpers there, although they may also meet individuals and animals with less power.

Bon Voyage

A good way to approach your initial journeys is to do what new travelers do—sample each new place briefly to see how you experience it. Notice the differences in the places and the people you meet there, and develop your own preferences about where you like to go and who you would like to meet again when you return.

When you take a shamanic journey to the upper world to meet a teacher or other spiritual helpers to seek power, insights, and information, view your journey as a way to gain wisdom and direction from whatever helpers or teachers you meet there. In turn, your own beliefs in the wisdom and guidance of this upper world will help to create the kind of place that offers the wisdom and guidance you need.

Taking a Middle World Journey

When you go on a middle world journey, basically to some place on earth, you typically go on one of three kinds of journeys: 1) to a sacred place; 2) to any place to contact the spirits there; 3) and to work with the elements of nature. It is also often a starting off point to travel into the past or future or into other worlds, such as taking a journey into outer space or to other planetary galaxies.

One of the most common destinations of a middle world journey is a sacred place. Traditionally, this is a real place considered sacred by the members of a community, and it may even be a place that people physically travel to, such as a sacred mountain, spring, or waterfall. An example is the sacred waterfall of the Shuar, which they call Tuntiak, the name of the sacred rainbow that forms there. This waterfall is regarded as the place from which the first Shuar man and woman emerged (Perkins, 1994, 26). Also, a sacred spot might be a place from which the spirits are believed to come to join with or help members of the community, such as the kachinas of the Hopi, who come from their sacred mountains. It may also be a site of vision quests, such as among the Lakota.

Then, too, many shamans travel to any number of surrounding places, from towns and villages to mountains, streams, and fields. These locations may not be singled out and identified as sacred sites, but a shaman will call on the spirits that reside there.

Finally, you might take a middle world journey to work with the basic elements—air, earth, fire, and water—that are all around us and represent different aspects of oneself. These elements can be a very powerful source of insight about your personal qualities and personality traits.

You can also use the qualities you associate with the elements to help you deal with various everyday situations. For example, you might see fire as representing aggressiveness, assertiveness, or spontaneity; associate air with enlightenment or fluidity; relate water to movement or flow; and link earth with strength and solidity. Then, by going on a journey in which you experience these qualities, this contact may help you recognize these qualities in yourself or take on these characteristics, so you can better use those traits in everyday situations. For example, if you don't feel strong enough to confront a difficult person or situation, a journey in which you visualize yourself connecting with the earth might help you feel stronger and enable you to draw on this increased strength to get what you want.

The main associations with the middle world are:

◆ Geological and natural features on the earth, like rocks, trees, plants, mountains, and valleys

◆ Power animals, spirits of sacred places, and teachers

- ◆ Associations with Mother Earth and the living things on Mother Earth
- ◆ Growth, harvest, the soil, plants
- ◆ Strength, solidity, being grounded
- ◆ A mix of masculine and feminine principles, being balanced
- ◆ The everyday ordinary world
- ◆ Everyday animals, humans
- ◆ Cycles of life and death, time
- ◆ Changing seasons and daily cycles

When you take a shamanic journey into the middle world, you can engage in a variety of activities, from contacting animals and teachers to seeking a balance between the various principles associated with the upper and lower worlds. In turn, as in the case of traveling to the lower or upper worlds, your own beliefs in the helpful qualities of the middle world will help to create exactly this kind of helpful environment you seek.

You can supplement middle world journeys with other activities that are practiced by shamans to get more in touch with nature and the environment. For instance, you might take a nature walk to become more aware of the plants and animals in your area. You might also become active in efforts to preserve the local ecology, as some traditional shamans are doing in areas under siege, such as the rainforest in South America. You might also apply the emphasis in traditional shamanism on helping others to find ways that you might help the needy in your community.

So What's the Difference? Journeying-Hypnosis-Dreaming-Trance

People frequently ask how journeying differs from hypnosis, trances, and dreaming.

It's helpful to think of the states of consciousness we experience while journeying, dreaming, or under hypnosis as part of a continuum. At the one end is everyday waking consciousness, which has been termed being in a *beta* state by many researchers and popular writers on the subject. This everyday waking state is characterized by a greater frequency of shorter, more frequent brain waves on a biofeedback machine. This beta state gives way to a greater frequency of slower, longer waves, which is popularly called an *alpha* state, associated with relaxation. Then, when you go into an even deeper state of relaxation, which gives way to sleeping, you get an increase in the frequency of the very long, slow waves, described as a *theta* state. Dreaming is associated with rapid eye movements or REMs.

Just as there is a continuum of consciousness, you can have a continuum of experiential states as you move from everyday consciousness into a light state of meditation or light hypnosis to an even deeper state of hypnosis that turns into trance. In most cases, journeying would fall on the continuum near the state of hypnosis, where you are aware of the experience and in control of it, although you might also feel a loss of control over it as you move into a trance.

> **Wise Ways**
>
> Neurobiologists, psychiatrists, and other scientists now have a number of tools to relate neurological activity in different parts of the brain to different types of thinking and feeling states. These techniques have greatly increased our knowledge about states of consciousness and how they relate to brain function.

Taking a Journey into Trance

People frequently find themselves in a state in which they are aware of their surroundings but not in control of themselves—essentially in a trance—after repeated dancing or chanting or after having ingested a strong drug like ayahuasca. They may still be very aware of what is happening and remember it, but not able to guide the process and guide and direct where they go and what they see.

> **CAUTION**
>
> **Off the Path** _____
>
> John Perkins, who took ayahuasca with the Shuar of Peru in the Upper Amazon, described his experience of a deep trance state. In contrast to a controlled journeying process, during which he fully entered another world with all his senses and could come out of the state and back to ordinary reality at any time, with ayahuasca, he could not (Perkins, 1994, 48). Instead, he found himself deep in another world where the Shuar goes to communicate with plants, animals, and even the earth, and he had all sorts of powerful visions of jaguars, waterfalls, and soaring birds. But he was unable to direct whatever visions came to him or leave the state until the power of the drug receded.

In some states of deep trance, you may not even be consciously aware of what is happening, such as in the trance state practiced by the dancers in the traditional ceremonies of Bali. The dancers dance to the point of ecstasy, fall down, and have no memory of what happened after they wake up. By contrast, the shamanic trance is more like a light meditation or hypnotic state, although in some cases a journey may deepen into such a trancelike state.

But Is It Hypnosis?

While journeying, you are usually aware of where you are going and you can pull yourself back at any time.

You usually want to cultivate a state of light hypnosis, keeping your conscious awareness alert to guide the journey. You also want to be able to remember your journey when you come back. The experience is like letting your mind go, while you are in a very relaxed, receptive state, yet remain in charge, so you are both observing and experiencing and guiding the process.

When you're on a shamanic journey, you're like a film director who is directing a scene. You choose the actors, decide on the setting, give the actors a general guideline to follow, and let them improvise. Yet, at any time you can interrupt to redirect and guide the action, and then return to observing again. Or imagine you are putting your car on automatic cruise control, where you can glide through the scene just observing and enjoying as the car zips along. But whenever you want, you can step in to use your manual override to stop the car or guide it in another direction. Importantly, too, whether you are a film director or driving the car, you can always stop the process at any time and simply go home, arriving there in an instant when you decide to stop.

Unless you are game for a far deeper trance, such as produced by ayahuasca, and willing to accept the potentially dangerous risks of such a ride, it is best to use the controlled and directed journeying state.

> **Wise Ways**
>
> One way to think of journeying is as a form of light or medium hypnosis in which you are traveling in your imagination to other worlds. Whether or not these experiences you have there involve contacting real spiritual beings or projections of your imagination, you can still use these encounters and the information you get there to guide you in your life.

Shaman Says

Here are a number of other names that might describe the usual state of journeying or are akin to what one typically experiences:

- Psychonavigation
- Creative visualization
- Mental imaging
- Light to medium hypnosis
- Mind power techniques
- Guided fantasy
- Active meditation
- Any other names you can think of ... add them here!

How Dreaming Is Different Than Journeying

In many ways, the shamanic journey is like dreaming, since your unconscious mind is also traveling. However, in journeying you normally are in control (except for very deep trances, such as those induced by very powerful drugs). Also, unlike most types of dreaming, you can will yourself in or out of the shamanic journey, because a conscious part of you is still in charge. Too, you usually have a clear memory of what you experienced, whereas dreams often fade quickly, unless you are especially attuned to them and engage in some quick, effective dream retrieval techniques.

In dreaming, you don't usually have control over where you go and the nature of the experience, although some people have developed an ability to control and direct their dreams through practicing a conscious or waking dream process, known as *lucid dreaming*. This is a kind of dreaming in which a part of you remains alert and aware you are dreaming. You can likewise develop this ability to enter and guide the dream, but it's a skill that requires much training and practice, and it can quickly slip away if you don't practice it regularly.

> **Shaman Says**
>
> **Lucid dreaming** is a kind of dreaming in which a part of you remains alert and aware you are dreaming. You can develop the ability to enter and guide your dreams. A **waking dream** is another term for a lucid dream, in which you are both awake and dreaming, since a part of you remains alert and aware that you are having a dream.

Because you are in control, shamanic journeying is usually safer than dreaming. You can easily change direction or stop the journey, so you don't get trapped in a journey you don't like. By contrast, at times you may become stuck in a dream, only to wake up in an upset and anxious state, as the dream tends to linger on.

Integrating Your Journeys and Your Dreams

Despite the difficulties of staying conscious and controlling dreams, you can create a bridge between your journeys and your dreams, so they influence and guide each other. You can create two key journey and dream connections by either using your journeys to influence your dreams or using your dreams to influence your journeys.

Use Your Journeys to Influence Your Dreams

In this approach, you notice issues or questions that come up in your journeys, particularly if there is something you are unsure about or you feel is unresolved. Before you go to sleep at night, or even before a daytime nap, take a few minutes to meditate on that issue or question. This way it is highlighted in your mind before you go to sleep; it is the last thing your conscious mind is aware of before it submerges and your unconscious mind takes over. By doing so, you are transferring this issue or question that's important to you from your conscious to unconscious mind, like a ferry transferring its passengers across a river.

To better make this transfer work, emphasize its importance in your mind by repeatedly telling yourself something like: "I will dream about this ____," "I will dream the answer to my question ____," "I will dream the resolution to my problem ____." Fill in the blanks very specifically and precisely, so your unconscious mind, which will later launch the dream, gets a very clear picture of what it should do.

Use Your Dreams to Influence Your Journeys

In this opposite approach, pay attention to your dreams for the issues or questions that come up. Then use your journeys to gain more information and answers. This is a particularly good approach to use when you aren't sure what your dreams are all about and you want some help interpreting them. For instance, if you aren't sure who a person is in a dream, why such an event occurred, why you encountered a particular person, or what some images in a dream mean, go on a journey to help you find out. To do so, ask your power animals, spiritual helpers, or teachers in the upper, lower, or middle worlds, wherever you prefer to go for that type of information, about whatever you saw in your dreams.

> **Wise Ways**
>
> It might be helpful to record your dreams and journeys, keeping track of when your dreams influence your journeys and when your journeys influences your dreams. You can then review your experiences and look for patterns.

Simply frame the question or goal to start your journey as you normally do. The only difference is you are asking about something you saw or experienced in your dream.

No matter where you journey or what shamanic practices you use to gain more fulfillment, satisfaction, joy, and love in your life, remember that you set the goals.

The Least You Need to Know

♦ Although there are differences from tradition to tradition, commonly the lower word is underground and is usually associated with power animals; the upper world is in the air and the clouds and is frequently associated with spiritual teachers and higher beings; and the middle world corresponds to the everyday natural world.

♦ Journeying differs from hypnosis, dreaming, and trance, in that a person taking a journey is in a waking altered state of consciousness and is both experiencing and guiding the process.

- ◆ When you take a shamanic journey, you are like a film director directing a scene, where you set the stage, give the actors general directions, and let them improvise. But at any time you can redirect or stop the action or even leave the set.

- ◆ You can combine and supplement your journeying with other activities, including dreaming, taking nature walks, helping to improve the environment around you, and working to help those in need in your local community.

14

Getting the Most Out of Your Journeys

In This Chapter

- ◆ Using multiple senses to experience more
- ◆ Keeping your experience positive
- ◆ Adapting the journey for you
- ◆ Using variety to enhance your experience
- ◆ Journeying in a group or on your own

There's nobody quite like you, right? You have unique interests and insights, likes and dislikes, tendencies and fears. You read different books, see different movies, like different songs. So it makes sense that your shamanic journey should be as individual as you are. In this chapter, you'll find tips and techniques for tailoring your journey to fit whoever you are.

Putting Your Best Sense Forward

People usually have one sense that is strongest—that they rely on the most. For example, you may not see images very well, but you have an excellent sense of hearing or touch.

The major distinctions in perception are as follows:

♦ People who are very visual are more likely to see pictures when they first get information.

♦ People who are more auditory or hearing-oriented are more likely to have thoughts or gain information through words.

♦ People who are more feeling-oriented are more likely to experience sensations and feelings.

In addition, some people have other well-developed other senses, such as for taste, touch, smell, and movement, that can be used to supplement the journey experience.

Most people are a mixture of types of perception, though in different degrees.

Your strongest perception will probably also influence how you experience your shamanic journey. Most people are visual, and so experience their journeys visually—a little like watching a movie unfold in the mind. Likewise, hearing-oriented people will be more likely to hear their spirit guides and the sounds of the world they visit rather than see or feel them. More feeling-oriented people will have a strong emotional response to their guides and teachers. However, you can create an even more intense journeying experience by engaging all of your senses—so you not only see, but also hear, feel, smell, and taste the experience. First, you need to figure out which sense is already your strongest. Then, you need to practice developing your other senses. Listen up, look ahead, and stay in touch to find out how!

> **Wise Ways**
>
> People differ in the degree to which they perceive information through their primary sources of perception—seeing, hearing, feeling. Although smell, taste, touch, and movement can add to your journeying experience, they play a more secondary role.

Can You Hear Me?

You're probably aware to some degree of your own sensitivity in each of these areas—seeing, hearing, feeling, and knowing or intuition. As you journey, you will become more aware of how you perceive, and you can work on developing your weakest sense so that you experience the journey more fully. You can develop your weaker senses by giving yourself mental directions during your journey and paying attention to what you experience with that sense.

Try developing your weaker senses with self-talk and self-direction. You become your own coach, guide, or mentor, advising yourself on what to do as you go. Here are some examples of what you might do:

♦ Instead of seeing a mostly silent film as you look around on your journey, focus on hearing more. Ask yourself if you can hear the sound the earth as you take a walk, as you listen to the movement of any nearby water, or as you become aware of the whistling of the wind. Take the time to stop and really listen to what you hear.

♦ If your journeying experience is like listening to a tape, with only occasional or blurry images, then spend more time looking at each image you see. Remind yourself to notice the colors, pay attention to the outlines. Imagine that you're a bug crawling around and closely investigating what you see.

♦ Add to what you see or hear by working on more intensely feeling and sensing the world around you. Pause in your journey and notice what sensations you feel. Reflect on what you just have seen or heard and how this might relate to your feelings.

Shake, Rattle, and Roll

You can also intensify the journey experience by using external sources of sensory input, such as rattles and drums.

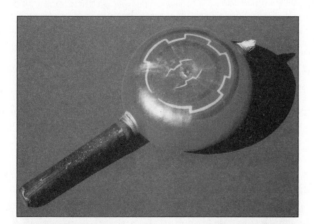

You can use rattles and drums to intensify your journey.

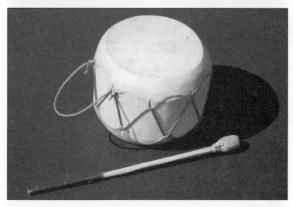

Off the Path

If external sounds are more of a distraction than an aid in achieving alternative consciousness, then don't use them.

Some of the external sensory sources you might use include:

◆ Beating drums or shaking rattles, or playing a tape of these sounds in the background.

◆ Chanting or singing a simple repetitive song, or playing a tape of you or someone else chanting or singing such a song.

◆ Burning incense or setting heavily scented flowers near you.

Know Your Sixth Sense

Apart from using and developing your most common senses—seeing, hearing, feeling, smelling, and tasting, you can use journeying to work with and increase what is popularly called your "sixth sense": knowing or intuition. Knowing is often linked with feeling in everyday conversation, such as when someone says they "feel" something will happen or they have a good or bad "feeling" about someone. However, knowing is more of a mental, intuitive awareness that something is, has been, or will be. It's like your inner truth detector—your inner source of wisdom and knowledge.

The shaman journey is ideal for working with your sixth sense, because it puts you in touch with your deeper consciousness, sometimes described as the "unconscious," which is a source of your inner creative powers and intuition. Of course, you don't need shamanism to work with these inner abilities, but shaman journeys provide an excellent vehicle for exploring your inner radar and fine-tuning it, so it becomes even more sensitive and accurate.

To develop your sixth sense, think of a question before you begin your journey—one that you can ask your spirit guides once you embark on your otherworldly trip. Make sure it's a question about something for which you can later find the answer from a reliable

Wise Ways

I discuss developing these inner abilities in more detail in two other books, *Mind Power: Picture Your Way to Success in Business* and *The Empowered Mind: How to Harness the Creative Force Within You.*

source. For example, you could go on a middle world journey to seek some information from your spirit guides about a situation or person you're not very familiar with. Or you might go on a journey into the future to find out about a particular event. When you return from your journey, take some time to reflect on what your experience was like when you received the information you were seeking. Consider how you felt, how your spiritual helper gave you the information, and whether your spiritual helper seemed certain or unsure, and so on.

Next, find out the answer to your question. How you go about doing this will depend on the kind of question you asked. If you asked your spirit guides to tell you a friend's favorite color, for example, you can ask your friend in person what his or her favorite color really is. If you journeyed into the future to find the answer to your question, then wait until you reach the point in time you visited on your journey to find out the answer to your question.

Once you find the real world answer to your question, think again about how you felt when you received the answer from your spirit guide. If you find out that the information you received on your journey is correct, you can use the way you felt and how your spiritual helper communicated the information to guide you on future journeys. Then, when you get these same feelings or your helper communicates this information in a similar way, that can be a sign this new information will be correct, too. After practicing this technique several times, you should begin to feel more confident about judging the information on journeys.

Alternatively, if the information your spirit guide gave you was incorrect, think again about the way you felt when you first received the information. Did you overlook any signs indicating that you shouldn't trust the information? For example, maybe you experienced a sense of uncertainty as you heard this information, so you wondered whether this information was correct. Or maybe you noticed your spiritual guide was hesitant or reluctant to give you the information before sharing it with you. If you can identify such a sign, then look for this sign in the future as a warning that information may not be accurate or may be uncertain.

Thus, a good way to be better prepared for future journeying is to not only notice such signs about whether your information is likely to be correct, but to write down the signs you get and your experience with them later. For example, you can keep a notebook and write down a "track record" of whether the intuitive information you received was helpful and accurate (or not) and what kind of indicators you noticed associated with the process of getting this information on your journey.

As you hone your skills with these techniques, you'll become more confident in your ability to find answers to meaningful questions on your journeys.

Off the Path _____

It's important to assess the validity of the information you get from your intuition, because you can't always trust all of the information you get from it. Sometimes your intuition is wrong.

Turning Off the Lights to Gain Enlightenment

Traditionally, shamans work at night, twilight, or in the darkness. For example, shamans in Peru and Ecuador don't even begin their all-night healing sessions until around 9 P.M.

at night, and they usually last until dawn, or first light. A reason for these late night sessions is that at night, shamans are less likely to be distracted by ordinary reality, so it's easier for them to enter an altered state of consciousness and to go on a journey. In other words, the darkness often enhances your other senses.

You can certainly go on a shamanic journey anywhere or anytime—even on a crowded bus, in a busy airport, or on a sunlit beach, particularly once you become comfortable using the journeying process. However, if you need help tuning out the people around you, it's best to find a dark setting, such as a dark room, or just cover your eyes with your hand or a blind fold. In the darkness, you'll see and experience more, because you can more intensely focus on your inner world and its nonordinary reality. The darkness acts like a filter, shutting out the distractions of ordinary reality.

Off the Path

Sometimes people associate the darkness with evil or negativity. You can readily tune out any negative associations with darkness by visualizing images of protection around you, such as a white light. Alternatively, try lighting a small candle to feel more comfortable.

The night sky often helps people get into an altered state, too. For example, some people feel they are more receptive to nonordinary reality when the moon is out, so they may time their journeying to coincide with such moonlit nights.

Lighten Up a Little, Will Ya?

Ironically, though the darkness will help you achieve an altered consciousness state, once you've entered an altered state, you may experience an infusion of light, bright light rays, a circle of light around you, or light flowing into you. Or you may feel yourself full of radiating light, experiencing a sense of enlightenment or illumination.

People of many religious backgrounds have experienced similar "enlightening" experiences, and these experiences often are associated with gaining wisdom or knowledge. Pictures of St. Theresa of Ávila, for example, a Carmelite nun who experienced the divine, often depict her as radiating light. In turn, many of the pictures of traditional shamans show them surrounded by a halo of light.

Illuminating Art

You'll find numerous examples of the light of wisdom and healing in shamanic art. For example, some of the yarn paintings of Huichol shamans, such as the one in Chapter 3, show them with brightly colored lines of energy radiating out from them. The energy lines symbolize wisdom the shaman is receiving or energy projected by the shaman to fend off any negative forces. One painting by a Peruvian shaman even shows a healing shaman counteracting a vampire bat spirit, which was sent by a rival spirit, with bright, luminous rays! (Vitebsky).

Examples of the importance of light to shamanism can also be found in modern art, according to Mark Levy in his book, *Technicians of Ecstasy: Shamanism and the Modern Artist.*

As Levy points out, many modern artists use shamanic practices to enter nonordinary reality without being aware they are doing this. The illumination they experience appears in their art. As Levy explains this process:

> Modern artists are using shamanic practices to enter non-ordinary reality … Artists need not be conscious of themselves as being shamans to employ shamanic methodologies. They may use shamanic imagery without being aware of its content. (Levy, 1993, xix)

Some such images include:

◆ *The Wheel of Light*, a photogravure by Max Ernst, which shows an eye with lines radiating from it (Levy, 1993, 124).

◆ *The Illumination*, a black and white photograph by Arthur Tress features the silhouette of a male figure with a cone of light pouring out of him (Levy, 1993, 127).

◆ *Round See*, an acrylic painting by Gordon Onslow-Ford, shows a series of circles, spirals, and lines that radiate like an explosion of energy and light (Levy, 1993, 125).

In some cases, as Levy points out, these artists may even get these insights in a trance-like or dream state that has parallels with the way shamans get their own insights.

Staying Positive, Getting Powerful, and Keeping Comfortable

It's important to expect your journey to be a positive, comfortable experience. The expectation will help make it happen. Furthermore, when you meet power animals, spirit helpers, and various other teachers on your journey, don't be afraid of them. Expect them to approach you in harmony and peace and they will be helpful and friendly.

Among the keys to having a good, positive and comfortable experience, as well as a powerful one, are to focus on the following:

◆ Keep your intent positive.

◆ Use a clear specific question to stay focused.

◆ Turn away from negative images.

◆ Find a good, comfortable location.

I'll describe each of these in more detail in the following sections.

Be Positive ... or Else!

A good, usually surefire, way to have a positive experience is to use power for positive ends. You're probably familiar with sayings such as, "What goes around, comes around," "What you put out, you get back," and the law of karma or cause and effect, in which you end up with good or bad consequences based on what you do. These effects and outcomes are even more magnified when you engage in shamanic practices, since you're working with powerful natural energies and magnifying them in your life.

Wise Ways

The power of positive thinking has a long history—maybe not so long by shamanic thinking, but at least back to the early twentieth century in the U.S. Numerous writers, religious thinkers, and business entrepreneurs developed a literature of success building on the idea of positive thinking. Norman Vincent Peale popularized the concept with his book, *The Power of Positive Thinking*, published in 1952. *Think and Grow Rich*, by Napoleon Hill, is another classic in this tradition.

These writers certainly didn't think of themselves as shamans, but they were promoting a change in consciousness, in which positive thoughts lead to positive results. Rather than the spirit guides of shamanism, they were seeking to tap the spirit of capitalism, so perhaps they might be regarded as something of shamanic practitioners in that they were also in touch with a spirit!

Just like in everyday life, with shamanism, positive thinking leads to positive results. The more powerfully you learn to use the techniques, the greater the rewards.

If you keep your intention positive and seek positive results, you'll have a better chance of having a positive experience.

What Do You Want?

Use a clear, specific question to begin your journey—and don't forget to phrase it positively! For example, instead of asking something like: "Why do I keep having problems with my partner?" Ask: "What can I do to improve my relationship with my partner." Focusing your question in this specific positive way, will help to keep your journey on target, keeping you on track as you look for the information and insights bearing particularly on that question. By focusing on a specific, positive question, you'll be less likely to wander off in other directions on your journey.

When any stray thoughts enter your mind, simply push them aside and remind yourself of your question. This should get you back on track in no time. The process I'm describing is similar to that used in many forms of meditation, where practitioners concentrate on a certain mantra, word, or concept, such as "ohm." Should their thoughts start moving away from that focus, students of meditation are taught to refocus on their mantra. It's the same in shamanism, except instead of a mantra, you have a question on which to focus.

Although you want to remain open and receptive to whatever comes on your journey, you mainly want to be open to the information relative to your question. After all, that's the purpose of your journey.

 Bon Voyage

To help you stay focused, think of your journey like watching a TV program. If you encounter any interference, adjust the antenna to bring the channel into focus. If you hit the wrong button on the remote, click back to the right channel so you don't miss part of the show. When you journey, your goal is to stay tuned to your spiritual programming.

Danger: Negative Experiences Ahead

Journeying is almost always a positive experience if you engage in the journey with a positive attitude. If you do feel uneasy or afraid of anything you see, just reject or turn away from it, and it will go away. It's really that easy! Some shamans take a power staff or object with them to ward off danger. If they encounter anything that bothers them, they point their staff of power object at what bothers them, and it disappears.

Don't dismiss fearful image altogether though, because they can sometimes give you a useful warning about possible future events and developments or insightful information about yourself. Should you want to explore these warnings or insights later, perhaps with the help of a more experienced shamanic practitioner or other professional, you can always do this.

If you experience something frightening, try to remember it with the part of you that is still directing and guiding the journey. After your journey's over, you can analyze your experience to determine if it can tell you about something you need to work on. On the other hand, if you don't want your journey to lead you in the direction of deeper psychological exploration, then push these images aside. As they say in the business world: "I don't want to go there." Likewise, in taking a shamanic journey, if you don't want to go somewhere, simply don't.

Wise Ways

It might be too scary to deal with frightening situations in your altered journeying state. But if you look at it later in a more analytical, rational light with your conscious mind, you may be able to deal with it effectively.

Different Strokes for Different Folks

Learning about the many different styles of journeying in different cultures and for different people can be a great source of inspiration, but you still need to make the journey on your own by adapting it to your own style and interests. From its earliest roots, shamans have adapted their practice to fit their needs at the time and the inspiration of the moment. Likewise, apart from guidelines on not having negative intentions or a negative attitude in your journeying, make the trip your own. Pack your own bags and create your own itinerary, so to speak.

Some key ways to adapt the experience to suit your needs include:

♦ Finding a setting that's ideal for you.

♦ Incorporating your own symbols and meanings

♦ Going with a group, on your own, or do both

Setting the Stage

You can enhance your experience and make it your own by journeying from real-world locations you like or that have special meaning for you.

Sometimes you'll discover these locations when you're learning about shamanism in a group or as part of a community of people practicing shamanism. If so, go back to that location later, either with others or on your own. Take some time before journeying to acknowledge and honor the spirit of that place. By doing so, you'll invite the spirits in the area to assist you in having a good, powerful, useful journey.

Once you get to an area to go on a journey, to find a location that feels especially right for you, stand or sit at the boundaries of the site. Then, get very relaxed, look around, and let yourself be drawn to a location. Don't try to actively choose it yourself; rather, let it choose you. Perhaps imagine that you're sending lines of energy radiating from your body; notice which area has the strongest pull on these lines of energy you send out. Then, move toward that area and experience the pull getting stronger as you go closer. You're responding to the pull of the place that has selected you.

> **Wise Ways**
>
> I describe how to find particularly powerful places in more detail in Chapter 11 and in my previous books on Shamanism: *Shaman Warrior* and *Secrets of the Shaman*.

Once you've felt a kinship or connection with a place, revisit it and, when you do, acknowledge and honor the spirit of that place, noting that you have felt a strong link to the place before. Note that you've had a good, powerful journey experience there before. Such recognition and reminders about the past will help you to have a similarly good and powerful experience again.

Don't overlook places in your house that might contribute to successful journeying. Maybe you have a certain room that you're drawn to, or even a particular corner or chair. Again, let your feelings or intuition guide you in choosing the spot the first time, or let it choose you. No matter how you're drawn to a location, once you find this spot, return to it to build on the power of that place for future journeying. When you do, as with other locations, take some time before you journey to acknowledge and honor that spot.

Bon Voyage

Returning to any place to which you feel a special connection can help increase the energy and intent of the journey. It's similar to going into a house of worship or a shrine. Try to think of your special place as your personal sacred place or shrine.

Once you've selected a special place for journeying, you can give it even more power by marking and honoring it in a special way. For example, have a symbolic dedication cere-mony, in which you honor the spirit of the place with some words, such as a poem or blessing, or perform ceremonial acts that are meaningful to you. Put some meaningful objects around the area, or even create a small altar or small space for an altar, making a mesa such as those used by many Peruvian shamans.

In short, by finding, repeatedly using, and adding meaning to the places you feel con-nected to, you can enhance the power of your journey.

You can also bring others with you to these places that are important to you and journey with them at times, as well as traveling alone there at other times. If you share your spe-cial place with other people, be sure they're also involved with shamanic practices and respectful of the place where you're going, so the location retains its special quality as a place for journeying. Otherwise it could lose that character—so, no, you don't want to bring the family or kids for a picnic on the site.

Alternatively, as you develop your own meanings and associations with these places, you may prefer to visit them alone, making them your own personal sanctuary for taking your journeys. Either way—going on a solo journey or inviting others to journey with you— will work if it feels right for you.

Choosing Your Own Symbols, Guides, and Teachers

Just as what you wear reflects your own tastes, so too should the symbols, guides, and teachers you use on your journeys. As you work with the journeying process, you'll find a myriad of symbols, guides, and teachers to choose from. Some will come from different traditions, some will be personal to you.

Wise Ways

Traditionally, certain symbols have been associated with certain cultures, such as the ancient Maya, Egyptians, and Greeks, with their panoply of gods and religious beliefs.

Off the Path

Some cult groups insist that their members use only certain symbols or teachers. It's fine to use someone else's symbols if you feel comfortable with them and can make them your own. But there's nothing magical or absolute about any particular system. They are all possible approaches you can use, but there is no single way.

This variety is to be expected for two key reasons.

- Shamans usually work with representations or aspects of the ultimate power, rather than the power of the universe directly, because this force seems too powerful, impersonal, or abstract. These guides can take many forms, and their names vary from tradition to tradition or for different individuals.

- The globalization of culture has put people in touch with a mixture of different traditions, so people usually have a multiplicity of symbols with which they are familiar. These symbols are different representations of aspects of the same basic force.

Feel free to use any symbols that you feel comfortable with or that are meaningful or helpful for you. If you've already developed associations with certain symbols, such as from your religious upbringing or a shamanic group you attended, work with those symbols. If you find others you like in the future, work with those, too. In short, consider that you can choose among many paths for your journey—they will all lead to your destination.

Just go with what happens. If you feel a special connection with one animal, teacher, or symbol, keep them around, work with them more, or treat them like a very close friend or guide. Conversely, with those animals, teachers, or symbols that come and go, simply draw on the information they offer when it seems useful and appropriate.

Bon Voyage

By cultivating a variety of spirit guides, you'll increase your chances of getting the help you need. That's because different guides and power animals are associated with different qualities.

Variety Is the Spice of Life—and Shamanism

While turning to a particular cadre of symbols and helpers is fine if you feel like working with them and want to deepen that relationship, recognize the value of variety, too. One advantage of being open to this variety, even when you most frequently turn to certain symbols and helpers, is that you often get different information and help from different sources.

As you go on journeys, expect to encounter numerous beings and symbols. As you journey more often, you'll discover which ones you feel most comfortable with and which ones you can use for different purposes. Choose and use whatever feels right for you.

Off the Path

If you find it difficult to get an answer to a question you've asked before, it may be because your unconscious has already answered it for you. In other words, you may be psychologically bored, since your unconscious thinks: "Oh, you asked this before," and isn't as engaged in finding an answer. Or your unconscious may resist, because it says to itself: "You already know the answer; why are you asking this question again?"

Thus, in seeking help for yourself, you may get better answers if you ask something you haven't asked before or ask about something you really don't know the answer to.

When it comes to journeying, the most important thing is to stay positive, and do what feels right for you at the time. Everything else will fall into place.

The Least You Need to Know

- You can increase the power of your journey by using a combination of senses.
- Another way to intensify the journey experience is by using external sources of sensory input, such as rattles and drums, though if you find these sounds distracting, do your journeying in a quiet place.
- You can develop your sense of knowing or intuition by testing yourself on how well you know something.
- Some other ways to have a good journey, including being positive, finding a setting that's ideal for you, and incorporating your own symbols and meanings.

Chapter

15

More Ways to Maximize Your Journeys

In This Chapter

- ◆ Preparing and purifying yourself
- ◆ Learning to let go and be receptive
- ◆ The need for humility in working with power
- ◆ Interpreting your journey experience

When you get in your car to go to the grocery store, you probably don't give much thought to the trip, except to perhaps take a shopping list. It doesn't matter if you're wearing old jeans and a sweatshirt or that you haven't taken a shower. And you probably don't think much about your route, either. So it is with practiced shamans taking regular journeys. They don't require a lot of effort and planning, since they have become a familiar routine.

Now consider another scenario: Instead of going to the grocery store to pick up whatever you need for the next day or so, say you have to organize a gala celebration for a friend's anniversary or an office party. You can't just stop off at the store to pick up a few things you need. Instead, the event requires extensive planning, including what you'll wear, what you'll have to eat, what you'll do at the event and afterward, and so on. Some shamanic journeys are the equivalent of this special event, requiring special planning and preparation.

Getting Prepared and Purified

One way to set the stage, particularly if you're planning an especially important journey, is to take some time before the journey to prepare and purify yourself. This can be a powerful step to take, whether you're going to take this journey yourself or in a group.

There is a long tradition of preparation and purification in shamanism. For example, the long journey the Huichol Indians of Mexico take to find the sacred peyote cactus, which they use in their ceremonies, is part of their preparation. And so are the trips Peruvian healers take to the lowlands to obtain the ingredients for making the ayahuasca brew or to the highlands to obtain sacred artifacts to be used in their healing ceremonies. Many modern groups, such as pagan and magical groups conducting elaborate ceremonies engage in extensive preparations, too.

Often journeys to gather ritual materials are preceded by or include some form of purification or cleansing as a way to make the journey and ritual materials gathered there even more sacred.

Douglas Sharon describes a purification process in *Wizard of the Four Winds: A Shaman's Story*. He traveled with shaman Eduardo Calderòn to the sacred lagoons, called Las Huaringas, in the Peruvian highlands to collect artifacts for Calderòn's mesa. Once they arrived in the highlands, they met up with a healer named don Florentino, who went through an extensive purification and preparation ceremony to cleanse himself and the others before they acquired artifacts from a sacred place:

> After the opening invocation, don Florentino approached all the participants and poured a small portion of herbal remedy from his seguro into their palms. This was imbibed through the nostrils by all present … Next don Florentino instructed us to prepare for the bath. Undressing to our underwear, we entered the water, tossing offerings of silver coins and sweet limes sprinkled with sugar into the lagoon. We were next instructed to wade ashore briefly and then return to the lagoon for a quick final dip. As we came out of the water for the second time, the curandero blessed each of us and then instructed us to jump up and down and wave our arms in order to get warm. Once dry, we were allowed to dress …

> Once dressed, each of us picked up the amulets and good luck charms we had brought with us and bathed them in the lagoon. Then, one by one, we took a turn before don Florentino for a "cleansing," or rubbing with his large sword … To end the ceremony, we brought our artifacts before the curandero to be blessed in the name of the lagoon—a process that consisted of invoking the lagoon, calling out our names, and then orally spraying the artifacts with the herbal liquid from the seguro (Sharon, 1978, 131).

Here's one pagan group that is staging an early morning ceremony in Tilden Park near Berkeley in Northern California. To set the stage for the ritual, the group members first purify and cleanse the area through ritually sweeping the ground and using smoke to purify the air. Then, they are ready to conduct their ritual.

In many cases, not only the preparation for a ceremony, but the ceremony itself, in whole or part, can be one of purification and cleansing. The result is that the ritual becomes even more sacred and the experience of it that much deeper and more powerful.

You can use purification and cleansing techniques, such as those pictured, wherever you perform a ritual.

Cleansing can take many forms, including fasting, sweating, bathing, coating your body with oils, getting a massage, or imagining a cleansing white or colored light surrounding you. No matter which method you use, you experience yourself being cleansed and purified; imagine any negative energies, any feelings of contamination being washed away or drained out of your body.

The process of purification and cleansing can even extend to the room or surrounding area where you are. In some cleansing and purifying ceremonies, whole communities, or even the nation and world, are ritually purified.

Given the power of purification and cleansing, take some time to do it yourself, especially before you go on an especially important journey or perform an especially important ritual. This cleansing can be for yourself, for the group, the area where you are going on the journey, or for other purposes. This way you invest whatever you will be doing with even more energy and power.

Take a Spiritual Bath

There are many different ways you can cleanse and purify yourself. Try the following in any combination:

♦ Brush your hands along your body, starting with your head and moving down to your feet. Visualize yourself cleansing your body and flicking off any negative energy. You'll feel refreshed and cleansed when you're finished.

♦ Visualize yourself brushing your hands along your body, as above, to cleanse yourself.

♦ Take a bath or shower, imagining that you're purifying your spirit as well as your body.

♦ Recite some affirmations, either in silent meditation or as you perform other purifying activities. Say something like: "Now I purify and cleanse myself." "I release and get rid of all negative energy from my body and spirit." "I am projecting this bright cleansing energy all around, cleansing this room, the environment around me, and I'm sending this cleansing, purifying energy out to the world."

♦ Brush with your hands any objects you're using in your shamanic rituals, and visualize yourself brushing away any negative energy.

♦ Go into a warm quiet place, like a sauna or kiva, and experience the heat taking any negative energy away as it rises. Then, as you open the door, watch this negative energy disperse into the outer air.

♦ Write down on a piece of paper anything you feel is negative and you no longer want in your life. Then, fold this paper and burn it. As it burns, visualize the negative energy dispersing into the atmosphere.

Think of other things you might do to cleanse and purify yourself and the environment around you.

Letting Go, So You Can Receive

Another key to having a positive experience is letting your mind go and releasing your ego. After you express your initial purpose or ask your initial question, let things happen as they will, like you're watching a movie you haven't seen before. Don't try to direct the sequence of events; instead, once you state your question or request, let the spirits tell you what you need to know.

The key to getting good insights is letting go and trusting the process, the spirits, and the wisdom you receive. Even if you don't initially understand the information you get, listen quietly and receptively. Don't try to question or resist. Later, after your journey, you can seek to interpret and understand.

The following principles are so important, they are worth repeating or even framing and hanging on your wall.

- ◆ Let go, let go, let go!
- ◆ Trust the process.
- ◆ Be open to receive.
- ◆ Listen to the answers you get without judgment.
- ◆ Look on the answers as wisdom from the spirits.
- ◆ Even if you don't understand at first, just listen.
- ◆ Interpret, analyze, and judge later.

To continue an example used in the previous chapter, think of yourself like a radio receiver, TV antenna, radar dish, or ship's radio. Your job is to pick up messages from the spiritual world. Your goal is to be very tuned in, so you get the best reception. If the message comes in an unfamiliar language or is clouded with static, adjust your focus to improve the reception, and stay tuned and listen. If you need to translate or figure out what the message means, save that for later. The first goal is to simply receive.

A good way to think of your inner receptivity is by thinking of a radio or TV antenna. Just tune in and listen closely, to hear more.

What If You Don't Get a Very Good Answer?

At one time or another most people engaging in shamanic journeying find that the spirit world holds back on answering their question—or at least they *think* it is. People's experiences are usually similar when this happens to them: They have trouble getting their power animals, teachers, or others they contact to respond to their query, or the guides say that they don't know the answer, that this isn't the time to ask, or the seeker isn't ready to know. What then?

Let's say it happens to you. You've asked your power animal and spirit guide whether a career path you're considering following is the right one. If your spirit guides don't answer your question after a few tries, don't try to force an answer. Rather, accept whatever they do tell you. You might find out later, either in the interpretation phase or later in your everyday life, that what your spirit guides are telling you is quite relevant to the original topic—it's just not what you expected to hear.

> ### Bon Voyage
>
> Because answers sometimes come in strange and unexpected ways, try not to cut off or block off the information you receive. Giving yourself over to the journeying process will help you understand the information, because when you're in this very receptive, non-judging, receive-whatever-comes mode, you'll experience your unconscious or subconscious talking to you. When it talks, pay attention and listen to receive these messages, so you can learn from them on your journey.
>
> Similarly, if you're seeking an affirmation of something you're doing, if that desired message doesn't come, acknowledge and accept whatever does. It may be that what you're doing isn't what you really want to do, that you're doing it because you think you should do it. So that's why you're not getting any inner support from your spiritual helpers. They think you should be doing something else, not something that's wrong for you.

By trusting your intuitive processes and the spiritual assistance you gain from this, you'll generally begin to recognize your inner truths, which may be different from what you consciously think or believe. These truths may be hiding from your conscious mind, but when you put that outer part of you aside on a journey, you can tune into your inner wisdom. Certainly, at times your intuition isn't always correct, but if you use some of the intuitive checking measures described in Chapter 14, you can improve your hits in listening to the intuitive, knowing part of you.

Staying Humble to Stay on the Path

To let go and be receptive, you need to stay humble in the face of power. Sometimes it can be hard to maintain this humility, as you work with shamanic techniques and start feeling a strong sense of increased power and control. It's not unusual to feel heady from the power and control that comes with access to this world of spiritual power and energy.

Humility is one of the strongest weapons in the face of power; without it, people risk losing touch with the source of power or its appropriate uses. Once people lose touch with the spirit world, they either eventually lose the power or, even worse, end up using it for negative ends, such as causing difficulties or harm to a rival. Of course, there's a good chance the power will eventually turn back against them, putting them in deep trouble.

Don't Sow Negativity, Or Else ...

If you seek negative ends, any negativity can eventually come back to you. It might not happen immediately, but in time, the infusion of negativity will snap back, much like stretching out a spring or a rubber band. Keep pulling it hard enough with enough energy, then suddenly, SNAP! All that negative force you've put out comes back to you. Ouch.

There are lots of reasons why working with negative energy in shamanism doesn't work. Many of these reasons also apply to personal relationships that fall outside of the realm of shamanism. However, when you work with spiritual energy, it's critical to avoid applying shamanic practice for negative ends.

Working with power in negative ways doesn't work, because it creates negative relationships with other people. For example, let's say you ask your spiritual helpers to help you thwart the goals of someone else or hold them back, so you can get ahead. Who knows, maybe you'll experience some success initially, particularly if you've used the journeying process to gain insight on how to influence and manipulate someone to your advantage. However, in the long term, such an approach will backfire, because if people feel manipulated, mistreated, or taken advantage of (and they will!), at some point, when given the chance, they will often turn against you.

Off the Path

Don't think negative things into reality. If you believe or expect something will happen, your belief or expectation can help to make it so.

Another reason using power for negative ends doesn't work is the backfire effect. You can become so steeped in negativity that it washes back over you like a returning tide. For instance, the negative intentions and thoughts you send out can return in the form of doubts and fears. Then, these doubts and fears can create the physical manifestation of what you doubt or fear. To take just one example, if someone starts needlessly worrying about what might go wrong with her health, she might end up making herself sick. Initially, there may be nothing wrong, but by focusing on these concerns, she soon discovers all sorts of real problems.

Thus, for a positive, productive shamanic experience, keep the negativity out of your journeying.

What Comes Around Goes Around

The danger that comes from not being humble and misusing power is illustrated in tale after tale about modern gurus—or more accurately, *former* gurus—who lost their way. Even if they started off with the best of intentions, they let their visions of power go to their head, and this backfired on them big time. Among other things, they got involved in sex with followers that led to sex scandals, abused alcohol, and were discredited by a barrage of negative publicity. So, to use the common expression: They lost their mojo.

Take the example of two therapists who started a healing center based on using feeling therapy in Los Angeles. At first, they and everyone else involved were filled with good feelings and love. Then, filled with power, they embarked on an ego trip. Immersed in their inflated sense of themselves, they began using that power to manipulate and control others. The outcome, as in so many groups that experienced a similar trajectory, was that many participants soon turned against them and the center, and the whole enterprise quickly fell apart.

Then there's the story of the Rajneesh Center, in Oregon, which was devoted to a sensual type of yoga that the founder called "rajneesh" yoga. It featured a kind of trance dancing, akin to the repetitive dancing, that might accompany shamanic drumming or the all-night house music at a rave. The idea was to open up the heart and sexual energy centers, called *chakras*, and let the energy flow. For a time the group claimed to experience a rapid growth in their mental and spiritual development. But after a few years, a leader's teachings led the group to become increasingly isolationist and paranoid, including stockpiling guns in case of attack from outsiders. They also sent recruiters and commercial busses around the country to bring homeless people to their center so they could gain residency to vote, so the group members could take political control over the town. Eventually, the group's activities so

> **Shaman Says**
>
> **Chakras** are the main energy centers that exist in the body from the base of the spine to the top of the head. In the Hindu and most New Age systems there are seven of these at the base of the spine, groin, abdomen, heart, throat, third eye between the eyes, and at the top of the head. They are called by various names including: base or root chakras, sexual or navel chakras, solar plexus chakras, heart chakras, throat chakras, third eye or brow chakras, and crown chakras.

Off the Path _____

All kinds of power, including shamanic power, has the potential to become like an aphrodisiac. Sniff it too long and hard, and the scent turns to poison, dooming you to destruction.

scared the neighbors that they complained to the police, and soon the leaders became the subject of a criminal persecution because of their stockpiled guns. The result was a blaze of publicity, and the group soon fell apart.

Again and again, spiritual leaders and teachers lose their power because they abuse it. They may shine for a time, but then they get off track by seeing themselves as so powerful that they can do whatever they want, with no thought as to whether their actions are right or wrong. They begin to see themselves as superior, and isolate themselves from others. They use their power for destructive ends. Eventually, they inflate themselves with so much destructive power that they burst like an overinflated balloon. It's a process that has occurred repeatedly, and not just in shamanism.

Be a Vehicle for Power, Not Its Source

As these cautionary tales illustrate, it can be easy to lose perspective and start to feel that the power source you're tapping into is your personal power and that it's yours to keep. The paradox is that once you start thinking that you permanently own this power or start doing negative things with it, it can easily disappear or turn against you.

The power you access through shamanic journeying and ritual is the power or energy of the universe. When you do positive things with this power and keep a sense of humility and perspective, you can generally continue to draw on it effectively. In a way, the spirits you are calling on in your journeys or other shamanic rituals are continuing to look on you with favor, since you are using the power they offer with wisdom and humility.

Rather than seeing yourself in charge of that power, see yourself as a vehicle for this power that comes from the universe.

Interpreting Your Shamanic Experience

After you have returned from your journey with a response from your power animals or spirit guides, the next step is interpreting your experience. This can be one of the most difficult parts of shamanic practice for people just beginning to journey. That's because it requires you to reflect on, explain, and sometimes look for symbolic meanings in images or a few words or phrases, and these are skills that are not often developed in our more pragmatic, action-oriented society.

Suspending Prior Judgments and Expectations

A key to successfully interpreting what you experience and how to apply that knowledge is to suspend any prior personal judgments on what you want to see or on the value of what you do see. Your goal is to seek to interpret the information you have brought back from your journey without the influence of your hopes and wishes shaping those interpretations. While these hopes and desires may have triggered the question that guided your journey, seek to put them aside, so you can listen to the knowledge you have gained from your journey, even if it runs counter to your hopes and wishes.

Ways to Recall, Reflect, and Interpret Your Experience

To better interpret your experience, start by recalling as much as you can and reflect on this. There are several ways to do this, depending on whether you are journeying on your own or with others.

If journeying alone:

1. Either write your recollections down in a notebook or talk about them into a tape recorder.

2. Next, review what you've written down and reflect on it; or play back your recollections and, as these trigger insights, stop the tape, and write down your reflections.

If journeying with others:

1. Either write down your recollections in a notebook or get together with a partner or small group and take turns sharing your recollections. If you discuss your recollections with others, ask your partner or someone in the group to take notes on what you say for you (and you can do the same for them).

2. Next, either review what you or someone else has written down and reflect on it, or share with the group what the experience has meant to you. The advantage of this group sharing is that it often serves as a "reality check," so that others can tell you if you have lost touch with reality in your interpretation or plans for action.

Bon Voyage

To help suspend your prior judgments and expectations, think of yourself as a blank slate on which the journey writes your experience. When you return to everyday reality, think about what is written on your slate without trying to edit or change it. Consider what's written about your experience as the message you need to know, and interpret the message's meaning in that light.

You'll find other suggestions for getting the most out of your journeying experiences in the next few chapters.

The Least You Need to Know

- ◆ If you are planning an especially important journey, take some time before you go to prepare and purify yourself. This practice of purification, along with cleansing, is widely used by many groups before major ceremonies and events.

- ◆ One way to cleanse and purify yourself is by taking a spiritual bath—either by actually bathing yourself or by visualizing yourself doing this.

- ◆ Let go of your ego, preconceptions, and expectations so you can better receive the insights and wisdom you seek on your journey.

- ◆ Remember to stay humble to stay on the path to both helping yourself and others, particularly as you gain power.

Chapter 16

Journeying into the Soul: The Psychology of Shamanism

In This Chapter

◆ The intersection of journeying with psychology

◆ Discovering the uses of journeying

◆ Comparing shamanism and psychology

◆ Using shamanism in psychological practice

In the first part of this book you learned about anthropologists' interest in shamanism as a traditional cultural practice. In the last 30 years, another group of social scientists have become very interested in shamanic practices, as well: psychologists.

It makes sense that psychologists would be interested in shamanism. Take just one aspect of it, entering an altered state of consciousness. As noted in previous chapters, this is similar to hypnotic states and light or deep meditative states that have been used by psychologists in their therapeutic practices for years. Furthermore, some branches of psychology, such as humanistic and transpersonal psychology, have emphasized self-improvement, personal development, and even infusing religious or spiritual elements into the understanding of the self.

In this chapter, we'll explore the connection between psychology and shamanism and consider the benefits that can result from a relationship between the two.

Psychology Meets Shamanism

The link between shamanism and psychology is in large part due to the exploration of shamanism by one offshoot of psychology, known as *transpersonal psychology*, which developed out of humanistic psychology, an approach based on a client-centered, holistic approach to promoting wellness and optimizing the human potential. Transpersonal psychology added the spiritual or religious dimension to personal development and growth. Besides focusing on the whole person, transpersonal psychology uses techniques of spiritual healing and explores alternate states of consciousness to promote wellness and resolve psychological problems.

When I participated in a variety of programs at Esalen in the 1970s and 1980s, this field of psychology was in full bloom, and many practitioners were offering workshops in hypnosis, dreams, and altered states of consciousness, which were closely related to the practices of shamanism. Although many of these workshop leaders didn't make the link themselves, there was clearly an overlap in the experiences of program participants. It was as if the programs on transpersonal psychology and shamanism were proceeding on two parallel tracks, using similar techniques to enter and explore alternate states of consciousness but using different terminologies. In time, though, these developments came more closely together, as transpersonal psychologists (or psychologists working with transpersonal techniques) more explicitly began to use shamanic terms and methods in their practice.

> **Wise Ways**
>
> Taking a shamanic journey is very much like using many other techniques for altering your state of consciousness and exploring your inner world. The use of shamanism for self-discovery, for example, is similar to hypnosis, trance dancing, meditation, and programmed or lucid dreaming. The terminology and symbols you use may differ, but the psychological effects are very much the same.

The emphasis at the time was on using these transpersonal-shamanic practices, both hypnosis and journeying, for individual self-discovery and personal growth. For people such as myself who were participating in workshops on both shamanism and transpersonal psychology, it was like going to a psychological and personal development buffet, where one could choose from a variety of approaches. All the approaches were different paths to discovering more about oneself and increasing one's awareness and sensitivity on all levels of development, resulting in greater personal growth and success.

Thus, for example, on one weekend, workshop participants might engage in a dance trance program (psychology), and on another, they might participate in a shamanic workshop that included an exercise in dancing their animals (shamanism). On one weekend, they might learn about techniques for deepening the hypnotic state (psychology); on another, they might travel to the upper, lower, or middle worlds of the shaman (shamanism). And on one weekend, they might learn how to guide or control their dreams through programmed or lucid dreaming (psychology); on another, they might use the dream state to supplement what they had learned on a shamanic journey (shamanism).

In the psychology workshops, the workshop leaders didn't use the term shamanism; whereas in the shamanism workshops they did. In both cases, my and others' experience of working with the altered state was very much the same. The terminology and concepts were different; but they pointed to essentially the same process: using an altered state of consciousness to go deeper into oneself; in other words, taking some kind of journey of self-discovery, by whatever name it was called.

Psychologists Embrace Shamanism

Another more recent development has been the use of shamanic techniques, particularly journeying, by psychologists and other therapists to help their patients overcome personal problems. In these situations, journeying becomes a path into the inner psyche to investigate repressed feelings and memories and uncover *developmental wounds*—the result of developmental wounding, such as described by licensed psychologist Jeannette M. Gagan, Ph.D. in her book: *Journeying: Where Shamanism and Psychology Meet.* Gagan combines the discipline of psychology and shamanism into methods that she uses in her clinical practice with both adolescents and adult clients and teaches to other therapists.

Shaman Says

Developmental wounds are the psychological injuries a person suffers while growing up, such as from abusive, negligent, or overprotective parents.

As Gagan notes, shamanism and psychology have generally been considered divergent, though they actually share certain features. For example, she finds shamanic techniques particularly useful for taking patients back into the past to discover the roots of the developmental wounds they received due to inadequate bonding with parental figures, including neglect or abuse. Then, she uses journeying as a way to repair developmental gaps and promote the development of new bonds—either with a parent or with someone else taking that parental role who might offer the support unavailable from the person's own parent. Also, she finds journeying useful to help patients get in touch with repressed feelings, such as their unexpressed anger, so they can rechannel those feelings in a positive direction. For instance, she describes how she helped one client take a journey to get in touch with his long-repressed rage due to a childhood illness and combat experience in Vietnam. With journeying, he was able to transform that rage by getting in touch with shamanic guides who helped him contain it (Gagan, 1998 1–3).

Bon Voyage

You can use the intersection of shamanism and psychology to help yourself by taking a deep inner journey to uncover and work through repressed feelings, such as feelings of anger or hostility. Or if you have experienced some kind of developmental wounding in your childhood years, such as a lack of bonding with your parents, you can use journeying and a relationship with shamanic beings to overcome and transform such wounds. Other woundings might include soul loss due to abandonment, sexual or physical abuse, or betrayal of trust. However, it's best not to try this inner journey on your own. Rather, look for a psychologist or therapist to help you take such a journey and work on transforming yourself based on what you discover.

Putting Shamans on the Couch

A third type of intersection of psychology and shamanism has come through the use of psychological techniques and analysis to better understand the dynamics and effects of shamanism and the development of the shaman.

For example, psychologist Stanley Krippner has explored such dynamics in investigating shamanic *epistemology* and how it is reflected in shamanic rituals and ceremonies. Krippner and others look closely at how biology shapes the way we think, feel, perceive, and know what we know; and how the changes in the functions of the brain during altered states of consciousness lead shamans and others to have the experiences they do. The results of this research might be used to help us better work with the shamanic state for personal development and healing purposes.

Shaman Says

Epistemology is an area of philosophical inquiry that focuses on the question: How do we know what we know? It is concerned with understanding the way we acquire and process knowledge and how we form our world view that frames the way we perceive and understand the world.

Some researchers engaged in studying imagery and hypnosis have suggested that shamans tend to be *fantasy-prone*. In other words, shamans may have an ability, possibly inherited, that enables them to better use their imagination. Certainly, everyone engages in fantasy and imagination from time to time, such as when children participate in play activities, when adults think of creative solutions in problem-solving, and when both children and adults engage in "role play," pretending they are someone else. Actors are especially good in using this skill for fantasy, and you let yourself go in a fantasy when you go to the movies, too. Then, too, some therapists help their clients use this ability to fantasize to understand their family members and their motives.

As researchers have found, shamans seem to be able to draw on this ability even more than other members of their community. In fact, shamans claim to be able to read peoples' minds, predict the future, and describe distant events; these claims are common among people who are fantasy-prone (Krippner, 2001, 6).

In turn, such research by psychologists might be helpful for those interested in using shamanic techniques. If we better understand these processes, such as fantasy-proneness, which contribute to the shamanic experience, we can help people better develop and use these skills. For instance, if you can better use your imagination to engage in fantasy, you might experience a deeper, more informative shamanic trip, whether you're using it for journeying on your own or working with a psychologist using shamanic techniques in his or her practice.

Shaman Says

Fantasy-prone is a term used by psychologists to describe a trait, which some individuals have, of being better able to use their imagination to exercise their imagination. Fantasy-prone people are more likely to engage in this activity more often than others, and to put it to practical use.

Or to take another example, one brain researcher, Steve Pinker, who wrote the popular 1997 book *How the Mind Works*, proposes that the mind is made up of many "modules" or units, which have different specialties when they interact with the world, such as to think, see, analyze, and understand input from others. These modules interact together in various ways, much like the interaction of separate software programs on a computer (Pinker, 1997, 24–25). More recently, anthropologist Michael Winkelman, writing in *Shamanism: The Neural Ecology of Consciousness and Healing*, has suggested that shamans may have learned to integrate these different modules or units in the brain better than other people, so they can more easily shift their consciousness between different worlds. Likewise, you may be able to learn to integrate these different elements in your own brain, so you can have a more productive journey of discovery and healing.

Shaman Says

Cognitive psychology is a relatively new field in psychology that studies mental processes to understand differences in how people in different groups think and process information. **Cognitive psychologists** study cognitive psychology.

In short, a growing body of research by brain researchers, *cognitive psychologists*, anthropologists, and others has been discovering more about the relationship between consciousness, brain functioning, and shamanic practice, which could have practical applications that professionals—and you, too!—can use to better apply shamanic techniques for desired goals.

Finally, some psychologists and therapists have begun to look more closely at the psychological factors that contribute to the personal development of a shaman. Cynthia Bend, a psychospiritual teacher and healer, writes of the transformation of one woman who moved from a difficult past, including blindness and epilepsy, to become a modern healing shaman in *Birth of a Modern Shaman*.

Psychological Journeying

How journeying can help in psychological discovery and healing is made especially vivid by Jeannette M. Gagan, who found journeying to be therapeutic for herself before she began using this approach with her own patients. As she describes in *Journeying: Where Shamanism and Psychology Meet*, her own discovery of shamanism began when she was 55, and her 32-year marriage was disintegrating. She was living alone, feeling very uncertain and despairing, despite all the past psychological work she had done. She felt a need to turn inward, and spent hours each day in deep reflection. Then, one weekend, at a workshop at a mountain retreat conducted by a Native American woman, Gagan had her first taste of shamanism, when the Native American woman went into a shamanic trance and blew a power animal she had retrieved on her journey into Gagan (Gagan, 1998, 5–7).

After that, at the Native American woman's prompting, Gagan began to work on her own in traveling into the lower world to meet with and gain answers from her power animal. The answers came either telepathically or from observing the animal's behavior. During these journeys, she felt a great sense of healing energy and relief from the emotional pain she felt as she wondered about her future. Her sixth journey proved especially healing. On that journey, she entered a garden, where she saw a circle of women caring for an infant—essentially her infant self. Then, in her next journeys, she felt a new sense of being cared for, as her power animal sat or lay nearby as "a defender and benefactor" of her well-being (Gagan, 1998, 7–8).

Eventually, this process brought her in touch with a long-buried rage she had, as she experienced and interpreted the symbols that appeared in her journeys or dreams, such as her power animal coming to her holding the bloody flesh of a lamb in its mouth (Gagan, 1998, 9).

The process soon led her to see parallels with the psychological processing she had done before. For example, she saw the discovery of her infant self as an experience of soul retrieval and compared soul loss to its psychological counterpart, called "dissociation" as she terms it, though it might be more accurately called a "dissociative disorder." In this harmful state of dissociation, parts of the psyche are split off due to a trauma the individual experiences (for more on soul retrieval and soul loss, see Chapter 6).

Gagan eventually went to a shamanic practitioner for a formal soul retrieval and began to go through shamanic training. The process led her to look for her other childhood parts besides her infant-self that might be "lost" to her (such as her very young child-self). Additionally, she used the process to recognize and release her long buried rage, and experience both emotional and physical release on each of her journeys. Gradually, she returned to her psychotherapy practice and began to incorporate some of the approaches of shamanism into her own clinical work. She was particularly interested in such questions as how shamanism can bring its healing power to the wounds the psyche experienced early in life (Gagan, 1998, 9–13).

Wise Ways

Just where is the shaman going when he or she journeys? Is it into the personal unconscious or collective unconscious or into a nonordinary reality or spiritual world? Psychologists may prefer to think of this journey as tapping into the personal unconscious or even into a collective form of unconscious. But there are parallels between the conceptions of the psychologist about the unconscious and the beliefs of the shaman about entering the world of the spirits. However you conceive of it, the shamanic journey will work for you.

The Many Parallels Between Shamanism and Psychology

As Gagan and others have noted, shamanism and certain branches of psychology share many ideas and practices. For example, they are both designed to overcome suffering and induce healing, they both explore altered states of consciousness, and they both involve the patient's active participation in the healing ritual (Gagan 35–40).

Given these parallels between shamanism and psychological practice, it is not surprising that a growing number of psychologists have found shamanic techniques useful in helping their clients and that I found many parallels in the workshops I attended on hypnosis and using altered states and imagery for personal development. The particular techniques and terminology may differ, but the overall approach shares many similarities.

The Least You Need to Know

- ◆ Many psychologists, particularly those influenced by humanistic or transpersonal psychology, have begun to use shamanic techniques in their practice.
- ◆ Psychologists have found many shamanic techniques to be useful for helping their patients explore their developmental wounds.
- ◆ Brain researchers have begun to investigate the biological changes in the brain that occur when a shaman goes into an altered state during a shamanic journey.

Part 4

The Well-Traveled Shaman

Once you've taken a few trips to the different shamanic worlds, the secret to getting things done effectively is to go back regularly and explore further. This way you become more familiar with the different sources of spiritual power in each of these worlds, and you become more comfortable working with them, like getting to know a long time friend more deeply.

In this section you'll learn how to become more attuned to the traditional associations with the lower, upper, and middle worlds, how to work with others to find information and empowerment, and other ways to get the most out of your journeys.

Chapter 17

Planning Your Itinerary

In This Chapter

- ◆ Two ways to seek help from the spirit world
- ◆ Some cautions about journeying for healing and therapy
- ◆ Using shamanism for personal growth and everyday situations
- ◆ More ways to maximize the shamanic experience

Because the journeying process can be used for many purposes and take many forms, before you go on your own journeys, you need to answer some questions: How do you want to use the journeying process? What's your purpose for using it? And how deep do you want to go? In other words, figure out what kind of trip you want to take; then plan your itinerary!

Planning Your Trip

The two most common ways to seek help from the three shamanic worlds is to go on a divination or healing journey.

In the *divination journey*, you go on your journey with a question in mind or a problem or situation about which you'd like advice either for yourself or

Shaman Says

A **divination journey** is a journey to get information, such as an answer to a question asked by others or yourself. A **healing journey** is a journey to seek an infusion of healing energy or insights about how to treat a particular problem for yourself or others (though seek specialized training in healing to do this properly).

another person. Then, when you meet your power animal or teachers and guides in these various worlds, ask your question telepathically, and wait for the answer.

Alternatively, in the *healing journey*, you go on the journey to experience a healing or infusion of energy. When you return from your journey, you'll typically feel very uplifted and powerful; and if you have been experiencing some problem, such as a headache or tiredness, you may feel healed.

Because you should seek specialized training or advice before taking a healing journey, the rest of this chapter will focus on divination journeys.

Multiple Choice Answers

The information you divine on your journeys may come to you in various forms, including:

♦ Directly, as advice about what to do, including some specific action to take.

♦ Abstractly, in the form of symbols, signs, stories, or experiences that you must interpret.

♦ As a process, since the journey may be a way to work out and release feelings you have about something. Once those feelings are released, you may feel a sense of completion or resolution, so there is nothing more to do. For example, a woman who was very angry at a neighbor who had damaged a tree on her property took a journey that helped her release her negative feelings toward her neighbor. On her journey, she saw herself taking revenge and cutting down her neighbor's tree. Such negative imagery doesn't mean you should actually take such actions; rather, the journey acts more as a form of psychological healing, in which you release feelings of anger and hostility. Later if such feelings come up again, you may take another journey to do more releasing in the future.

Bon Voyage

By symbolically acting out what you can't do for real, you can release your pent-up feelings and go on to other things. The process is like writing an angry letter to someone, but not mailing it. The writing process gets out the anger; but since you know you would create even worse problems by mailing it, you don't send it. However, you feel better for having written down your thoughts and feelings in your letter.

Journeys of Personal Growth and Discovery

People typically use divination journeys as ways to achieve personal growth and handle issues in everyday life. In particular, you can use shamanic journeys for the following:

- Improving relationships
- Resolving conflicts
- Developing personally and professionally
- Solving problems
- Setting goals
- Making decisions
- Increasing your creativity
- Anticipating the future
- Better understanding others
- Making plans to achieve your goals

Bon Voyage

Before starting a journey decide what kind of trip you want to take—your purpose for journeying. Then determine how to get there, what to explore or what beings to meet once you've arrived, and how long to stay.

More Ways to Maximize

Okay, so if you're ready to go on a shamanic journey, here are some ways to maximize the experience, so it's as an intense, yet controlled, event for you.

Stay Alert During the Experience

People sometimes have difficulty entering an altered state of consciousness. They might have trouble keeping their minds off events of the day or get so relaxed that they drift off to sleep. If either drifting or falling asleep becomes a problem, you can do two things to stay focused:

Shaman Says

A **trigger** or **triggering device** is an indicator, such as a sound or motion, you can use to cause you to do something, in this case to pull you out of a shamanic journey experience. You might use such a trigger to stop a difficult experience or redirect your thinking from negative to positive thoughts.

- Instead of lying down when you go on a journey, try sitting up. This will help you pay attention and stay focused, and if you start to drift off to sleep, your body may react naturally to jerk you awake.
- Use a trigger for yourself, so if you start to drift off or fall asleep, your trigger will wake you up. For instance, hold your hands in a

certain way, such as touching the tips of your fingers. Then, program yourself in advance with the suggestion that if the triggering event happens (i,e., the tips of your fingers come apart), that's a signal to pay attention again and stay awake.

Adjust the Speed of the Experience

Different people have different paces when they journey. Some like to move quickly through wherever they are; others like to take their time, moving slowly and looking closely at their surroundings. If you're journeying in a group guided meditation or listening to a taped visualization, the journey might go too fast or slow for you, since it's hard for any leader to moderate the pace to suit everyone. There are two ways to adjust the speed for yourself, if you're listening to a guided meditation or visualization:

> **Bon Voyage**
>
> Another key to having a good experience when you're led on a guided journey is don't worry about following every word or image. Just respond to the ideas or images that are meaningful for you and let go of the others. This way, you can adapt the journey to your own needs and desires, much like you can adapt the journey to suit your own speed.

- If it's too fast, feel free to stay and linger if something is especially interesting to you. Then, when you are ready, simply leap past the next parts of the journey to catch up with the leader or group.

- If it's too slow, and you feel the visualization is staying too long in one place, go off on your own side trip. Then, when the group gets ready to move on, quickly report back, and be ready to go on.

Decide Whether to Observe or Participate

Many people feel more comfortable observing their surroundings on a journey rather than actually engaging with spirits. In particular, beginners, who might not be sure what is going to happen, might prefer to observe for a while.

How involved and active you are in your journey is totally up to you. Typically, as people get more experienced in journeying and feel more comfortable with the process, they participate more. But as soon as things get difficult or even a little scary, it's fine to pull back a bit to gain more detachment from the situation.

Going Places Faster and Better

Whenever you go to different worlds, it can help you get there more quickly and easily if you use the following travel tips:

◆ Use the same starting off place each time, although you can leave from anywhere. The value of starting from the same place is that it's a way of conditioning yourself. In other words, using the same starting point—such as a particular cave to the lower world, tree to the upper world, or path to a middle world location—acts as a mental trigger, which tells you that you're about to go on a journey to these worlds. Then, this message to you will help to immediately put you in the focused mental state needed to go on a journey.

◆ Feel free to go quickly in all directions, since you are not limited to staying on one level or moving in real time. As you prefer, r walk, ride or fly around on your own. You can even ride on or be carried by your animal guide if he is big enough, or conversely, if you make yourself small enough to hop on a small animal. Or move instantly from place to place. Just see yourself there in your imagination, and there you are.

◆ Create your own safe and comfortable reality, so you feel free to imagine the shamanic world where you're going however you want. It may correspond to a familiar place or it may not, but most importantly, it should feel safe and comfortable for you for everyday traveling. If something is scary or makes you feel uncomfortable, turn away (the exception is if you are working with shamanism for therapeutic healing and seeking to overcome blocks—but that's another kind of traveling, and you should be working with a trained practitioner in that case).

◆ Go back to where you have been before, so this location becomes a familiar place that you get used to visiting. This familiarity helps to make journeying a comfortable habit, and you may meet many of the same animal helpers, teachers, or guides there again and again. Like familiar friends, they can become especially helpful and supportive.

◆ Make a mental map of wherever you go to help reinforce the reality of that place. Perhaps reflect on your journey there later, or even make a drawing of that place and what you experienced there. This mental map or drawing will not only help you better understand your experience, but it will make it even more vivid for you, so you can more quickly and easily revisit the area.

◆ Don't try to question or analyze the experience while it is happening. Doing so will only break into your altered consciousness state and bring you back to everyday reality. Just give yourself over to the experience.

Off the Path

You may find that it takes quite a while to develop abilities for journeying. People have different capacities for visualization, fantasy, and using their imagination, and some people may feel inhibited or uncertain about exploring other worlds in nonordinary reality. Just keep practicing, and eventually you'll get there!

- Feel free to meet whomever appears on your trip, because there are no particular spirits, animals, or other beings who exist in any particular place. And even if you see unusual or unexpected beings, such as cartoon animals, humorous characters, or unlikely teachers and wise beings (such as Hugh Hefner in a bathrobe, as one person experienced), don't question the experience. Rather, meet whoever is there and later think about what you can learn from that being.

- Don't be concerned about the reality of the beings you meet, because it doesn't matter whether you believe these are real beings or think of them as aspects of yourself. Or maybe this reality contains a mixture of both. Use whichever perspective you feel most comfortable with; the experience has power to help you either way.

- Preferably, go back the way you came in, since that will ease the movement from one world to another. However, if necessary, a quick return is possible, such as when you have a scary encounter or when everyday reality intrudes, such as when the phone suddenly rings or someone interrupts you. Then, you can quickly snap right back to deal with the everyday intrusions. Then, afterwards, as you prefer, go immediately back to where you left off in your journey, or if it's more comfortable for you, go back more gradually by returning via your trail in.

Experiencing the World of the Shaman More Fully

Finally, a few last travel tips so you have an even more pleasant intense experience:

- Use all your senses, once you are in this other shamanic reality, to make this an even richer sensory experience. Don't only see or listen, but use your sense of smell, touch, and taste. For instance, smell the flowers, touch and feel the walls of a cave, notice the taste of any food your teacher gives you. In fact, as you become more experienced in shamanic traveling, you are likely to naturally become more aware and experience even more with all your senses in everyday life, as well as on your journeys.

- Be satisfied with whatever you experience, even if you get only a slight glimpse of this other world or have trouble entering it, especially when you are first starting to work with journeying. Just take whatever you can from whatever you experience, and realize that the more you work with these techniques, the fuller and richer your experience will become.

Bon Voyage

Don't worry if you don't see vivid imagery or have dramatic results right away. If you get a worthwhile idea, the experience is still a valuable one for you.

- Have a purpose or question in advance of your journey, so that you don't wander around aimlessly. Your question or reason for going is what helps to direct you. It is a way to trigger yourself in advance of your journey, so you can direct and guide the overall process, while you let go and experience it.

◆ Feel free to ask whatever kind of question you want. As long as you have some question to guide you, it can be anything. For instance, it can be a deeper, more profound question, such as "What should my goal in life be?" or it can be something very mundane and day-to-day, such as "What should I do tomorrow?" or "What should my priority be at work?" The one exception is don't ask deeply probing questions to open up your inner psyche unless you are working with an experienced practitioner or therapist who can guide you in processing such material and overcoming any resistances that come up for you.

◆ Let go to experience and enjoy while you direct. Use your initial question or purpose to give a specific reason to guide and structure your journey. But then, relax, so you are receptive to what comes. By combining an initial structure with receptivity, the two parts of you—the rational and the intuitive; your conscious and your unconscious—work together harmoniously to create a satisfying whole. While the one part of you directs and guides the show, the other is listening, receiving, and responding spontaneously to whatever you experience when you are there.

So now, get ready to go, experience, learn, and enjoy. The next three chapters will help to guide you in traveling to the three main shamanic worlds … and beyond.

Bon voyage!

The Least You Need to Know

◆ A divination journey is one that you go on to get information or advice for yourself or another person; a healing journey is one you take to experience a healing or infusion of energy.

◆ The information you get on your journeys may come in multiple ways, including as signs, symbols, stories, and experiences you have to interpret.

◆ You can use shamanic journeys for a number of purposes, including improving relationships, resolving conflicts, developing personally and professionally, solving problems, setting goals, making decisions, and increasing your creativity.

◆ There are several techniques you can use to maximize your shamanic journey.

Chapter 18

Looking Low and High: Lower and Upper World Journeys

In This Chapter

- ◆ Taking a lower world journey
- ◆ Taking an upper world journey
- ◆ Comparing worlds

In Chapter 7, you were introduced to the idea of power animals of the lower world and spiritual guides and teachers of the upper world. In this chapter, we'll return to the lower and upper worlds to learn even more about these powerful shamanic resources. The more often you visit these worlds and interact with your power animals and spirit teachers, the more you'll get out of your journeys.

Let's return to the lower world first.

Trips Down Under: Lower World Journeys

To begin your journey to the lower world, you'll need to find an opening to it. Ideally, this should be a natural passage that goes down into the earth. Traditionally, shamans entered the lower world through caves, ponds, springs, lakes, rivers, tree stumps, hollow trees, whirlpools, waterfalls, wells, gopher holes, or holes of other burrowing animals, depending upon what natural features were present in their environment. If you prefer, though, you can use a more modern entrance, such as a basement or a mine.

After you go through the opening of your choice, you'll encounter a tunnel or tube. These passages are very spacious and easy to move through. If, for some reason, you encounter any obstacles in the tunnel, look for a crack in the obstacle or some other potential alternate path you can use to maneuver around the obstacle. The obstacle may take the form of a membrane between the tunnel and the shamanic world, like a real world–spiritual world barrier. Just keep going and generally you'll pass right through.

> **Wise Ways**
>
> Sometimes this tunnel or tube, or the opening at the end, may resemble a wheel, circle, or mandala.

Finding Insight and Information

You can use the same basic exercise for contacting your power animal for information as described in Chapter 7. As you return and get more acquainted with this new world, it might become increasingly easy to go there and get information. It's a case of familiarity breeding more insight and accuracy. So plan to go back again and again and get to know, trust, and work with your power animal even more closely.

In general it helps to cultivate a particular animal as your personal power animal, much like you may seek out a close friend or relative you've come to know and trust intimately over time.

Shaman Says

People often associate the various worlds as representing different aspects of consciousness or different qualities of life, as follows:

- **Lower world:** physical qualities, nurturing, support, unconscious, strong desires (sometimes called the id) Often, but not always, associated with power animals.
- **Upper World:** mental and/or spiritual qualities, direction, guidance, rule, law, superconscious, superego. Often, but not always, associated with teachers and spiritual guides.
- **Middle World:** emotional qualities, caring, common-sense, conscious, ego. Often, but not always, associated with the elements of nature and ancestor spirits.

Meeting Other Animals to Help You

While you may find meeting and working with your primary power animal ideal for you, as many people do, you may also find it helps to meet different animals depending on what you want or need at the time of your journey. For example, if you need strength, you might seek out an animal you associate with strength, whereas if you want to work on an issue involving a relationship, look for help from an animal that suggests those qualities.

For instance, in one workshop, some of the participants met panthers, which they associated with power or strength when they were seeking answers to money or work related questions. However, when one woman was looking for information about personal relationships and feelings, she encountered a tiger, which she associated with softness and femininity.

Or perhaps you might encounter an animal who can offer a mix of qualities you need, such as the woman who encountered the gorilla. She felt he was not only a strong animal, but an intelligent one, who could understand complex human emotions, like a desire for revenge. She felt she had encountered this particular animal because her unconscious mind knew what she needed and what her animal would have to do, so it provided the gorilla to serve these purposes. As she put it:

> I feel like I met the gorilla because I was looking for certain things in my animal. I associate the gorilla with beating his chest, being very strong and powerful, and then he's very intelligent … He was intelligent enough to understand all these complicated human emotions, like the desire for revenge, and he understood I was upset about my tree.

The power animals you meet can take many forms, such as a gorilla who helped one woman, and a panther who helped another.

Tips for Interacting with Your Animals

Approaching your power animals in the right way can make a big difference in how helpful they are. Follow these suggestions to create a pleasant relationship with your power animals:

◆ Look on the animals and other spiritual beings you meet as friends, and when you go back, say hello from time to time, like dropping in to keep up your ties with your friends or neighbors.

◆ Don't always ask for help and favors when you journey. Rather, take some time just to be friendly and get better acquainted with the spirit beings you meet. This way, your power animal and other helpers will remain more receptive to helping, just like a friend with whom you've nurtured the relationship.

◆ From time to time, ask your animal if it has any tasks for you. This can good way to remind yourself of responsibilities or roles you might perform.

◆ Try asking your animal if it has any additional suggestions for you, beyond what you have asked or your animal has already told you—much like you might do in conducting an interview with someone in real life. Then, if you find these suggestions useful, put them into practice.

> **Wise Ways**
>
> Even when you have limited ongoing contact, you will usually find your animals and helpers receptive if you're seeking help for others. It's like asking them to do a public service, and they'll usually be happy to lend a helping hand.

Want Better Trips Underground?

You'll have better results working with the lower world in the future, if you make regular visits there and stay in touch with your power animal or other spiritual powers that reside there. The lower world will be more open and accessible to you, because the world will seem more familiar.

You'll get to better know the lower world and its resident power animals each time you go, much like meeting up with an old friend time and again. Plus, you can get there faster and you'll notice more, because the way is more familiar. For example, you may zip through the tunnel down more quickly, and you may find your animal right there waiting for you. You will usually get your answer more quickly and clearly, too.

How often should you take these journeys? A good rule of thumb to keep the connection open is to take a journey to the lower world—or whatever worlds you prefer to visit— once to a few times a week. If you don't visit regularly, you'll start to lose touch with the beings who live there and your ability to get there. As a result, you may have to start the journeying process again, as if you are taking a journey for the first time.

As you journey more often, you may start interacting with a number of different animals and spiritual helpers who can help you with different things.

Some of the benefits to keeping up this regular contact include:

- It can make you feel powerful and pro-tected. It's like having a special retreat or place where you have helpful friends you can turn to.
- It can give you a sense of assurance that you have a source of knowledge and wis-dom you can turn to when you need infor-mation.
- It can energize you.
- It can make you confident enough to con-front problems and seek answers for yourself and others.

Bon Voyage _____

Don't wait until you have a problem to take a journey. It's more difficult to get clear answers when you're under pressure, and it's even harder when you haven't already built up a familiar con-nection with the other world.

Reaching for the Stars: Upper World Journeys

When you go to the upper world, you can use any number of entry points. Some tradi-tional pathways or entry points have included any type of tree, house posts, poles, smoke—either going through a smoke hole, or rising up from a campfire. Another possi-bility is going up a chimney or using a fireplace to go up to the upper world.

Wise Ways
The main pathways or entry points to the upper world include the following:

- Trees
- House posts
- Poles
- Smoke, smoke holes, and fires
- Animals you can ride or fly
- Ladders
- Whirlwinds and tornadoes
- Mountains
- High buildings and bridges
- Anything else that gets you high (physically, that is!)

High places are another traditional site of entry to the upper world, such as climbing to the top of a high mountain and jumping off into the clouds or heavens. You can also use animals to ride up into the upper world, such as the Siberian shaman who rides a horse or reindeer into the spirit world. Even the image of Santa Claus has its roots in the shamanic vision, for in some pre-Christian European traditions, a Santa Claus-type figure would travel with his reindeer and sleigh around the winter solstice to visit the sun god and ask for a blessing for the people.

Ladders are another common means of entry, and you might think of the rungs on the ladder corresponding to the levels of the upper world. The higher you go on the ladder, the higher you climb into the other world.

Whirlwinds and tornadoes are still another possible point of entry. For example, consider the *Wizard of Oz*, in which Dorothy is suddenly caught up in a tornado and finds herself in another world. Some cultures have also used rainbows as a way of going up.

You can incorporate more urban heights, such as going up to the top of a tall bridge or a high building, especially one with a high point, like the Transamerica Pyramid building in San Francisco, the Empire State Building in New York, or the Eiffel Tower in Paris.

In short, there are all sorts of possibilities that people have used or can use. Choose any point that feels comfortable for you.

When you reach the upper world, it can take various forms, such as being on the top of something (like the top of a mountain, cliff, or building) or you may experience yourself floating in the clouds. Sometimes when you get there, you may enter a high enclosure or building, even a magical castle. Wherever you are, think of it as the home of the spiritual beings or teachers you have come to see.

Off the Path

Sometimes, because teachers are often viewed as much higher, wise, powerful beings, they may seem more distant or hard to meet and talk to. Don't let that dissuade you. Instead, show serious commitment and respect, as you might with any real-world teacher. Generally that attitude will make your teacher more receptive and more helpful for you.

If At First You Don't Succeed ...

Many people meet a teacher and get an answer to a question they have on their first visit to any world they visit. However, sometimes those new to journeying report more difficulty meeting with upper-world teachers, as compared to meeting their power animal in the lower world, since they experience these teachers as higher, more distant, harder-to-contact beings.

Even if you don't get an answer, especially in the beginning, don't feel discouraged. Sometimes the difficulty is because you experience these beings as more revered or distant, or perhaps they may appear to be testing you before they reveal themselves. Or sometimes you may not get an answer because you're tired or are distracted by other things.

If the beings you encounter in the upper world seem especially distant, or unfriendly, or seem to be testing you, try another path or opening to get there the next time you visit. Also, to facilitate your meeting, before you go on your journey, suggest to yourself that you will meet helpful, friendly teachers on your trip.

Try to think of a journey in which you don't get any information as helping to prepare the way for next time. Then, the next time you go, you'll find it easier to get there and will be more likely to get answers and information, since you have already been there once.

Shamanism Meets Other Spiritual Beliefs

The upper world is often associated with the sky, stars, or heaven, and is thought to be the home of higher beings from sky gods and star deities to beings associated with the major religions, such as Christianity, Judaism, and Islam, where they are called by various names, such as God, Jesus, Jehovah, and Allah. Also, angels, guardian spirits, prophets, and other heavenly or celestial beings are also thought to reside in this realm, as are the sky father or grandfather spirit.

If you already hold spiritual and religious beliefs about higher beings, feel free to contact those beings as your teachers and spiritual helpers and work with them. Or work with other beings, especially as you learn more about traditional shamanism. Try to think of your shamanic practices as an addition or supplement to beliefs you already hold; they don't need to pose any kind of conflict with these currently held beliefs.

If it feels comfortable to you to contact these beings from your religious traditions on your journeys, then do so. Otherwise, work with whatever beings present themselves as helpers, guides, and teachers. Or perhaps contact a combination of these beings. What's most important is that you do what feels comfortable for you, since that will provide you with the best insights and answers when you seek help.

> **Bon Voyage**
>
> Think of the reality of your experience in the way that is most comfortable for you, whether you think of it as a journey in your imagination, a way to contact your higher self, or a way to contact real spirits, beings, or energies. At different times, you may think of the upper world journey in different ways—whatever way feels right for you will work best.

Messages from On High

As with any journey, you may get clear direct messages, or you may have to interpret images and meanings from your experience and what you see. Sometimes these may be symbols and metaphors coming from your unconscious that you have to unravel the meanings of by reflecting on them. The process is much like what you may experience in traveling to the lower world, except the particular images and messages may be different, since your destination is different.

> ### Wise Ways
>
> As in working with animals and helpers in the lower world, your teachers in the upper world may communicate with you in various ways. They may tell you something directly to give you advice, or they may show you images or give you experiences you need to reflect on to understand. However, the particular images, symbols with deeper meaning, and experiences will generally be different in these two worlds.

Also, keep in mind that you may not always see your teacher or spiritual helper immediately, whereas your power animal is often waiting there for you and the first animal you see. That may be because the higher spiritual beings or teachers are often experienced as more reserved. Then, too, as higher beings, they may have assistants and helpers who will meet and greet you first, much like a king, village chief, or high ranking government leader will have courtiers and administrators to make the initial introductions.

Be Nice to Your Teachers

As in working with your power animal or other animal helpers, once you have met your teachers, you can continue to work with them in the future. Often, when you go back, you will come across the same teachers again and again and will get to know them better and better, though you may meet other teachers, too.

Sometimes, because teachers are seen as powerful, wise beings, shamanic practitioners use a special courtesy to recognize and honor them. For example, once a shaman meets a teacher on a journey, he will go to see that being on his next journey, and if he wants to seek another teacher, he will ask the first teacher's permission to work with someone else.

If you like the idea of doing this, on your next journey after meeting your teacher, return to say hello, ask your teacher how he or she is, and show your respect. Then, you can ask this same teacher for help or ask permission to go on to get help from another teacher.

Normally you will receive permission as a matter of course. It's not absolutely necessary to ask permission, and you may prefer to view whoever shows up on your visit as your teacher. But asking for permission is a nice approach, and you may find it makes your teachers more responsive to helping you in the future, much like a real-world teacher might be more available and helpful when you show such respect.

These teachers and guides are commonly viewed by shamanic practitioners as deserving of this respect, as very powerful, wise beings in a higher spiritual realm. Likewise, you should look up to them as beings who are wiser and more knowing than you.

Also, many shamanic practitioners, such as in many Western adaptations of traditional shamanism, view the beings in the upper world as more powerful and wiser than the animals and other beings who reside in the lower world. That's because these teachers are seen more like parent or authoritarian figures, in contrast to the animals and other lower world beings, who are viewed more like friends and may have a playful quality about them. However, if you find your upper world teachers are more like friends or comrades, that's fine. Although it helps to know about the traditional associations with these teachers, you should work with what feels most comfortable for you.

> **Bon Voyage**
>
> Just as you do in the real world, show your teachers honor and respect. Regard them as high, wise, powerful beings, and they will be more available and helpful, just like real-world teachers.

Because of these upper-world associations, which have become common today, many people who journey to the upper world encounter teachers who are well-known wise figures, such as Mother Teresa or Gandhi; wise spiritual beings, such as angels; or birds or animals associated with spiritual power or heights, such as an eagle or hawk. Still, who you meet can be quite unpredictable, so you may meet people you don't normally think of like teachers, such as a high-profile celebrity or wealthy businessman.

Don't be concerned if the teacher doesn't seem wise or not the type of person who you expect to be a teacher, because anybody can have something to teach you—even a dragon, as one woman reported in a workshop: "He taught me not to be so serious," she said. Certainly, traditional shamans had a more limited view of who they might contact in the upper world, such as when they went to meet their ancestor figures or the deities of the sky or stars as conceived of in their culture. But modern shamanism has become very influenced by Western notions about the upper world as a higher world, so feel free to choose as you will, incorporating traditional or modern notions or a combination of both.

> **Wise Ways**
>
> Many people have preconceptions of who their teachers should be, because of upper-world images and associations with wise teachers and spiritual beings. But put those preconceptions aside, so you can accept anyone as your teacher and look to what that teacher has to tell you.

If you experience any resistance to accepting someone as your teacher, try to let that go, because that resistance is usually coming from your conscious, guiding mind, and is caused by preconceptions of who your teacher should be. For instance, in a workshop on journeying to the upper world, one man met a monk, and his first reaction was that this person seemed too drab; the man thought he should meet someone who was more assertive and colorful. It turned out, though, that the monk had some valuable things to teach him about acceptance and humility.

So put aside any preconceptions of who you want to teach you and accept whoever you meet.

Ways to Work with the Upper World in the Future

Besides going to the upper world for information for yourself and others, some other ways to work with this world in the future include the following:

> **Bon Voyage**
>
> If you have an encounter with a teacher or guide or have seen an image that makes you feel really good, peaceful, and enlightened, such as an image of the sun that evokes a feeling of love and warmth, return to the upper world to re-experience that. By returning to meet with that teacher or guide or going back to where you saw that image, you will trigger that same feeling.

- Because the upper world is thought of as a place where teachers are especially wise and powerful, go there to get insights into the major developments in the world generally.

- Because the upper world is often associated with the future, go there to make predictions about future events for yourself or for the world as a whole.

- Because the teachers in the upper world are commonly associated with such qualities as enlightenment, uplift, or spiritual protection, go there if you want to feel enlightened, uplifted, and protected.

- Because the upper world is frequently associated with intellectual development and creativity, seek support for your ideas or a charge of creative energy to have more ideas.

Keep Coming Back

As in the case of going to the lower world, it's important to stay in touch with the upper world occasionally, to facilitate your ability to go there and get information in the future. By the same token, it helps to treat your teachers with respect and establish an ongoing friendship with them by occasionally going to visit them or occasionally acknowledging and thinking about them during the day. This way, you can better keep the connection open, so they are there when you need them, just as with real-world teachers and friends.

As part of this process of showing respect or building a friendship, you might go back sometime and tell them something like: "This is what I learned from you," "Thanks for your help," or "This is what I am doing now."

Why Travel to Different Worlds?

Although some people may find that they can contact power animals in the upper world, just as they can contact teachers and higher spiritual beings in the lower and middle world, it's generally helpful to go to different places for different objectives. Think of it as a way of expanding and differentiating the way you use shamanic techniques or as expanding your repertoire, much like you might look to different friends and associates for different types of help in the everyday world.

Furthermore, you will often get different types of information in different places and from different types of helpers. You can choose among the different worlds and energies you prefer to work with for help in different situations.

Try to look on the different techniques and journeys to different worlds as a way to open more doors to knowledge and other types of help. You'll probably find you prefer taking some types of journeys and working with certain animals and helpers. As you work with different approaches, pick those that work the best for you and use them in the future.

You may be drawn to a particular approach for a number of reasons—from your own personal style to your past experiences and influences. For instance, in some cases, people have worked with certain beings, spirits, or guides in the past, and find them again on their journeys, so they find it comfortable and familiar to work with them. By contrast, other people may not have had such an experience or be more open to new experiences. Also, different people relate more strongly to different things, because of different personalities, attitudes, feelings, backgrounds, experiences, and ways of relating to the world.

You may also find the personalities of the people or beings you meet in different places more appropriate for dealing with different kinds of questions. Or maybe you like going one place more than another because it feels more like home to you.

Whatever the differences for you, use this knowledge to help decide where to go in the future.

> ### Wise Ways
>
> Just like you might visit a specialist for a particular health problem instead of going to your family physician, so you might look to the different worlds and helpers you meet there for different types of help.

> ### Bon Voyage
>
> As you travel to these different worlds, notice the qualities you associate with them. Pay attention to the kinds of beings you meet and types of information you receive. Your observations will help you to decide where it's best to journey for different types of information and advice.

Getting a Second Opinion

Yet another reason for going to two different places is to get two different opinions, so you can compare them. It's like going to a doctor for a second opinion, before you take some major step like surgery. If you get the same opinions or advice in both places, as with going to two doctors who make the same diagnosis and recommendation, you feel more comfortable. The views reinforce each other and can strengthen your confidence and resolve in making a decision or embarking on a particular action.

If you get different opinions—such as one upper-world teacher telling you to do to one thing, while a lower-world animal helper advises you to do something entirely different, then a good option might be to get a third opinion. To do so, you might return to the upper or lower world or both for additional insights. Or perhaps go to the middle world, as discussed in the next chapter, for still another viewpoint to help you choose.

The Least You Need to Know

- The lower world is often associated with the physical aspects of life and with power animals.
- The upper world is often associated with the mental or spiritual aspects of life and with wise teachers and guides.
- If you already have spiritual and religious beliefs about higher beings, feel free to contact them.
- Try not to have preconceptions about what beings you will meet on your various journeys. Just be receptive to learning whatever they have to teach you in these different worlds.

Chapter 19

Staying Close to Home: The Middle World Journey

In This Chapter

- ◆ Keys to a successful middle-world journey
- ◆ Working with your middle-world journey
- ◆ Applying associations with the elements
- ◆ Working more closely with the elements
- ◆ Seeking balance

The third world of shamanic reality is the middle world, or earth itself. Because this world includes the natural world and world of everyday experience, you'll work with this world differently than with upper and lower world. As with the other worlds, you can meet experts and teachers, but you can focus on working with the elements or forces of nature to gain power and emotional support, too.

Also, experiences or materials in the middle world, namely earth, can be used to supplement journeys to the other two worlds. For instance, a practicing shaman might go on a walk in the nearby woods or on a long hike to a place considered sacred to collect plants for healing or visions. You can do the same by finding places you can go in the natural world around you or on a journey to a power place.

Alternatively, a shaman might take a journey in an altered state of consciousness to travel to distant worlds to invite his ancestor spirits or the spirits of the mountains, rivers, or other areas to return with him to help with a ritual or healing. Likewise, you can take a middle world-journey in an altered state of consciousness to call on the spirits of these areas, contact your own ancestor spirits, or become more aware of and feel closer to the plants, animals, rocks, or surrounding environment. In doing so, you combine journeying in an altered state of consciousness with real-world journeys to get more in touch with these elements. For instance, take a walk in the woods or on the beach to contemplate and possibly collect objects of nature that have particular meaning to you.

Wise Ways

The four elements in nature are earth, air, fire, and water, according to many systems, and are widely used in modern shamanism and in many Native American traditions. They frequently have these associations:

- **Earth:** stability, solidity, strength
- **Air:** lightness, insight, awareness
- **Fire:** heat, energy, power, aggressiveness, excitement
- **Water:** flexibility, flowing, adaptability, calm

Bon Voyage

A good way to work with middle-world journeying is to combine a shamanic journey with real-world travels before or after your journey. For example, take a hike into nature and tune into the objects you see that are especially meaningful to you. Or you can collect and later work with the objects themselves, if you can bring them back with you without disrupting the natural environment.

Trips to the Heart

The middle world is often associated with the emotions, especially in modern Western shamanism. Thus, a middle-world journey can be ideal for working with emotional issues and feelings and working with the elements of nature to support these efforts. It might be useful to think of it as the world of the heart.

Although you can meet spiritual beings in the middle world just as in the upper and lower worlds, this chapter focuses on working with the four elements of nature: air, earth, fire, and water. Working with the elements involves looking more closely at what the different qualities or energies of these elements and how to incorporate them into yourself and apply them to your life. The process is much like what happens when a traditional shaman puts certain plants or stones on his altar because they have certain symbolic meaning to him or her, such as described in Chapter 8.

Use your initial middle world journey to contact and understand the elements. Then, in later journeys, you can work with these elements for a particular purpose. For example, because fire is commonly associated with aggressiveness or energy, get in touch with and work with that element to reinforce or develop those qualities in yourself. Or because the earth is generally associated with stability and solidity, contact and work with the earth to feel more stable or solid about something you are doing where you need that strength, such as moving to take a job in a new community.

Among the many ways you can work with the middle world are going out into nature by simply taking a hike and becoming aware of nature or honoring the earth through ritual.

The Nature of the Middle-World Journey

Although you can go anywhere on earth, even to a city street to meet a teacher ("Hey, dude? What you got to teach me?"), traditionally, middle-world journeys have involved going into a setting in nature, such as when the members of some American Indian tribes go off by themselves to a quiet isolated place to seek a vision. Some common settings to visit on these journeys include wooded groves, caves, or mountains, or other places you think of as places of spiritual connection or power. Particular rocks, plants, and other natural objects may be sources of power, too.

> ### Wise Ways
>
> You can think of the middle-world journey as a trip to become more in touch with the elements of nature. Each element—earth, air, fire, and water—has different energies of the universe, and you can access those qualities or energies to develop those qualities in yourself and increase your personal power as a result.

A goal of the middle-world journey is to tune into the basic energies of the universe reflected through the natural elements and use these energies to help develop and empower yourself.

Getting There

To get to your destination, you follow a path, much as in lower- and upper-world journeying. However, in the middle world, you stay on the surface of the ground.

In the following exercise, you will get acquainted with the four elements. Once you're acquainted with each of the elements, you can use them to create more intense experiences and to achieve particular ends:

To start, focus on your breathing going in and out, in and out. You feel very comfortable, very relaxed. Yet you are awake and alert. Take a few moments to focus on your breathing and get ready to begin the journey.

Now, see yourself walking down a path that leads to a meadow. You reach the meadow and are standing in the green grass, and it's a very sunny, warm day. You feel very comfortable there and very safe.

Next, you notice a path leading from the meadow, and it goes down toward the beach. Follow that path.

At the end of the path you reach a beach. Pay attention to the feel of the sand and stones under your feet. You can move around on it very easily. As you walk on it, you may notice that on parts of the beach, the sand is very soft under your feet. In other areas where the beach is wet, the sand is firmer and harder. If you move toward the edge of the beach away from the water, you can feel the very firm earth surrounding the beach.

Stand wherever you feel most comfortable and experience the earth under your feet. As you do, think about the qualities that you associate with earth. You might notice that it has some qualities such as stability, strength, and firmness, associated with it. You might experience yourself becoming like that earth or experience the earth as part of you.

Imagine that you're drawing those qualities you associate with earth up through your feet. If you want those qualities for yourself at any time, just visualize these earth qualities flowing into you and surrounding you. It's like you feel yourself becoming the earth because it's part of you.

Now let that association go, and look ahead of you and notice the water. It may be a lake, river, ocean, or other body of water. Whatever type of water it is, you notice that it's flowing gently by you or in front of you. If you want, step into that water and experience yourself flowing with it, maybe even swimming in it like a fish.

Think about the qualities you associate with water. You may associate it with fluidity, with motion, with movement. The water may have a sense of calm or peacefulness about it. Or maybe you associate it with purification. Whatever qualities you think of, as you move in the water, experience those qualities becoming part of you. Be aware that you are those qualities. As you're feeling those qualities, flow with the water and feel it around you. As you do, you feel very comfortable and very safe. Whenever you want to have a quality or have more of a quality you associate with water, just visualize yourself moving in the water. Swim back to the beach where you started and let those associations with water go.

Step back on the beach again. Now look up and notice the air around you. As you do, you might feel the wind flowing by. Think about those qualities you associate with air. They may be qualities like lightness, enlightenment, a feeling of creativity, or a sense that your imagination or spirits are soaring.

Now experience yourself moving up into the wind and move with it like you are flying—perhaps see yourself like a bird and feel that quality of being lifted up. You feel very light and airy. You feel all those qualities you associate with the air.

As you notice these qualities, be aware that these qualities are within you, and you can call on them when you want them. If you feel like being light, airy, creative, or whatever qualities you associate with air, you can experience that. Continue to experience those qualities around you and within you, and know you can draw on those qualities as you need them, because they are all around you and part of you.

Bon Voyage

To get in touch with water, try to imagine yourself like a fish swimming through it. To experience fire, try staring into a fire in a campfire or fireplace. As you do, imagine yourself as one of the flames and feel yourself move with the flames.

Bon Voyage

To experience air, imagine yourself as a floating cloud or flying bird. To experience the earth, as you stand, focus on the solidity and firmness of the ground under your feet.

Let go of those associations and settle back down on the earth. Next, look to your left or right, and notice a small campfire or barbecue pit. You see a small fire there. Go over to it and gaze into the fire for a while. As you do, notice the flames moving up and down, and think about the qualities you associate with fire. Maybe you think of qualities like excitement, energy, assertiveness, aggressiveness, unpredictability.

If you feel comfortable doing so, imagine yourself stepping into those flames, feeling very safe and very comfortable. Then, if you wish, experience yourself being like the fire and feel that movement and energy of fire all around you. You're aware that those qualities are a part of you, too. You can call on these qualities to help you to be more assertive, aggressive, or have more energy. Now let that association with fire go, step away from the fire, and follow the path back to the meadow.

When you get back to the meadow, you notice a large tree and go over to that tree. As you stand or sit under it, you feel very relaxed and comfortable.

Now think about some question, problem, or conflict in your life that you want to ask about to get answers on what to do. As you listen for an answer, be aware that you can tap into the different energies of earth, air, fire, and water, which you have just experienced, for help. Think about how you can draw on these qualities or what qualities you can apply to your question, problem, or conflict. Then see yourself drawing on these energies and using them in this situation.

Meanwhile, as you draw on these energies, notice a screen in your mind's eye, which shows how you might use these qualities. Then, continue to observe that screen or, if you prefer, see yourself stepping into it and becoming part of that situation. As you observe or play out the scene, you can draw on these qualities, and notice how they help you find a solution or resolution, whether you are observing or are part of the scene. In the future, you can use this screen and draw on the qualities you need for help in any situation.

Watch the scene draw to a close and let the image go. Then, leave your tree by the meadow, knowing you can always return to all the places you have just visited. You can always go back to the meadow or the beach. And you can always draw on the elements experienced on your journeys in the future.

Now follow the path you came in on out of the meadow, and start counting backward from five to one. As you do you'll come back into the room. Five, four, more and more awake. Three, two, almost back now. One, you're back in the room. When you're ready, open your eyes.

Working with Your Middle-World Journey

Working with this kind of visualization can be very powerful, because it helps you feel a strong connection with the four elements and realize how they can help you.

For some people, getting in touch with and working with the elements helps to trigger an awareness that leads to greater integration and balance in life. The process is like seeing the four elements unified in nature, and then applying this model to your own sense of a more unified self.

A good analogy for how the process of working with the four elements contributes to personal integration and harmony comes from music. Think of a symphony, orchestra, or any type of musical group. The different notes, rhythms, tones, instruments, and voices blend together to create a whole. So the musical piece works well when you have the different contributions combining to create a rich, blended whole, where everything is in harmony, yet dynamic, because of the diverse elements that are joined together.

 **Bon Voyage**

One way to think of these elements is as different sounds and voices that you can integrate and blend to create a harmonious melody. Another way to think of them is as different colors or shapes you can bring together to create a balanced composition.

Putting the Elements to Work

You can use the images and associations you receive on a middle-world journey in two key ways:

◆ To help you decide what to do in a situation. For example, if thinking about the element air makes you feel lighter and less weighed down by stress or emotions, this might be a clue that you need to lighten up a little and stop worrying so much about things you can't change.

◆ To help you take action more effectively, by drawing these images and associations when you act. For example, suppose someone makes you mad by triggering your hot buttons. If you notice that this person is doing something to anger you, visualize an image or association that conveys peacefulness or calm to help you lighten up. For instance, see yourself surrounded by air and feel the air cooling you down.

 **Off the Path**

Should you notice feelings of discomfort associated with a particular element or place, when you're going somewhere on a journey (such as to the ocean, because you fear the high waves and sharks), don't go there unless you want to work through the issue causing the reaction. Instead, go someplace equivalent where you feel comfortable (such as a lake or river).

Resisting Resistance

Occasionally you may experience resistance to working with particular elements or going to places associated with certain elements. This resistance may suggest there is something in yourself you need to work with more to better balance the elements within you. To overcome such resistance, a good method is to gradually approach what you initially resist, so you go closer and closer each time, and feel more confident you can do whatever this is, as you approach. This process works much like any sensitizing method that is designed to help one overcome everyday fears, such as a fear of heights or fear of flying.

You can return to the middle world as many times as you want to work through the issues causing your insecurities or fears.

Elements of Everyday Life

The three major ways you can work with the elements in your life are to:

♦ Develop the qualities you need or desire.

♦ Ask questions and get answers.

♦ Better understand and relate to people with different qualities.

We'll investigate each of these ways in turn.

Develop the Qualities You Need

You can develop these qualities you need by visualizing yourself surrounded by or infusing the elements with those qualities into yourself. Then, use that extra dose of those qualities in a particular situation, such as at work or in a relationship. For example:

♦ Say you associate the earth with qualities like being more solid, secure, stable or strong, and you seek strength and stability, such as at work, where you have a lot of work to do. To reinforce your commitment to stick with it, which requires the qualities of perseverance and endurance, you might visualize or feel the earth around you to help get through the project.

♦ Or say you associate water with a sense of calm and flowing with things like a gently flowing river, and you're in a situation where things are in turmoil and you are facing new situations and aren't sure what to do. Visualizing water around you or seeing yourself pleasantly swimming in it might give you a sense of calm and help you adapt as things change.

♦ As for air, suppose you associate it with creativity or enlightenment and feel you could use more of these qualities in your life. You might imagine yourself in the air or experience yourself flying like a bird, which might lead you to feel more inspired to come up with new ideas.

♦ Finally, you might use your associations with fire to help you in a situation where you need to feel more energy or feel more spontaneous, aggressive, or assertive. For example, if you are going to a job interview and want to come across as very strong and dynamic, visualize the fire and draw it into yourself.

If you're not certain which qualities you need, try visualizing yourself sitting in the meadow under a tree or see a mental screen in your mind's eye to help you reflect on the situation. Then visualize the situation in your mind's eye or on the screen, and ask your question: "What qualities do I need to help me deal with this situation?" to help you figure out what qualities you need.

Ask Questions and Get Answers to Help Make Decisions

You can use the elements instead of a shamanic journey to find the answer to questions you may have about your life. Using the elements instead of a journey can be especially good for getting quick answers rather than taking a more extended journey to meet with your animal helpers or teachers and guides.

Bon Voyage

Try this experiment to see how you relate to different elements. Ask yourself the same question as you:

♦ Hold a rock and look at it.

♦ Gaze into the clouds.

♦ Look into a pool of water.

♦ Look into a fire.

Then notice and compare your answers. What differences were there? And which element did you feel most drawn to as you asked your questions? Which answer felt more accurate or comfortable for you?

Better Understand and Relate to Other People

By recognizing how you react to and associate with the elements, you can better understand how you relate to other people and even improve upon your relationships. Just as the elements each have their own unique qualities, people have different personality types, taking into consideration that they can reflect both positive and negative qualities associated with each element. You can use the four elements to characterize people into types. For instance:

♦ Some people are more earthlike, such as by being very down-to-earth and solid on the positive side. But on the negative side, they might be so solid that they become overly rigid.

◆ Some people are more like water, in that they flow with events and are more adaptable and flexible. But on the negative side, they might have a tendency to flow and shift too much, frequently changing course and not sticking to anything.

◆ Some people are more airlike, such as the person who is very creative and full of ideas. But on the negative side, that person might turn out to be very flighty and overly prone to unrealistic fantasies—sometimes called an "airhead" because of the strong associations with air.

◆ Some people are more fiery, such as people who are very energetic, dynamic, volatile, easily excitable, passionate, and emotional. On the positive side, they can be fun and exciting to be with; but if they express too much emotion, they can be quick to anger and erupt.

◆ And, of course, some people are a varying combination of these different characteristics.

Once you use the elements to characterize people, think about how you feel drawn to or more comfortable with people with certain qualities, just as you feel more comfortable with certain elements. You can work with the elements to develop qualities in yourself to better relate to those people.

Wise Ways

When you work with the elements to ask questions and get answers, you may find certain elements are more responsive to you, because you feel more linked to those elements. If so, you might continue to work with those elements, although it's helpful to develop closer connections with the other elements, to gain more balance, so you have a greater repertoire in dealing with situations, getting answers to questions, and better relating to people of all types.

Hey, Element, Can I Get Some Advice?

To ask the elements a particular question and to determine which elements you prefer to work with, return to the guided visualization at the beginning of this chapter. Start the visualization as described. Then, do the following:

1. When you are on the beach, first ask a question of the earth. Then, watch the answer form in the sand or in any energy you see rising up that may take human or animal form.

2. Turn to the water and ask that same question or another question. Then, watch for the answer to appear on the surface of the water, in a wave, or in any energy you see rising up that may take human or animal form.

3. Look up and ask the same or another question to the air. This time, your answer might come in the wind, which might say yes by moving faster or no by slowing down. It might move back and forth to tell you "maybe" or "not sure." Or maybe your answer might appear in the clouds, or you might observe a bird or spirit being appear with an answer for you.

4. Then, go to the campfire and ask the same or a different question to the fire. This time, the fire may say yes by rising up, no by quieting down, or move up and down to say "maybe" or "not sure." Or the answer may appear in the flames or you might see a spirit or being appear in the flames to give you your answer.

5. Return to the tree in the meadow, sit under it, and think about your answers. Choose which one you prefer or which is the most practical. Notice which answers seem least useful or which you might want to reject. And think about the element or elements you prefer to work with.

6. Finally, take the path back from the meadow to where you began and return to the everyday present.

Making Sense of Your Answers

Once you get your answers from a journey or visualization, it's time to interpret your answers, whether they came to you as clear statements telling you what to do or how to think about something or as symbols or images you have to interpret. You may have been able to do some interpretation in your visualization when you were sitting under the tree reflecting on what you experienced. However, often the message may still not be clear and you may have to think about the meanings you received in a conscious state.

Sometimes you can readily interpret these images and associations yourself. But at times, the message will be unclear to you but crystal clear to someone else. For example, try describing your experience to someone who knows how to work with symbols and images (such as a member of your shamanic group, if you have one), and ask

Bon Voyage

Although you can interpret your experience on your own, it can help to get an outside opinion from others. So when you work with the elements, try sharing your experiences with a partner or a group involved in exploring shamanism.

Off the Path

Are you getting the same messages or different ones from different elements? If the messages are same, that's a sign of certainty, because you're getting reinforcement from different sources. If different, that could mean the situation is unclear or uncertain, and you should look at the reasons more closely to decide what to do.

this person for feedback on what the message may mean. Of course, you are the ultimate interpreter in deciding what the images and associations mean to you and the value of the answers you get from different elements.

But I Didn't Ask a Question!

Generally, it will be clear what your message or images are in response to, because you will have asked the elements a specific question. But even if you don't clearly ask a question on a middle-world journey, you can still interpret whatever experience you have by relating that answer to your current concerns, although you might not be clear enough about them to put them into words.

One woman who participated in a workshop on middle-world journeys reported that she didn't ask any questions on her journey, but the elements gave her answers, anyway. As she reflected on these answers, she began to realize that she was, indeed, searching for the answer to the question: "What should I do to make my life more satisfying?" As she described her experience:

> My answer was that I should take little trips somewhere when I thought about the earth. Then, when I looked at the water, I thought of swimming. And at the fire, I thought of spending more time socially with people, since campfires make me think of people getting together around a fire and enjoying themselves. So when I put these experiences all together, I feel like I should lighten my burden and be freer. I guess the air told me that, too, since when I looked up in the air, I got a sense of lightness, of being less serious, in what I do.

Concluding that this information from the elements was good advice, she decided to make some changes in her life to feel freer, such as by thinking of ways to lighten up. For starters, she decided she should get out more and spend more time with people in a light, fun context.

Even if you're not sure you have a question or if you know you have one but aren't sure how to formulate it, you may still get useful answers. Always interpret any answers you get and, if it feels right, put what the answer tells you into practice, just as you would if you were clear about the question you asked in the first place.

Unmixing Mixed Messages

What if you get mixed or contradictory messages from different elements?

Sometimes this occurs because the situation is unclear and a number of possible outcomes are possible. In this case, knowing which elements are giving you which messages might help you understand the alternatives, such as when you wonder about whether to do something, and you get "no" and "yes" from different elements.

One woman received mixed messages when she asked whether a man she loved would love her back. She got yes from the water and earth, but no from the fire and air. At first, she was very confused. But when she thought about it, she recognized that she had long associated herself with the elements of water and earth, so she realized that her own elements were saying yes. Conversely, she identified the man with the other elements, fire and air, because he was a very creative, passionate person, and she recognized that his elements were saying no. As a result, she realized that she was doing a lot of wishful thinking in hoping that his resistances toward getting more involved in a relationship would come down. She realized she might have to accept the reality that the relationship might not happen, and she might have to learn to live with the currently limited relationship as it was.

Likewise, if you get contradictory messages, this could be because the situation you are asking about is unclear or because the people involved have different expectations or intentions. Thus, view these contradictory messages as a way to better understand an uncertain situation or recognize your own ambivalence. Then, you can use this understanding to help decide what to do to resolve the situation now or whether to wait until the situation becomes clearer and you are more certain about what to do.

Getting a Little Closer to the Truth

Working with the elements can also help you overcome any preconceptions you have about yourself or others, as you let go of the expectations and images of your conscious mind to explore with and listen to your unconscious or inner self.

For example, one woman, who thought of herself as a very practical, rational person, consciously identified with the traits she associated with earth and air, such as being very solid, stable, and intellectual in her outlook. But when she took the journey to work with the elements, she found herself much more in tune with the water and fire and felt that meant she needed to release her emotions and passions more. She realized she had been holding these back, since they conflicted with her outer image of herself as a highly logical, productive professional person.

Similarly, you may gain such discoveries about yourself in working with the elements, since often our preconceptions about ourselves shape our outer or conscious self. These preconceptions often come from being brought up to believe you should be a certain kind of person. But if you let your intuitive unconscious part go, you may discover and connect with this other side of yourself, so you experience a greater sense of balance—it's like you are more closely unifying the inner and outer parts of you.

You can achieve more balance by working closely with the elements to draw on their different qualities. Then, you can further develop the qualities you need more of, such as seeking a balance in the polarities of earth (representing solidity and strength) and air (representing lightness and creativity) or the polarities of water (representing calmness and flow) and fire (representing excitement and aggression). As you work with the elements, you will become more aware of these different qualities and associations and can apply them in your life to achieve a greater balance.

The Least You Need to Know

◆ One way to work with the middle world is to work with the elements of nature—commonly described as earth, air, fire, and water.

◆ You can combine journeying to work with the elements by going on trips into the natural environment.

◆ The different elements have different associations, such as earth with solidity, water with flexibility, air with creativity, and air with lightness, that you can use in understanding other people and developing different personality traits in yourself.

◆ An advantage of working with all of the elements is you can use them to develop increased balance and integration in yourself.

Chapter 20

Traveling in Twos: Journeying with a Partner

In This Chapter

- ◆ Why two is sometimes better than one
- ◆ Working with strangers
- ◆ Seeking answers for a partner
- ◆ Working together to interpret a message

Surprisingly, it's often easier to go on a journey to seek information for someone else than for yourself. That's because the question you ask for another person doesn't pertain to your life, so you won't have a preconceived expectation or hope of what the answer might be. Also, your ego isn't involved in the outcome, as it might be when you ask your own question. Thus, you'll be better prepared to let your unconscious go and trust whatever information you receive.

In this chapter, you'll find out how to journey for someone else to find answers for them, and vice versa. Not only taking such journeys a fun way to socialize, but the information your partner obtains might help you solve problems you can't resolve on your own. After all, you've got the benefit of another opinion.

Partner Up for Improved Power

Partnering up for a journey is a great way to hone your divination skills, particularly if you work with someone you don't know very well. When you work with a partner, you both go on a journey in which you ask questions and seek answers for each other. After you each get your answers, you check with each other about how suitable those answers seem to be.

> **Wise Ways**
>
> You'll find that you get more confident and more accurate the more you seek answers for others.

Later, you can use this process to get information for friends or associates—the person doesn't even have to be present to be the subject of your journey, as long as you picture him or her in your mind as you go.

Generally, when you seek feedback from the other person about your answers, you'll find the information is quite accurate. Just as with most things, the more you practice getting information for others, the better at it you'll be.

Hey Stranger, Wanna Take a Trip with Me?

Even if you don't know the person you're seeking an answer for, the information you get might be right on target. This is because your higher or unconscious self can tune in to the person's energy or essence on a symbolic level. As you practice finding answers for people, you'll become even more accurate at it.

Fortunately, your practice in getting help for others can improve your ability to get help for yourself when you need it, because it gives you experience in letting go of your conscious control.

The following exercise shows you how to work with a partner to seek answers to each other's questions.

When you ask a question for yourself, look for the answer from your power animals, guides, or teachers in two forms:

- What they tell you
- Where they take you and what you see

Feel free to go to whichever world seems most appropriate to answer the question your partner has, just you seek answers to your own questions in different places.

Working with a partner also is ideal for journeying in a natural environment, where one person goes on the journey, while the other observes the area to make sure everything is comfortable and safe for the person taking the journey. Then, as necessary, should potential distractions or problems arise, the partner can tell the person taking the journey to return to everyday consciousness.

To start the journey, you and your partner should each choose a question you want the other to answer for you and tell the other person what this question is. Then, you each take a journey into whatever world makes the most sense to seek an answer to that question from the beings you meet. You may encounter a being you've worked with before or meet another one. Either way, ask it the question, and then listen to it and/or observe what happens. When you come back, you and your partner should discuss your different experiences and how they relate to the questions you each asked.

Use the same basic approach for entering the lower, upper, or middle world, as described in Chapters 18 and 19, except now ask your question for your partner rather than for yourself.

Bon Voyage

A good way to develop your ability to gain accurate information about yourself or others on a journey is to work with a partner. Then, you go on journeys to ask questions for each other, share the result, and reflect on the information your partner brings back for you.

Reflect On Your Answers

Discussing your experiences with your partner and reflecting on the feedback you get is an important tool for recognizing and improving your accuracy in taking a journey to gain information. A few examples from a workshop I taught on seeking help from the lower world illustrate how to make the most of a divination journey with a partner.

For the most part, the workshop participants reported on their journeys by describing them and telling their partner what they saw. But a few drew pictures to show what they observed, because they found it difficult to put the experience or the images they saw in words. You can similarly use either—or both— approaches in sharing your journey experiences to divine answers for each other.

For instance, when two women partnered up to divine information for each other, one woman asked her partner to seek the answer to the question: "How can I break through my money blocks and gain more prosperity?" By a "money block," she meant she felt she had a psychological barrier to earning money, such as a fear of success or a feeling she didn't deserve to earn more money

Bon Voyage

When you share the details of your journey with your partner, you can describe it in words or draw the images you saw in your experience. Then, you each react to this description or image, as you consider how it relates to the original question you asked.

than she did. After her partner journeyed to the lower world, she reported back the following experience:

> The animal I met told me that [my partner] needed to value her contribution and know that she was making a contribution. Then, it took me to this African village, and I saw her there making this beautiful ornate basket. Then, she told me that she had baskets all over her house. It was like she was feeling very needed, very important here, since she was making these baskets that the villagers could use … And I felt that was her answer: that she needed to find something that she loved to do to fulfill a need, so she would feel she was making a contribution. Then she would feel it was okay to receive money in compensation, and she would receive it, too.

The woman who sought the answer to the question about her financial life related to the experience her partner reported, because she felt she had been doing work she didn't really like to do. She really did want to shift into a job or lifestyle where she could express her more creative side, so the other woman's journey helped to confirm her own yearnings and leanings. As she stated:

> I feel the journey [of the other woman] was very good, because I feel I do want to make a contribution that involves my aesthetic part. I'd like to find something I can create where I will fulfill a need for somebody, maybe even doing art therapy.

Thus, while the two women had met for the first time in this workshop and hadn't gotten to know each other before their journeys, one woman had picked up very accurate and helpful information for the other.

The second woman sought the answer to the following question: "How can I resolve my own money question and find my right work?" Here, her issue related to her feelings of tension around earning a lot of money and not enjoying the work. So she had a very different concern about money, and the answer her partner found for her was quite different, suggesting a return to a simpler, less hectic life. The response seemed to be exactly what she wanted. Here's how her partner described the journey:

> **Wise Ways**
>
> Though you might not know the partner you're journeying for very well, you can get very accurate and helpful insights from your unconscious. In fact, working with a partner you don't know very well can help you improve your accuracy.

I visualized her on a farm, and I saw her working on the farm and feeling very relaxed. She had jeans on and seemed right at home. She had horses and even a nice young man there with her, and she was right into it. It was the perfect setting for her.

At first I worried how is she going to make a living doing this, knowing that the farmer makes less. But then, I tried to stop getting analytical, and I saw that she was very, very happy. It seemed like all her money problems were taken care of. The farm seemed so peaceful, and it seemed to be encircled by a pale-shade of gold.

The woman whose question it was responded favorably to the description her partner brought back from the lower world, saying that she found the farm image very appealing:

> The journey was very interesting, because I've been thinking about how I would like to get out to the sea or to the country. Ever since I was little, I wanted to live on a farm. I wanted horses. As I was growing up, it's like I was fixated by the horses in the country and the land. I can't quite see making money there, but I've always had that strong desire to get back to the land.
>
> But then, maybe I wouldn't need to make money. Maybe that would somehow be taken care of if I did get back to the land. Maybe there might be things I could do, and it would all fall into place. Because I love horses, and my guiding picture has long been to live on a farm with a man.

Off the Path

In some cases, your experiences might not immediately make sense to you or your partner, particularly when you're new to journeying. No matter how confusing what you see or hear seems to be, work on interpreting the meanings in light of the question you asked. Be receptive to whatever words or images come to you on your journey.

Spirit Beings Have Common Sense, Too!

In other cases, your or your partner's reports or interpretations of these reports may seem to be simply common-sense suggestions. They may not seem like you would need to travel to the spirit world to obtain this information. For example, one woman in my workshop was seeking information about how to feel younger. Her partner journeyed to the lower world to seek an answer, and reported back that the power animals she visited said her partner should think about or do more youthful things to feel young. The woman seeking advice was disappointed, saying, "Oh, this is really accepted wisdom. I've heard people tell me this before in different ways."

Bon Voyage

Even if your insights seem like ordinary common sense, they're still important bits of knowledge. They can remind you to pay more attention to something you need to focus on now.

However, a journey isn't any less valid just because it reports back common-sense suggestions. Such suggestions might be quite appropriate for the person at this time, and thereby serve as a reminder to pay attention to something which can provide the help he or she needs.

One Question, Two Answers

Sometimes when you journey to learn answers for a partner or yourself, the spirits may not only answer the question you asked, but another related question, which the person wants to know, too—maybe even more than the question they asked.

Don't worry if this happens; rather, consider the additional answer to be a bonus, like getting bumped up to first class on an international flight!

You Can Borrow My Symbol, But I Want It Back

It's also important to realize that the information you receive about the other person may come to you through your own symbols and meanings. You can interpret what these personal images mean to you to learn what they are saying about the other person.

For example, one woman in my workshop saw images of clothes when she journeyed to seek an answer for her partner. It turned out that the woman who took the journey worked as a fashion model and spent a great deal of time around clothes, so clothes were important symbols of work to her, even though her partner had little interest in clothes.

> **Wise Ways**
>
> Is an image you or your partner gets for you on a journey especially meaningful for you? Does it have a strong resonance or feeling for you? If the answer is yes to either question, consider how you might work with that image in the future to guide you in daily life.

When the model went about interpreting the clothes in light of her partner's question—"What should my priorities be now over the next year?"—she was tempted to say that her partner should focus on work. After giving it some thought, though, she realized that although clothes were a powerful symbol of work for her, they probably meant something completely different to her partner, who had little interest in clothes. Here's how she interpreted her journey:

When you asked me about your priorities, I saw my little dog, and then he led me to a closet, where I saw a lot of formal wear. At first I was thinking, gosh, I spend all day around clothes, I see all these clothes. But then I saw these other images of pants stacked on top of each other making a design, which looked like paper clips linked together. Then, when I connected that image with the types of clothes I saw—mostly formal wear and sun dresses, I surmised that maybe you should think about putting more of your priorities toward relationships.

And the other woman agreed, replying:

Yes, I really can relate to that, because I know I'm spending time working quite a lot, and I thought I should think more about having relationships. This is a part of myself I need to develop more of in my life.

As these examples indicate, the understandings you get from these journeys can be very accurate, even if you don't know the partner for whom you are seeking answers and even if you have worked with this process for the first time. That's because your unconscious or higher self triggered through journeying has a great deal of inner wisdom. It can pick up information for others on a symbolic or metaphorical level, which when interpreted contains important truths.

You can develop your abilities to see more and more accurately and better interpret the symbols you receive, as you increasingly work with the process.

Brainstorm with Your Partner

Another way to use the messages and images you get on a journey—whether for someone else or for yourself—is to view them as a starting point for either of you to make associations. Even if either of you don't initially see any connections between the messages and the question, give the experience the benefit of the doubt and use it as a trigger to suggest other meanings. To do so, use the experience as a focus for brainstorming, and ask questions like: "What does that mean to you? How can you relate to that?"

Even if the messages or images don't seem to mean much at first, as you think about them, they will suggest other things to think about and will help you break through the barriers of your logical mind to gain insight from your unconscious.

Develop Particularly Strong Experiences

If someone goes to a place in their journey and brings back especially insightful information for you, try going there in your own journey to get even more information.

That's what one woman did in a workshop after her partner traveled through a series of rooms to answer the woman's question: "Where will I find my soul mate?" On the journey, the woman's partner obtained some very accurate information. Later, by visiting the rooms herself, the woman seeking information about her soul mate sought additional information about him and was able to develop her own images and associations that could guide her.

You can use the same journeying processes, which you use to get answers for others to find them for yourself. For example, go to the same place you went before and meet the same teacher or teachers that gave you helpful answers for the other person. And if someone else has gone on a journey to get information for you, consider incorporating the images they saw or the places they went in your own journey.

Finding Fellow Travelers

Just as you can work with a partner, you can similarly work in a small group or as part of a larger group event or program. For example, many shamanic drumming groups have sprung up around the country, and a number of leaders, locally and nationally, have programs on shamanic journeying techniques and shamanic healing practices. Other options include finding a teacher, coach, mentor, or other leader you can work with personally to expand your skills

Appendix C lists a selection of shamanic groups, programs, nationally known leaders, Internet sites, and related organizations and programs. You can use it to help you find other shamanic paths.

The Least You Need to Know

◆ Working with a partner to find an answer can help you break through preconceived ideas that are preventing you from finding the truth.

◆ You don't have to know someone well in order to obtain an answer for them on a journey.

◆ Sometimes you might use symbols that are powerful for you in order to interpret the answer to your partner's question.

◆ Don't hesitate to return to a place on your own, if your partner found good information for you there.

◆ Consider working with a shamanic group to maximize your experience.

Chapter 21

Modern Shamanism and the Future

In This Chapter

- ◆ The varieties of modern shamanism
- ◆ Why some traditional shamans are angry
- ◆ The future of shamanism

Modern shamanism has come a long way from its origins as a traditional system of healing, counseling, and wisdom. Classically, shamans have been the tribal or village wisemen or wisewomen who have not only healed and counseled individuals suffering from illness, relationship problems, or just feeling blue, but have sometimes acted to help the whole tribe or village.

As described in the first part of the book, shamanism has undergone major transformations. It has become part of an increasingly urban and global world, gained growing interest and acceptance from medical practitioners and psychologists, and has been adopted and adapted by the New Age and self-help movement. Although traditional shamanism may continue in isolated pockets of the world—such as in the far reaches of rural Siberia and back country of the Amazon in Ecuador and Peru—mostly shamanism today has become a blend of many elements that are growing and further blending and morphing in multiple ways.

The Five Branches of Shamanism Today

The result is essentially five branches of modern shamanism, which are intertwined with one another. Though I've listed the branches chronologically as they developed, the later types of shamanism are growing faster than their traditional counterparts:

- ◆ Traditional shamanism in rural isolated communities. Increasingly, it is being impacted by modern influences, such as tourism and economic development.

- ◆ The use of traditional shamanic practices for healing and counseling in the developing world and in ethnic communities in the U.S. and other developed countries. Here shamans are occasionally full-time practitioners, though usually they combine shamanic practices with other everyday occupations to work with individual clients or to conduct group healing sessions.

- ◆ The incorporation of elements of shamanism, such as using traditional medicine herbs, into modern medical practices. Many medical practitioners are also becoming more sensitive to the alternate perspectives and belief systems used by shamans which contribute to healing. These medical practitioners are adapting their explanations of illness and treatments to incorporate these ideas from traditional healing systems, such as the Mexican notion of hot and cold illnesses, which are treated by shamans in different ways.

- ◆ The use of shamanistic journeying techniques in modern psychological practice to guide individuals to journey deep into their own psyche. Patients may go on the same kind of journey to contact spirits that others might take for personal and professional development. But they are guided to do deeper inner discovery and analysis by trained psychologists and psychiatrists.

- ◆ The adoption of shamanic journeying and healing methods by the New Age, self-help, and personal development movements. Here practitioners have used a mix of traditions, ranging from the fairly pure adaptation of traditional techniques to a mélange of techniques from varied sources. Such shamanic techniques are mixed together, often in combination with other New Age methods, many drawn from humanistic and transpersonal psychology. Here it's sometimes hard to sort out what is really traditional shamanism and what is self-development or holistic healing techniques under another label.

Likely Future Developments

What is likely to happen next? Probably, given the increasing pace of globalization and change, more *syncretism*, or intermingling of approaches. In turn, traditional shamans or modern shamans practicing traditional shamanic techniques are likely to increasingly incorporate other counseling and healing practice in their own work, especially with the arrival of tourists and government efforts to bring economic development and moderniza-tion. Moreover, when traditional shamanic practices are advertised on the Internet, such as the Siberian shaman who promotes her family's shamanic tradition online, can the modernization of most forms of shamanism be far behind?

Even the books that are about using traditional shamanic practices today have this *syn-cretistic* flavor. For instance, in *Magical Passes*, Carlos Castaneda, who gained fame through his ongoing conversations with don Juan, reportedly a Yaqui Indian from Sonora, Mexico, describes a series of bodily movements which don Juan calls "magical passes."

The book looks very much like many other New Age exercise, fitness, and yoga books. The text is accompanied by a series of pictures of a man and woman in tights performing various movements, with comments about how don Juan encouraged deep breathing and the impor-tance of focused intent. Yet, exactly the same type of advice is offered by many other books about fitness and self-development. Thus, this book illustrates still another example of how the bound-aries between shamanism and modern fitness and health techniques have become inextricably tan-gled and blurred.

> **Shaman Says**
>
> **Syncretism** is the com-bining and merging of different elements or factors together; a combination of one from the many. If something is character-ized by this blending together it might be considered **syncretistic** or **syncretic**.

Or take a recent book about using shamanic practices to heal yourself and others, described as using a traditional "energy medicine" by Alberto Villoldo in his book *Shaman, Healer, Sage*. In his prologue he describes how he learned about these techniques in the Amazon and Andean Highlands of Peru with an old Inca guide, Antonio Morales (Villoldo, 2000, 1). The book is devoted to describing how to use the "Luminous Energy Field" which surrounds the physical body like a magnetic field organizes iron filings to line up in the same direction (Villoldo, 2000, 42). Yet, as Villoldo describes this magnetic field, it sounds very much like the aura, which has been widely written about by New Age writers.

And Villoldo's discussion of the *chakras* sounds very similar to the version of Hindu and other Eastern traditions taught in several New Age workshops. The difference here is that Villoldo is linking this knowledge to what he calls "a nearly forgotten Inka practice for healing through the Luminous Energy Field" (Villoldo, 2000, 1). Whether this knowledge is or is not, in fact, from the ancient Incas, the discussion of techniques sounds much like what one might learn about in many New Age workshops on healing.

So where is the shamanism in these modern practices dubbed "shamanism"? Where is the New Age? Again, they seem almost completely blended together, while the practitioners are using new terms and definitions and claiming ancient links. They are essentially repackaging as shamanism modern-day teachings about health, wellness, and holistic healing that have been circulating since the 1970s during the heyday of Esalen. That's when the humanistic and transpersonal movements in psychology swept from the West Coast through much of America, and now they seem to have swept up shamanism, too.

Wise Ways

Some of the major ways in which modern shamanism has changed from traditional shamanism and is likely to keep changing are these:

◆ More syncretism based on the blending of many influences

◆ More individual use for self-development and self-healing

◆ More secularization, in taking shamanism out of a religious or spiritual context, so it is turned into a self-help practice, used for pragmatic ends.

◆ More use for personal and professional purposes

It's All About Me

Still another major development is the increasing individualizing of the shamanic tradition. At one time, shamanism was a practice which one went into much like one might become a doctor, priest, counselor, or other kind of helper and healer—to help individual patients, groups of patients, or the whole community. But increasingly, shamanism has become used more for one's personal development and healing.

Although shamanism is still used for helping others, such as by modern shamans serving special communities or when you take a journey to help a partner, (see Chapter 20), you have to be careful about assisting others without the appropriate training. In fact, there are many cautions in the popular literature and in popular workshops about doing this until you are fully trained to take on a medical or therapeutic role toward someone else. So mostly, people today are participating in shamanic programs or getting books about shamanism to help or heal themselves. In turn, this reflects the personal development/self-help thrust of the New Age and humanistic/transpersonal psychology movements. There's nothing inherently wrong with this individualistic development, but it further demonstrates how traditional shamanism is changing.

Where's the Sacred?

Another big change is that traditional shamanism has become increasingly secularized, as it has been adopted by a more secularized, modern culture. At one time, shamanism was closely integrated with the community's religious and spiritual traditions, and often shamans made contact with sacred spirits, whether of ancestors, deities, or spirits of nature. Also, many of the shamans using traditional practices to help clients in developing countries or ethnic communities in developed countries have incorporated religious imagery into their healing rituals, such as the way the shamans in Peru and Ecuador use images of Catholic saints or other deities on their mesas.

But in modern workshops, a sense of the sacred or spiritual is often missing, as people make contact with animals and other beings that have meaning only to them. As a result, unless someone is already immersed in a religious tradition and encounters religious leaders from that tradition, the teachers and guides are often everyday people or celebrities. For instance, in workshops I have led, people have reported getting quite good assistance from such teachers as Hugh Hefner and Donald or Ivana Trump. Again, this isn't to criticize this development; rather, it is intended to point out how shamanism has and continues to change.

The Practical Shaman

Finally, there has been an increasing use of shamanism for more practical, pragmatic concerns, from goal setting to problem solving to resolving conflict to bringing the troops together in the workplace. Traditionally, shamanism was sometimes used to help heal relationships and make people feel better, but that was an offshoot of treating physical symptoms that resulted from interpersonal or community problems. Now shamanic techniques are often used exclusively for personal and professional success and for improving relationships and motivation in the workplace.

But Is It Shamanism?

With all these changes in shamanism in response to changing times, and with all this blending of shamanism with other practices, the big question becomes: Is it still really shamanism? Or has it become something else, in which shamanic techniques have been so changed and blended that they have become something entirely new.

Sure, if the changes or combination of techniques works for you, that's fine. But is it shamanism?

I'm not really sure myself anymore, and I throw the question out there to stimulate thinking about the future of modern shamanism. Yes, it certainly still is shamanism when shamans in isolated communities and modern healers and counselors use

> **Wise Ways**
>
> As shamanism has been transformed, is it still shamanism? What makes it shamanism and not something else? These are questions that are being debated, and different people are defining shamanism differently, as it continually undergoes more change.

shamanic practices in developing countries or ethnic communities. But in the other instances, such as when medical practitioners, psychologists, and New Age leaders and followers blend shamanism with other traditions, maybe the changing and blending will become so great that, at best, we can say they involve shamanic roots. Or maybe what's emerging is a new, modern form of shamanism that is becoming an umbrella to absorb a mix of other traditions into its shamanic core.

Why Some Traditional Shamans or Groups Are Mad

Unfortunately, as modern shamanism has developed, borrowing techniques from traditional sources or changing and adapting them, some traditional shamans or the members of groups with a shamanic tradition have become angered. These people feel that Westerners from the United States and other developed countries are taking their information and material culture, often without permission or adequate compensation.

People from traditional cultures also object to others from outside their culture taking or using shamanic materials out of context. They argue that doing so causes the objects to lose their sacred character, particularly when the items are used for personal gain rather than to benefit others, which is their traditional use. Other people simply feel like they've been taken advantage of or exploited. They are particularly put out by Westerners who spread their teachings and practices, and they feel a loss of control or ownership over what were once special or sacred teachings limited to those who felt a calling or spent years learning how to become masters of shamanic techniques.

Off the Path

Some members of ethnic or tribal groups even accuse their own members of selling out when they use their group affiliation to popularize shamanic techniques. A number of anthropologists, including Marlene Dobkin de Rios, have objected to the growing popularity of what is called "shamanic tourism," where tour guides hire shamans to give tourists ayahuasca sessions. You'll even find some of these advertised on the web. The danger is untrained individuals representing themselves as shamans and bad trips from the ayahuasca. One result can be psychological damage from the visions individuals see and a lack of proper counseling and support when an individual does have a disturbing experience.

I saw some examples of this anger myself in the mid-1990s when I attended a shamanic conference in San Rafael. One of the presenters had adopted a Native-American sounding name, let's call him Eagle Father, and was leading people on vision quests. A few participants at the conference raised some concerns, while nationally there was a growing uproar from a number of Native Americans from different tribal groups, including pickets at some of his workshops and articles about his misuse of their culture in the Native American press. They protested that Eagle Father was appropriating their culture and was appealing to people to go on these vision quests based on their thinking he was a Native American. Plus these protesters objected to anyone, even a Native American, drawing on their traditional ways to turn them into commercial products and share them with ordinary tourists.

Eventually, Eagle Father did back down and change his name, and he stopped saying that he was leading Native American vision quests. But getting him to back down was just one of many cultural battles over the popularization of traditional shamanic techniques that took place and are still taking place. Furthermore, it's not just the Native Americans whose cultures have been appropriated by others. Groups around the world have seen their traditional shamanic practices misused and popularized.

A related concern is that by secularizing and popularizing these techniques and turning them into tools for self-development rather than helping and counseling others, modern practitioners have trivialized or undervalued the true meaning of shamanism, at least as it once was practiced.

Who's Really a Shaman?

This concern over devaluing traditional shamanism is particularly heightened by the spreading use of the term "shamanism" to refer to these changed and blended practices and by individuals simply calling themselves "shamans," although they have little training or knowledge. At one time the term was used to refer to one or a small number of people in a community who were regarded as having a specialized kind of wisdom and healing ability. But as a growing number of untrained or inadequately trained people start calling themselves "shamans"—particularly in the case of lay practitioners in the New Age movement, it undermines the status of "shaman" for others who have been trained.

Unfortunately, the problem is that anyone can call themselves a "shaman" or claim to be practicing "shamanism," because there is no formal or official licensing agency for shamans, no organized body that can indicate that a particular person is qualified or not. About the closest the field comes to an imprimatur, or official sanction, is that some groups, like the Foundation of Shamanic Studies, offer a training program for teachers or counselors leading to a certificate. But beyond that, it is often unclear what someone means when they call themselves a shaman.

> **Wise Ways**
>
> There is a lot of controversy over who should and shouldn't call themselves a shaman. You can avoid angering traditional shamans by simply saying that you use shamanic practices and concepts. Don't claim to be a shaman yourself.

There are no simple solutions to any of these problems, and shamanism's boundaries will probably continue to blur as globalization is increasingly connecting us all in a modern, high-tech world. Perhaps the best approach is simply to be aware of the issues and concerns. Instead of calling yourself a shaman or saying that you practice shamanism, instead think of what you are doing as drawing on shamanic practices and concepts. In other words, leave wholesale shamanism for the traditional shamans.

So bon voyage. Have a good journey, wherever your shamanic travels take you.

The Least You Need to Know

- Some traditional shamans are unhappy about the popularization of their traditional shamanic techniques.
- As it is practiced today, shamanism can be broken down into several different categories.
- Rather than call yourself a shaman, think of yourself as drawing upon shamanic practices.

Speak Like a Shaman: A Glossary

alpha state   A state of consciousness characterized by longer, slower brain waves, called alpha waves. It is associated with a state of relaxation.

alpha waves   These are the longer, slower brain waves that are associated with an alpha state of consciousness.

altered state of consciousness   A nonordinary state of consciousness that can range from states of light meditation and hypnosis to states of trance.

alternative healing   The use of nonbiomedical healing practices, such as using herbs, touch, and spiritual methods to heal.

animal helper   The animals that shamans call on for assistance when they are seeking knowledge or attempting to do a healing. Another term for these helpers are power animals.

animism   The notion that all things in the world have a spiritual essence or spirit, including all animals, plants, landforms, bodies of water, and elements.

archetypes   Deeply held symbolic images that are common in all cultures, such as the image of the "hero" or "mother. They are part of the collective unconscious, which is why they are common to all cultures and are such powerful, deeply held images.

ASC   The abbreviation for altered state of consciousness, which is frequently used by professionals in the field of psychology and other academics.

aura   This is the electromagnetic energy field surrounding the body, which you can learn to see through various techniques, such as in doing psychic work or working with shamanism.

ayahuasca   A brew, called by various names, such as "yage" or "yaje" in Columbia and "ayahuasca" in Ecuador and Peru, which is made from the vine *Banisteriopsis Caapi.* Sections of this vine are boiled with the leaves of a number of other plants, and drinking the brew produces a hallucinogenic effect.

behaviorism   A psychological approach founded by John B. Watson in the early 1920s that is based on measuring, predicting, and controlling behavior. Behaviorists have been particularly interested in examining the relationship between how a stimulus produces a particular response.

behaviorists or behavioral psychologists   Psychologists who study behaviorism, whereby they seek to measure, predict, and control behavior.

Beltane   The halfway point between the spring equinox and summer solstice, which is celebrated on May 1 as May Day.

beta state   A brain-wave state characterized by shorter more frequent brain waves called beta waves on a biofeedback machine. It is associated with a state of everyday alert consciousness.

beta waves   The shorter more frequent brain waves that characterize the beta state of consciousness.

biomedicine   The practice of ordinary, modern medicine based on a biological understanding of disease.

Candlemas   The halfway point between the winter solstice and spring equinox, around February 1, when the light and energy is growing stronger. It is also referred to as the Festival of Bridget.

chakras   The main energy centers that exist in the body from the base of the spine to the top of the head. In the Hindu and most New Age systems there are seven of these at the base of the spine (root chakras), groin (sexual or navel chakras), abdomen (solar plexus chakras), heart, throat, third eye between the eyes (third eye or brow chakras), and at the top of the head (crown chakras).

chants   Repeated words or sounds. They are used in shamanic practice to help produce a trancelike effect or carry the shaman on a journey.

cognitive psychology   A relatively new field of psychology that studies mental processes based on the model that the mind functions much like a computer.

cognitive psychologist   A psychologist who studies cognitive psychology.

collective unconscious   A pool of group thought composed of instincts and archetypes that are shared by all humans, though individuals may not be aware of this influence. It is like the unconscious of the group.

core shamanism   An approach to shamanism, originally developed by Michael Harner, in which certain key elements have been drawn from traditional, indigenous shamanism around the world and developed into a modern-day spiritual practice.

cross-quarters   The four half-way points between the four quarters—Candlemas, Beltane, Lammas, and Samhain. It is a term used by those in the modern Pagan and Wiccan traditions, and others.

curandero   A spiritual healer or healing shaman in Latin America.

developmental wounds   A term that psychologists use to refer to the psychological injuries that an infant or child receives in growing up, generally due to problems in the care received from a parent, such as abuse or neglect. The process is called **developmental wounding.**

divination journey   A journey to get information, such as an answer to a question. You can use it to get information for others as well as for yourself.

dowsing   The technique for sensing and working with the energies of a place by using a dowsing rod to pick up the various positive and negative energies of the earth and sense their power.

dowsing rod   The stick or metal rod used in dowsing to sense the intensity and positive or negative qualities of energy in a place.

drumming circle   A group of people who get together to participate in drumming, usually to induce a shamanic journey for one or more participants in the group.

elements of nature   The four major forces or ways of classifying nature: earth, air, fire, and water.

epistemology   Area of philosophy is devoted to investigating the nature and origins of knowledge. It seeks to understand how we know what we know.

Esalen   A major center for personal growth and spiritual learning that grew up in Big Sur, California, in the late 1960s and flourished especially in the 1970s and 1980s and still offers workshops today. Many programs in transpersonal psychology, as well as shamanism, have been held here.

ethnomedicine   The term used to refer to the approach to treating disease based on the beliefs and practices of the members of a particular culture.

ethnopsychiatrists   Psychiatrists or anthropologists with a psychiatric background who study ethnic groups.

fall equinox The time when the sun and earth are once again perfectly aligned, so that the days and nights are the same length. This occurs around October 21 or 22.

fantasy-prone A term used by psychologists to describe a trait that some individuals have of being better able to use their imagination to engage in fantasy. Such individuals may also be more likely to engage in this activity more often.

Feng Shui An ancient Chinese technique that involves sensing the natural forces associated with a place and using these as a guide as to where to build a house, how to build it, and what direction it should face.

folk medicine The term used by anthropologists and biomedical practitioners to refer to the treatments for illnesses as they are defined by the people in the community, rather than by the biomedical practitioners who are part of the medical mainstream.

guide(s) The beings who assist shamans. They may take many forms—from real people to ancestors to angels to guardian spirits. They are also called spiritual guides and teachers.

hallucinogens or **hallucinogenic drugs** Drugs that have the ability to produce an altered state of consciousness characterized by visions. Some examples of these drugs are ayahuasca, mescaline, peyote, LSD, and psilocybin.

healing journey A journey to seek an infusion of healing energy or to gain insights about how to treat a particular problem for yourself or others (but seek specialized training in healing to do this properly).

healing plants Plants that have healing properties in their leaves, roots, or bark, which you can access by chewing them, swallowing them, boiling them as a tea, using them as a salve, or burning them to release beneficial odors.

herbalist A healing practitioner who specializes in plants and their medicinal properties. Some shamans may also be herbalists, and others may refer patients to herbalists or work with them in treating the patient.

higher world The spiritual realm that is located in the air or above the earth, also referred to as the upper world. It is often where teachers, spiritual guides, and spiritual helpers reside.

holistic healing An approach to healing that emphasizes healing the whole person, rather than only treating specific symptoms. It is a type of alternative healing.

Homo sapiens The early humans, who date back to about 125,000 to 200,000 years ago, and are characterized by a growing brain size and an ability to make better tools from stone and bone.

Homo sapiens The first modern humans who emerged about 35,000 to 40,000 years ago, who are characterized by having fluent speech, expert toolmaking, and the expression of human creativity through art and religion such as reflected in the early cave and rock art. These are the first humans who are biologically identical to ourselves and have the same intellectual abililities.

humanistic psychology   A movement within the field of psychology that focuses on developing the whole person; the emphasis is on personal development and growth rather than on treating problems. It grew up in the 1960s and 1970s and was founded by Abraham Maslow.

humanistic psychologist   A psychologist who practices humanistic psychology.

hynogogic state   A light groggy or drifting state which you are in while you are falling asleep. It is a state between waking consciousness and sleep.

hypnopompic state   A light groggy or drifting state which you are in when you just wake up and have not fully achieved your waking consciousness.

inipi ceremony   A Lakota ceremony, also called the "stone-people-lodge" ceremony, that involves purifying oneself by sweating, singing and praying.

initiation   A ceremony in which one is introduced into new learnings or a new stage in life. It is often used to refer to the passage from one stage to another in learning the secrets or techniques of a religious, spiritual, or magical system or of a secret society.

journey   The trip a shaman or individual engaged in shamanic practices takes when he or she goes into an altered state of consciousness or trance in order to communicate with or contact the spirits in the spirit world. It is often referred to as a shamanic journey.

kachinas   The spirits of the Hopi Indians, which include spirits of the ancestors, corn, clouds, and other aspects of nature who reside in the sacred mountains, lakes, and canyons. They take human form and are imagined as having a variety of characters, costumes, and functions, reflected in the popular kachina dolls, used in Hopi ceremonies.

karma   The law of cause and effect that originally derives from Hindu religious thought. According to this doctrine, if you engage in negative actions, they will eventually trigger a negative harmful effect. Conversely, if you engage in positive actions, they will lead to positive, favorable consequences. This doctrine is actually quite a bit more complicated than this, but this is the gist of it.

kiva   An underground or partly underground room used by the Hopi and other Pueblo Indians for ceremonies or council meetings. People who follow many New Age philosophies also use kivas.

Lammas   The halfway point between the summer solstice and fall equinox, around August 1. It is also called August Eve.

ley lines   The lines, also called meridians, which are believed to crisscross the earth, much like acupuncture lines radiate through the human body. These are believed to be lines of power, and the intersection of these lines is thought to be especially powerful, so places of power are often located along these lines or at these intersections.

lower world   The spiritual realm that is located underground or below the earth. It is also referred to the as underworld. It is often the area where power animals are found in addition to being on earth.

lucid dreaming   A kind of dreaming in which a part of you remains alert and aware that you are dreaming.

mandala   A design in which the shapes and colors radiate out from the center, which becomes like the bulls eye of a target for directing one's focus. The design derives from Oriental art and religion, where it represents the universe.

meditation   The practice of engaging in a focused and relaxed concentration, where you are in a receptive mode, letting in whatever thoughts and perceptions come to you.

meridians   The lines, also called ley lines, which are believed to crisscross the earth, much like acupuncture lines radiate through the human body. These are believed to be lines of power, and the intersection of these lines is thought to be especially powerful, so places of power are often located along these lines or at these intersections.

mesa   The altar on which the shamans place their power objects. While the word means "table" in Spanish, the term is used in this special sense by shamans.

middle world   Another term for the planet Earth, as distinguished from the upper world and the lower world.

Mide Society   A society among the Objiway Indians that is focused on gaining a knowledge of herbs and plant medicine.

midewiwin ceremony   A key ceremony of the Mide Society in which new shamans are initiated. Over an 8-day period, a structured trance is used to give the initiate the vision of the society through cosmological stories, sacred chants, herbal lore, and other shamanic methods.

Neolithic Revolution   The time, starting about 10,000 years ago, when humans developed agriculture, which enabled people to grow and store food and settle down. They also began to domesticate animals and to form villages, some of which expanded into the beginnings of cities.

neo-shamanism   The term used, primarily by academics, to refer to the adoption of shamanic practices by modern-day Westerners, who are mainly using these practices for personal self-development and self-healing. The term also includes the many new teachers, workshop and seminar leaders, and group organizers who have developed modern versions of traditional shamanism.

New Age   The popular term used to refer to the growth of a movement or community of people, primarily modern-day Westerners, who are using a mix of practices drawn from humanistic and transpersonal psychology and teachings on success and self-fulfillment, for personal self-development and self-healing. The term also includes the teachers, workshop and seminar leaders, and group organizers who have developed modern versions of traditional shamanism. The term has been embraced by publishers and the media, although the use of the term has been fading, as many New Age activities are becoming incorporated into the mainstream today.

nonordinary reality   The reality that exists outside of our beyond the everyday or mundane world. It is the world where the spirits live and the world which a practitioner of shamanism contacts and communicates with when taking a shamanic journey. Often a shaman fully enters this world in order to meet with these spirits.

peyote   A hallucinatory drug made from the buttons of a cactus that can be found in Mexico and the Southwest. It has been used by a number of Native American groups in their ceremonies. Among other groups, it is used by the Huichol Indians, who have an annual pilgrimage to collect peyote.

power animal   The animals that shamans call on for assistance when they are seeking knowledge or attempting to do a healing. This is also called an animal helper.

power object   An object considered to have a spiritual force or energy that shamans can use in a ritual. Also called a sacred object.

power place   A place that is considered especially powerful; often it is a place where very powerful or sacred spirits reside. Sometimes a power place is also called a sacred place, although some locations may simply be considered places of power.

power spot   A particular location, often found at a power place, which is considered to be especially powerful because of a concentration of energy there.

prayer   A expression or thought of hope or supplication, which may be conveyed in a song or chant, or expressed internally in one's thoughts. The term refers to both the underlying intent of appealing to a higher power and to the way that appeal is expressed in words through a song, chant, statement, or in thoughts.

priest   A religious figure who is part of the religious establishment and gets his or her position and authority through training and the performance of established rituals and rites. A priest is not to be confused with a shaman, who gains his or her position and power from being able to go into an altered state and communicate directly with the spirits.

psychonavigation   A controlled journeying, in which you are fully in charge and in control of the experience.

quarters The four major divisions of the year—the winter solstice, spring equinox, summer solstice, and fall equinox. It is a term used by those in the modern Pagan and Wiccan traditions, among others.

REMs The rapid eye movements that occur when an individual is dreaming. They are found in sleeping animals, too.

Rorschach test A psychological test for interpreting the meaning of images seen in an inkblot.

sacred object *See* power object.

sacred place *See* power place.

Samhain The halfway point between the fall equinox and winter solstice, which occurs on October 31. It is sometimes called Halloween, although Halloween is a separate holiday with roots in the pagan celebration of Samhain. It is sometimes described as the time when the veil between the worlds of spirit and everyday reality are considered the thinnest, and it is thought of as the beginning of the New Year in the Pagan and Wiccan traditions,

San Pedro A type of cactus that is the source of the power hallucinogen used by many shamans in South America, including Peru.

seeing The process of deep looking that the shaman or practitioner of shamanism engages in, so that he or she can look into a nonordinary reality and truly see and understand what is there in this other world.

seguro A glass jar which the shamans use for collecting the magical herbs used in their rituals.

shaman A religious or healing practitioner who practices shamanism.

shamanic The characteristics of someone who is using the techniques of shamanism or the qualities of beliefs or techniques that make them part of shamanism. This term is also used to refer to techniques and practices that are "shamanistic," meaning that they are like shamanism or adapted from it, but the person using them isn't actually a shaman.

shamanic journey The trip a shaman takes when he or she goes into an altered state of consciousness or trance in order to communicate with or contact the spirits in the spirit world.

shamanism A deeply rooted traditional system for healing and solving personal and community problems, in which a religious or healing practitioner contacts the spirits for wisdom and advice, usually through going into a trance or other altered state of consciousness.

shamanistic   A term that refers to techniques or practices that are like shamanism or adapted from it, but that aren't actually shamanism; however this term is often used as an alternate term for shamanic.

shamanizing   A term sometimes used to refer to the activities of the shaman when he or she is engaging in the religious or healing practices of shamanism.

somatization   A term used by medical practitioners to refer to the process of expressing a mental or emotional condition as a disturbed bodily function. It is especially common in nonindustrialized societies where people don't recognize mental illnesses or deal with psychological problems as medical conditions.

sorcerer   An individual who works with negative, destructive forces and uses them to harm others, such as by causing them to suffer an illness, lose their job or loved one, or even die.

sorcery   The use of negative and destructive forces to harm others, such as by causing them to fall ill, experience bad fortune, or die.

soul travel   A term that is sometimes used to refer to going on a shamanic journey or journeying, though it is most commonly used by groups with a particular religious or spiritual orientation; it is not as common as the other terms: shamanic journey or journeying.

Soyal ceremony   A ceremony among the Ojibwa Indians which begins the ceremonial year, when the seed corn is blessed during the winter solstice in the hopes it will bring a good harvest in the coming year. It is led by the Soyal chief and priests.

spirit   A being or entity who has no physical or bodily form and is believed to exist in the spirit world. An essential element of shamanism is being able to contact and communicate with these spirit beings.

spirit world   The world of spirit beings, who exist in a nonordinary reality.

spiritual guide(s)   Beings who assist shamans and which may take many forms. They are also called guides and teachers.

spiritual healing   A type of healing in which the healer draws on the help of the spirits, deities, or God to heal a patient. Traditionally, shamans have called on individual spirits or a group of spirits, while many modern practitioners call on the help of God.

spring equinox   The time when the sun and earth are perfectly aligned, so that the days and nights are the same length. This occurs around March 21 or 22.

summer solstice   The height of summer, when the days are the longest and the nights are shortest—generally around June 21 or 22. It is sometimes called the Festival of Midsummer.

syncretism   The combining and merging of different elements or factors together; a combination of one from the many.

teacher(s)   Beings who assist shamans and who may take many forms. They are also called guides or spiritual guides.

theta state   A state of consciousness characterized by even longer, slower waves called theta waves. It is associated with a very deep state of relaxation or trance or with sleeping.

theta waves   The long, slow waves that are associated with the theta state of consciousness.

traditional   When referring to shamanism, the practices and beliefs that are rooted in the past, when people lived in tribal societies or small rural or village communities. It also, refers to the continued practice today of these past techniques, usually by healers living in communities in developing countries or in ethnic communities in developed countries, though sometimes modern Western practitioners may claim they are using traditional methods.

trance   An altered state of consciousness in which an individual loses touch with everyday reality and enters another world of seeing. Often individuals in this state may feel they can see and communicate with spirits, and they may or may not remember what they have experienced in this alternate state of conscious.

transpersonal psychology   A movement in the field of psychology that is based on bringing in a spiritual or religious dimension to personal development and growth. Besides focusing on the whole person, it uses techniques of spiritual healing and explores alternate states of consciousness as a source of promoting wellness and resolving psychological problems.

transpersonal psychologist   A psychologist who is involved in the practice of transpersonal psychology.

trigger or **triggering device**   An indicator, such as a sound or motion, you can use to cause you to do something. You might use it in shamanism to stop a difficult experience or redirect your thinking from negative to positive thoughts.

Tunkashila   The Lakota name for the Creator.

underworld   The spiritual realm that is located underground or below the earth. It is also referred to as the **lower world**. It is often the area where power animals are found in addition to being on earth.

upper world   The spiritual realm that is located in the air or above the earth. It is also referred to as the **higher world**. It is often the area where teachers, spiritual guides, and spiritual helpers are found in addition to being on earth.

Urban Revolution   The third major change in the history of humanity. It began in about 3000 B.C.E., initially in the river valleys where the agricultural revolution first began, and then independently developed or spread to other areas around the world. It marks the beginning of civilization as we know it today.

visionary plants   Plants that have hallucinogenic properties, such as ayahuasca, peyote, datura, and psychedelic mushrooms.

waking dream   Another term for lucid dreaming, in which you are both awake and dreaming.

Wheel of the Year   The movement of the year through the four seasons.

wiiwuchuim ceremony   The annual ceremony of the Hopi in which the young men who have reached the age of puberty are initiated into manhood.

winter solstice   The height of winter, when the days are shortest and the nights are longest— it generally falls on December 21 or 22.

world tree   A tree that Mayans and other groups believe stands at the center of the cosmos and connects the lower, middle, and upper worlds. This concept is called by various names and takes different forms in different traditions.

More Mind Journeys: Further Reading

There are hundreds of books and articles on shamanism. These divide roughly into the three major types of shamanism—traditional shamanic practices, many written by anthropologists and other academics; modern shamanism, as practiced by traditional healers; and New Age shamanism, primarily for personal development and self-healing. There are also many accounts of personal journeys to meet with traditional shamans by both academics and popular authors. Other recent books are by psychologists, psychiatrists, therapists, counselors, and medical doctors seeking to incorporate shamanic practices into modern psychology or holistic medical treatments.

I have tried to group writings on shamanism into these major categories. Because there are so many books and articles, this is a selective bibliography. Mostly, I have included books, though I have noted a few especially interesting articles. All of the books cited in the chapters are included here, along with many others. Mostly I picked these books from the top 100 or so bestsellers at Amazon.com and Barnesandnoble.com, plus recommendations from researchers studying shamanism today. For more listings, you can go to the many websites described in the Appendix C.

Traditional Shamanism and Historical Sources

Alekseev, Nikolai, "Shamans and Their Religious Practices," originally published in 1987, in Marjorie Mandelstam Balzer, ed. *Shamanic Worlds: Rituals and Lore of Siberia and Central Asia*. Armonk, New York: 1997.

Baldic, Julian. *Animal and Shaman: Ancient Religions of Central Asia*. New York: New York University Press, 2000.

Balzer, Marjorie Mandelstam, ed. *Shamanic Worlds: Rituals and Lore of Siberia and Central Asia*. Armonk, New York: 1997.

————. *Shamanism: Soviet Studies of Traditional Religion in Siberia and Central Asia*. Armonk, New York, 1990.

Basilov, Vladimir, "Chosen by the Spirits," originally published in 1984, in Marjorie Mandelstam Balzer, ed. *Shamanic Worlds: Rituals and Lore of Siberia and Central Asia*. Armonk, New York: 1997.

Bastien, Julien. *Drum and Stethescope: Integrating Ethnomedicine and Biomedicine in Bolivia*. Salt Lake City: University of Utah Press, 1992.

Brown, Peter. *Understanding and Applying Medical Anthropology*. Mountain View, California: Mayfield Publishing Company, 1998.

Burkert, Walter. "Shamans, Caves, and the Master of Animals" in Jeremy Narby and Francis Huxley, *Shamans Through Time: 500 Years on the Path of Knowledge, 223-226*. From his book: *Structure and History in Greek Mythology and Ritual* (Berkeley: University of California Press, 1979).

Coe, Michael D. *The Maya*. New York: Thames and Hudson, 1993.

Dioszegi, Vilmos. *Tracing Shamans in Siberia: The Story of an Ethnographical Research Expedition*. New York: Humanities Press, 1960.

Drury, Nevill. *The Shaman and the Magician: Journey Between the Worlds*. Boston: Routledge & Kegan Paul, 1982.

Eliade, Mircea. *Shamanism*. Princeton, NJ: Princeton University Press, 1972. (Originally published in French in 1951).

Erowid, "Ayahuasca & DMT Snuffs: Plant Species & Terminology," from *The Vaults of Erowid: Plants & Drugs, Mind & Spirit, Freedom & Law, Arts & Sciences*, article on website: www.eorwid.org/chemicals/ayahuasca/ayahuasca_terminology.shtml.

Espinoza, Luis. *Chamalu: The Shamanic Way of the Heart: Traditional Teachings from the Andes*. Rochester, Vermont: Inner Traditions, 1995.

Fagan, Brian M. *People of the Earth: An Introduction to World Prehistory, ninth edition*. New York: Longman, 1998.

Feinstein, David, and Stanley Krippner. *The Mythic Path*. New York: J. P. Tarcher, 1997.

Friedl, David A., and Linda Schele and Joy Parker. *Maya Cosmos: Three Thousand Years on the Shaman's Path*. New York: William Morrow, 1995.

Gillete, Douglas. *The Shaman's Secret: The Lost Resurrection Teachings of the Ancient Maya*. New York: Bantam Books, 1998.

Grim, John A. *The Shaman: Patterns of Religious Healing Among the Ojibway Indians*. Norman, Oklahoma: University of Oklahoma Press, 1990.

Halifax, Joan. *Shamanic Voices: A Survey of Visionary Narratives*. New York: Viking Penguin, 1994.

Harner, Michael, ed. *Hallucinogens and Shamanism*. New York: Oxford University Press, 1990.

———. *The Way of the Shaman*. San Francisco: Harper San Francisco, 1990.

Heinze, Ruth-Inge, ed., *The Nature and Function of Rituals: Fire from Heaven*. Westport, Connecticut: Bergin & Garvey, 2000.

——— *Proceedings of the 1st-19th International Conferences on the Study of Shamanism and Alternate Modes of Healing*, Berkeley, California: Independent Scholars of Asia, 1984-2002.

——— *Shamans of the Twentieth Century*. New York: Irvington Publishers, 1991.

Humphrey, Caroline. *Shamans and Elders: Experience, Knowledge and Power Among the Daur Mongols*. New York: Oxford University Press, 1996.

Huxley, Francis, "Drugs," in Arthur C. Lehmann, and James Myers, eds. *Magic, Witchcraft, and Religion*. Mountain View, California: Mayfield Publishing, 1985.

Jakobsen, Merete Demant. *Shamanism: Traditional and Contemporary Approaches to the Mastery of Spirits and Healing*. New York: Berghann Books, 1999.

Joralemon, Donald. *Exploring Medical Anthropology*. Boston: Allyn and Bacon, 1999.

Katz, Richard. *Boiling Energy*. Cambridge, Massachusetts: Harvard University Press, 1984.

Kenin-Lopsan, Mongush B., "Tuvan Shamanic Folklore," originally published in 1987, in Marjorie Mandelstam Balzer, ed. *Shamanic Worlds: Rituals and Lore of Siberia and Central Asia*. Armonk, New York: 1997, 110-152.

Konner, Melvin, "Transcendental Medication," in Peter J Brown, *Understanding and Applying Medical Anthropology*. Mountain View, California: Mayfield Publishing Company, 1998.

Krippner, Stanley, "The Epistemology and Technologies of Shamanic Studies of Consciousness," Unpublished paper, 2001.

——— "Integrating Individual and Community Wellness: The Shamanic Approach to Healing, Parts I and II," in *Alternative and Complementary Therapies*, August & October, 1997.

——— "The Shaman as Healer and Psychotherapist," in *Voices*: Winter, 1982.

Larsen, Stephen. *The Shaman's Doorway: Opening Imagination to Power and Myth*. Rochester, Vermont: Inner Traditions, 1998.

Larsen, Stephen, et. al. *Forest of Visions: Ayahuasca, Amazonian Spirituality, and the Santo Daime Tradition*. Rochester, Vermont: Park Street Press, 1999.

Lehmann, Arthur C., and James E. Myers, eds. *Magic, Witchcraft, and Religion: An Anthropological Study of the Supernatural*. Mountain View, California: Mayfield Publishing Company, 1985.

Lewis, I.M. *Ecstatic Religion: A Study of Shamanism and Spirit*. New York: Routledge, 1989.

Lyon, William S. *Encyclopedia of Native American Shamanism: Sacred Ceremonies of North America*. Santa Barbara, California: ABC-CLIO Incorporated, 1998.

Malotki, Ekkehart and Ken Gary. *Hopi Stories of Witchcraft, Shamanism, and Magic*. Lincoln, Nebraska: University of Nebraska Press, 2001.

Marks, Tracy. *"Elemental: The Four Elements: From Ancient Greek Science and Philosophy to Ancient Sites Poetry."* Article on website: www.geocities.com/tmartiac/thalassa/elemental.htm.

McClenon, James M. *Wondrous Healing: Shamanism, Human Evolution, and the Origin of Religion.* De Kalb, Illinois: Northern Illinois University Press, 2001.

Meyerhoff, Barbara. *Peyote Hunt: The Sacred Journey to the Huichol Indians.* Ithaca: Cornell University Press, 1974.

Narby, Jeremy, and Francis Huxley, ed. *Shamans Through Time: 500 Years on the Path to Knowledge.* New York: Putnam Publishing, 2001.

Perkins, John. *Spirit of the Shuar: Wisdom from the Last Unconquered People of the Amazon.* Rochester, Vermont: Inner Traditions, 2001.

———. *The World Is As You Dream It: Shamanic Teachings from the Amazon & Andes.* Rochester, Vermont: Inner Traditions, 1994.

Pinker, Steven. *How the Mind Works.* New York: W. W. Norton, 1997.

Ripinsky-Naxon, Michael. *The Nature of Shamanism: Substance and Function of a Religious Metaphor.* Albany, New York: State University of New York Press, 1994.

Sabina, Maria. *Maria Sabina: Her Life and Chants.* Santa Barbara: Ross-Erikson Publishers, 1981.

Sandner, Donald F., "Navaho Indian Medicine and Medicine Men," in Sobel, D., *Ways of Health.* New York: Harcourt, Brace and Jovanovich, 1979.

———. *Navaho Symbols of Healing.* New York: Harcourt Brace, 1979.

Schaefer, Stacy B. *People of the Peyote: Huichol Indian History, Religion, and Survival.* Albuquerque, New Mexico: University of New Mexico Press, 1998.

Swan, James A., ed. *The Power of Place: Sacred Ground in Natural and Human Environments.* Wheaton, Illinois: Quest Books, *1991.*

Taussig, Michael T. *Shamanism, Colonialism, and the Wild Man: A Study in Terror and Healing.* Chicago: University of Chicago Press, 1991.

Thomas, David Hurst. *Archaeology, Third Edition.* New York: Harcourt Brace College Publishers, 1998.

Turner, Victor. "Religious Specialists," in Arthur C. Lehmann, and James E. Myers, eds. *Magic, Witchcraft, and Religion: An Anthropological Study of the Supernatural.* Mountain View, California: Mayfield Publishing Company, 1997, 78-85.

Underhill, Ruth M. *Red Man's Religion*. Chicago: University of Chicago Press, 1965.

Vitebsky, Piers. *Shamanism*. Norman, Oklahoma: University of Oklahoma Press, 2001.

Wilcox, Joan Parisi. *Keepers of the Ancient Knowledge: The Mystical World of the Q'ero Indians of Peru*. New York: HarperCollins, 1999.

Winkelman, M. *Shamanism: The Neural Ecology of Consciousness and Healing*. Westport, Connecticut: Bergin & Garvey, 2000.

———. "Altered States of Consciousness and Religious Behavior," in S. Glazier, ed. *Anthropology of Religion: A Handbook of Method and Theory*. Westport, Connecticut: Greenwood, 1997.

———. *Shamans, Priests and Witches: A Cross-Cultural Study of Magic-Religious Practitioners*. Tempe, Arizona: Anthropological Research Papers, Arizona State University, 1992.

Modern Shamanism by Traditional Healers

Bend, Cynthia, and Tayja Wiger. *Birth of a Modern Shaman*. St. Paul: Llewellyn, 1987.

Black Elk, Wallace. *Black Elk: The Sacred Ways of a Lakota*. San Francisco: Harper San Francisco, 1991.

Calvo, Cesar, and Kenneth A. Symington, (translator). *The Three Halves of Ino Moxo: Teachings of the Wizard of the Upper Amazon*. Rochester, Vermont: Inner Traditions, 1995.

Freke, Timothy. *Shamanic Wisdomkeepers: Shamanism in the Modern World*. Boston: Standard Publishing, 2000.

Joralemon, Donald, and Douglas Sharon. *Sorcery and Shamanism: Curanderos and Clients in Northern Peru*. Salt Lake City, Utah: University of Utah Press, 1993.

Kalweit, Holger, and Michael H. Kohn, (translator). *Shamans, Healers, and Medicine Men*. Boston, Massachusetts: Shambhala Publications, 2000.

Lake-Thom, Bobby. *Call of the Great Spirit: The Shamanic Life and Teachings of Medicine Grizzly-Bear*. Rochester, Vermont: Bear & Company/Inner Traditions, 2001.

Lamb, Bruce. *Wizard of the Upper Amazon: The Story of Manuel Cordova-Rios*. Berkeley, California: North Atlantic Books, 1974.

Lunda, Luis E. *Ayahuasca Visions: The Religious Iconography of a Peruvian Shaman*. Berkeley, California: North Atlantic Books, 1999.

Nicholson, Shirley. *Shamanism: An Expanded View of Reality*. Wheaton, Illinois: Theosophical Publishing House, 1987.

Sharon, Douglas. *Wizard of the Four Winds: A Shaman's Story*. New York: The Free Press, 1978.

Thomas, Nicholas, and Caroline Humphrey. *Shamanism, History, and the State*. Ann Arbor, Michigan: University of Michigan Press, 1996.

Popular Books About Shamans

By or About Carlos Castaneda

Castaneda, Carlos. *The Wheel of Time: The Shamans of Ancient Mexico, Their Thoughts About Life, Death and the Universe*. New York: Washington Square Press, 2001.

———. *Magical Passes: The Practical Wisdom of the Shamans of Ancient Mexico*. New York: HarperCollins, 1999.

———. *The Eagle's Gift*. New York: Pocket Books, 1982.

———. *The Fire from Within*. New York: Simon & Schuster, 1984.

———. *Journey to Ixtlan: The Lessons of Don Juan*. New York: Touchstone, 1972.

———. *The Second Ring of Power*. New York: Washington Square Press, 1977.

———. *A Separate Reality: Further Conversations with Don Juan*. New York: Pocket Books, 1972.

———. *Tales of Power*. Washington Square Press, 1974.

De Mille, Richard. *The Don Juan Papers: Further Castaneda Controversies*. Belmont, California: Wadsworth Publishing, 1990.

———. *Castaneda's Journey: The Power of Allegory*. New York: iUniverse.com, 2000.

By Lynn Andrews

Andrews, Lynn. *Tree of Dreams: A Spirit Woman's Vision of Transition and Change*. New York: J. P. Tarcher, 2001.

New Age Shamanism

Arrien, Angeles. *The Four-Fold Way: Walking the Paths of the Warrior, Teacher, Healer, and Visionary.* New York: HarperCollins, 1992.

Berggen, Karen A. *Circle of Shamans: Healing Through Ecstasy, Rhythm, and Myth.* Rochester, Vermont: Inner Traditions, 1998.

Blain, Jenny. *Nine Worlds of Seid Magic: Ecstasy and Neo-Shamanism in North-European Paganism.* New York: Routledge, 2001.

Conway, D. J. *Advanced Celtic Shamanism.* Santa Cruz, California: Cross Press, 2000.

Cowan, Tom. *Fire in the Head: Shamanism and the Celtic Spirit.* New York: HarperCollins, 1993.

———. *Shamanism: As a Spiritual Practice for Daily Life.* San Cruz, California: Crossing Press, 1996.

Goodman, Felicitas D., *Where the Spirits Ride the Wind: Trance Journeys and Other Ecstatic Experiences.* Bloomington, Indiana: Indiana University Press, 1990.

Ingerman, Sandra, and Michael Harner. *Soul Retrieval: Mending the Fragmented Self.* San Francisco: Harper San Francisco, 1991.

———. *Welcome Home: Following Your Soul's Journey Home.* New York, HarperCollins, 1993.

King, Serge Kahili. *Instant Healing: Mastering the Way of the Hawaiian Shaman Using Words, Images, Touch, and Energy.* Los Angeles: Renaissance Books, 2000.

———. *Urban Shaman.* New York: Simon & Schuster, 1990.

———. *Kahuna Healing: Holistic Health and Healing Practices of Polynesia.* Wheaton, Illinois: Theosophical Publishing House, 1983.

Lawson, David. *So You Want to Be a Shaman: A Creative and Practice Guide to the History, Wisdom and Rituals.* Berkeley, California: Conari Press, 1996.

Meadows, Kenneth. *Shamanic Experience: A Practical Guide to Contemporary Shamanism.* New York: HarperCollins, 1998.

Mindell, Arnold. *The Shaman's Body: A New Shamanism for Transforming Health, Relationships, and Community*. San Francisco: Harper San Francisco, 1993.

Penczak, Christopher. *City Magick: Urban Rituals, Spells, and Shamanism*. Boston: Samuel Weiser, 2001.

Roth, Gabrielle, and John Loudon. *Maps to Ecstasy: A Healing Journey for the Untamed Spirit*. Novato, California: New World Library, 1998.

Ryan, Robert E. *The Strong Eye of Shamanism: A Journey into the Caves of Consciousness*. Rochester, Vermont: Inner Traditions, 1999.

Rysdyk, Evelyn C. *Modern Shamanic Living: New Explorations of an Ancient Path*. Boston: Samuel Weiser, 1999.

Sanchez, Victor, and Sonya Moore, and Robert Nelson. *The Teachings of Don Carlos: Practical Applications of the Works of Carlos Castaneda, Vol.1*. Rochester, Vermont: Bear & Company/Inner Traditions, 1995.

———. *The Teachings of Don Carlos: Practical Applications of the Works of Carlos Castaneda, Vol.2*. Rochester, Vermont: Bear & Company/Inner Traditions, 1997.

Sarangerel. *Chosen by the Spirits: Following Your Shamanic Calling*. Rochester, Vermont: Inner Traditions, 2001.

Scott, Gini Graham. *Secrets of the Shaman*. Tempe, Arizona: New Falcon Press, 1993.

———. *Shaman Warrior*. Tempe, Arizona: New Falcon Press, 1989.

———. *Shamanism for Everyone*. Atglen, Pennsylvania: Schiffer Publishing, 1988.

———. *Shamanism and Personal Mastery: Using Symbols, Rituals, and Talismans to Activate the Powers Within You*. Minneapolis: Paragon House, 1991.

———. *Mind Power: Picture Your Way to Success*. Paramus, New Jersey: Prentice Hall, 1987.

———. *The Empowered Mind: How to Harness the Creative Force within You*. Paramus, New Jersey: Prentice Hall, 1994.

Scully, Nicki. *Power Animal Meditations: Shamanic Journeys with Your Spirit Allies*. Rochester, Vermont: Bear & Company/Inner Traditions, 2001.

Stevens, Jose L., and Lena S. Stevens *Secrets of Shamanism*. New York: William Morrow, 1988.

Thorsson, Edred. *Northern Magic: Rune Mysteries and Shamanism*. St. Paul, Minnesota: Llewellyn Publications, 1998.

Wolfe, Amber. *In the Shadow of the Shaman: Connecting with Self, Nature, and Spirit*. St. Paul, Minnesota: Llewellyn Publications, 1989.

Personal Journeys to Meet Traditional Shamans and Healers

Jacobs, Don Trent. *Primal Awareness: A True Story of Survival, Transformation and Awakening with the Raramuri Shamans of Mexico*. Rochester, Vermont: Inner Traditions, 1998.

Perry, Foster. *The Violet Forest: Shamanic Journeys in the Amazon*. Rochester, Vermont: Bear & Company/Inner Traditions, 1998.

Pinkson, Tom Soloway. *The Flowers of Wiricuta: A Journey to Shamanic Power with the Huichol Indians of Mexico*. Rochester, Vermont: Inner Traditions, 1997.

Prechtel, Martin. *Long Life, Honey in the Heart: A Story of Initiation from the Shores of a Mayan Lake*. New York: J. P. Tarcher, 1999.

Prechtel, Martin, and Robert Bly. *Secrets of the Talking Jaguar: Memoirs from the Living Heart of a Mayan Village*. New York: J.P. Tarcher, 1999.

Odigan, Sarangerel, and Julie Ann Stewart. *Riding Windhorses: A Journey into the Heart of Mongolian Shamanism*. Rochester, Vermont: Inner Traditions, 2000.

Villoldo, Alberto. *Shaman, Healer, Sage: How to Heal Yourself and Others with the Energy Medicine of the Americas*. New York: Harmony Books, 2000.

Villoldo, Alberto, and Stanley Krippner. *Healing States: A Journey into the World of Spiritual Healing and Shamanism*. New York: Simon & Schuster, 1987.

Villoldo, Alberto, and Erik Jendresen. *Dance of the Four Winds: Secrets of the Inca Medicine Wheel*. Rochester, Vermont: Inner Traditions, 1994.

———. *Island of the Sun: Mastering the Inca Medicine Wheel*. Rochester, Vermont: Inner Traditions, 1994.

Wesselman, Hank. *Medicinemaker: Mystic Encounters on the Shaman's Path*. New York: Bantam Books, 1999.

Psychology and Shamanism

Achterberg, Jeanne. *Imagery in Healing: Shamanism and Modern Medicine*. Boston: Shambhala Publications, 2002 (originally published in 1985).

Gagan, Jeannette Marie. *Journeying: Where Shamanism and Psychology Meet*. Santa Fe, New Mexico: Rio Chama Publications, 1998.

Sandner, Donald F., and Steve Wong, eds. *The Sacred Heritage: The Influence of Shamanism on Analytical Psychology*. New York: Routledge, 1996.

Smith, C. Michael. *Jung and Shamanism in Dialogue: Retrieving the Soul/Retrieving the Sacred*. Mahwah, New Jersey: Paulist Press, 1997.

Winkelman, Michael. *Shamanism: The Neural Ecology of Consciousness and Healing*. Westport, Connecticut: Greenwood Publishing, 2000.

Other Books of Interest

Levy, Mark. *Technicians of Ecstasy: Shamanism and the Modern Artist*. Norfolk, Connecticut: Bramble Books, 1993.

Wolf, Fred Alan. *The Eagle's Quest: A Physicist's Search for Truth in the Heart of the Shamanic World*. New York: Touchstone, 1992.

Shamanism Sites and Sitings: Groups, Organizations, Practitioners, and Websites

There are so many groups, organizations, and websites devoted to different types of shamanism, along with a myriad of shamanic practitioners, that it is impossible to provide a complete resource guide. Also, as interest grows in shamanism, and the field is marked by change, it can be hard to keep up, particularly with new developments. And many shamanic listings are local ones.

Accordingly, this is a partial listing of the groups and individuals I am most familiar with and some drawn from a list of shamanic practitioners and alternative healing centers provided by Stanley Krippner (designated with a *). Most of these groups or individuals have a national presence or reputation. Plus, I have included a selection of websites that provide a range of information and/or have links to many other shamanic sites—like a portal into the world of shamanism—much like shamanism provides a doorway or tunnel into another world of consciousness. You'll also find information on shamanism, photos, and links at my own website at www.giniscott.com/shamanism.

Groups

Foundation for Shamanic Studies
P.O. Box 1939
Mill Valley, CA 94942
415-380-8282
info@shamanicstudies.com
This is the group founded by Michael Harner; one of the largest and most established organizations, since the 1970s.

American Holistic Health Association*
P.O. Box 7402
Anaheim, CA 92817
714-779-6152

Monterey Institute for the Study of the Alternative Healing Arts*
400 Virgin Avenue
Monterey, CA 93940
408-646-8019

Spiritual Emergence Network*
SEN at CIIS
1453 Mission Street
San Francisco, CA 94103
415-648-2610
SEN@CIIS.edu.

Institue for Contemporary Shamanic Studies
238 Davenport Road
Box 393
Toronto, Ontario
Canada M5R 1J6
416-603-4912; Fax: 416-603-4913
jump@icss.org
www.icss.org/home.htm

Universal Holistic Healers Association*
P.O. Box 2022
Mt. Pleasant, CA 29465
803-849-1529

Ayahuasca Spirit Quest
U.S. Coordinator
Box 1704
Boulder, CO 80306-1704
www.biopark.org/sprtqu3.html

Individuals

Merry Browne, shamanic healer*
4550 Gills Court
Louisville, KY 40219

Kenneth S. Cohen, shamanic counselor*
P.O. Box 234
Nederland, CO 80466
303-258-0941

Leslie Gray, Ph.D., shamanic counselor*
26 Allen Street
San Francisco, CA 94109
415-928-4954

Graywolf, shamanic counselor*
1480 Dutcher Creek Road
Grants Pass, OR 97527
503-476-0492.

Fawn Journeyhawk-Bender, shamanic healer*
Carson Indian Colony
461 Oneida Street
Carson City, NV 89703

Ralph Metzner
Green Earth Foundation
P.O. Box 327
El Verano, CA 95433
metzner@svn.net
www.rmetzner-greenearth.org

Janet Piedilato, Ph.D., shamanic healer and herbalist*
600 Forest Avenue
Staten Island, NY 10310
718-447-7200

Alberto Villoldo, Ph.D.
The Four Winds Society, Inc.
P.O. Box 680675
Park City, UT 84068-0685
435-647-5988; Fax: 435-647-5905
fourwinds@thefourwinds.com

Sarangerel
SiberianShaman
2634 West River Parkway
Minneapolis, MN 55406
888-645-0542
lydia@siberianshaman.com

Brant Secunda, shamanic healer*
Dance of the Deer Foundation
P.O. Box 699
Soquel, CA 95073
831-475-9560; Fax: 831-475-1860
shamam@shaminism.com
www.shamanism.com

Phillip Scott, shamanic healer*
#216, 310 Channing Way
San Rafael, CA 94903
415-479-5002

Thunderbird Starwoman, shamanic healer*
37 Clark Road
Cummington, MA 01026
413-634-0262

Publications

Shaman's Drum: A Journal of Experiential Shamanism & Spiritual Healing
P.O. Box 97
Ashland, OR 97520
sdrm@mind.net

Websites

Buryat shamanism
www.geocities.com/gulamta

Shamanism and Earth Mythology
www.r.metzner-greenearth.org/myth_orginfo.html

Native Web: Resources for Indigenous Cultures Around the World
www.nativeweb.org

Shaman Speaks: Shamanism Groups, Organizations, and Foundations
members.tripod.com/~shamanspeaks/instr_grps.html

Shaman Links
www.geocities.com/athens/troy/7922/SHAMLINK.html

Shamanic Organization
home.att.net/~pichowsky2/Lighthouse/g05ag4.html

Native American and Shamanic Healing—Spiritual Connections
www.newagedirectory.com/native.htm

Gini Graham Scott
www.giniscott.com/shamanism

Index

K

L